INVISIBLE POWER INVINCIBLE WEAPON

INVISIBLE POWER
INVINCIBLE WEAPON

The Cross

MARIE ROBERTE JOSEPH

Excerpt from Oswald Chambers' devotional classic, taken from My Utmost for His Highest® by Oswald Chambers, © l935 by Dodd Mead & Co., renewed © 1963 by the Oswald Chambers Publications Assn., Ltd. Used by permission of Discovery House, Grand Rapids MI 4950l. All rights reserved.

Scripture quotations taken from the King James Version
Public Domain
Some words have been updated from the 1611 Elizabethan English terminology. Such as "Thou, thy, shalt, hast, ye, saith, believeth, etc. This is done to render the verses more comprehensible.

Published by The cross triumphant ministries
Copyright © 2016 Marie Roberte Joseph

Website: www.thecrosstriumphant.org
Email: gloryatthecross@gmail.com

ISBN-13: 9780997227727
ISBN-10: 0997227729

Acknowledgment

I thank my Heavenly Father for His Son Jesus Christ.

I thank my Lord and Savior Jesus Christ for His blood that was shed on the cross for the salvation of my soul.

I thank the Holy Spirit for guiding me into the whole truth, "Christ crucified!"

TABLE OF CONTENTS

INTRODUCTION

THE BEGINNING OF humanity's history is a story of love, treason, pain, deep regrets, accusations, reconciliation and restoration. From the beginning, God showed the depth of His love for mankind when He went looking for Adam and Eve after their disobedience, which caused a separation between the first couple and Jehovah God their Creator. The separation was led by Satan, who used the serpent as an instrument to arrive to this end. Since then, man has fallen into a deep dark hole of endless despair. God revealed to Adam and Eve the plan of salvation by promising them that the posterity of the woman, who is Jesus, would crush the head of Satan, thereby destroying his power. And Satan would bruise His heel meaning Jesus would shed His blood on the cross for the forgiveness of sins in order to reconcile man with God, and finally bring Satan into the bottomless pit.

It is an intriguing story, which shows us the power of the cross of Calvary, the place where the biggest battle was fought between the forces of darkness, and God for the redemption of man. The power of the blood of Jesus can deliver at any time, in any season, and in any generation. It is also important to comprehend that the understanding of the purpose of the cross is necessary for the Christian to live victoriously in Christ.

Questions like:
What did the bronze or brazen altar of the Old Testament represent?

Why did God use the word "continual" meaning perpetually when He gave instructions to Moses concerning the sacrifice of the lambs on the brazen altar, when He knew that the death of Jesus would put an end to this practice?

What is the gender of the serpent who tempted Eve in the Garden of Eden?

The answers to these questions, along with the abuses, the false doctrines, the spiritual and moral degradation affecting the church, are topics that are addressed. And more importantly the solution to remedy these problems is presented. There are so many truths to uncover in the pages of this book, so take your time to read it entirely. Please, read on!

THE GARDEN OF GOD

WHEN I IMAGINE the Garden of Eden I see flowers of all kinds, Lily of the valley, roses, tulips, morning glory, hibiscus, lavender, ylang-ylang, and jasmine, just to name a few. The flowers exhaled their perfumes, night and day. There was a marriage of color and of perfumes, the sweet-smelling aroma of fruits of all kinds, as well as the song of the nightingale, the turtle dove, the cardinal, the garden warbler and others who took turns serenading Adam and Eve with their sweet melodies. They say that birds sing in their mating season. That melodious season never had an end in the Garden of Eden. With the addition of the uninterrupted presence of God, there was not another name more suitable to name this place than "Paradise." God put everything in its place, the firmament, the earth, the sea, the trees, the sun, the moon, the stars, the birds, the fish and the animals. There was one last thing He didn't create yet, a being in His image and likeness. *"And God said, Let us make man in Our image, after our likeness: and let them have dominion over the fish of the sea, and over the fowl of the air, and over the cattle, and over all the earth, and over every creeping thing that creeps upon the earth." (Genesis 1:26)*

God chose to give the garden to Adam, whom He had created in His image and likeness, so that he would cultivate, and kept it; in other words, so that he would watch over it. And He gave him specific instructions concerning one of the trees of the garden. *"And the LORD God commanded the man, saying, of every tree of the garden you may freely eat: But of the tree of the knowledge of good and evil, you shall not eat of it: for in the day that you eat thereof you shall surely die."(Genesis 2:16–17)* Adam was the governor of God's creation. God had left it in his care to name the animals over which he was going to have dominion.

"And out of the ground the LORD God formed every beast of the field, and every fowl of the air; and brought them unto Adam to see what he would call them: and whatsoever Adam called every living creature that was the name thereof." (Genesis 2: 19)

The animals were created before Adam, yet they still did not have names. It had already been in the mind of God that He would give the responsibility of naming the animals to the man He would create after them, from the tiny ant to the elephant, from the eagle to the quail. Consequently, He endowed Adam with an intelligence that was impossible to compare to any other man after him, whatever his intellectual level. After all that, He told Himself that it was not good for man to be alone, so He caused, a deep sleep to fall over Adam, and took one of his ribs to form Eve. Then God introduced to him this woman, made by His own hand created in His image and His likeness. No words could describe her beauty, and her kindness. I know that everything God makes is marvelous. She was the ideal woman, whom every man would have liked to have as a wife. Perfect harmony reigned between Adam and Eve his wife. They lived in abundance. The love that exuberated from this environment made it feel like it was an eternal spring.

⋏　⋏　⋏

Adam and Eve benefited from the permanent presence of God and their relationship was perfect. They did not need to contact God, for anything that they needed or wanted. God had put at their disposal everything that they needed. Their relationship to their Creator was flawless. Their motives to communicate with Him were pure. It was an unsurpassed love story which evolved into an atmosphere of perfect peace. In the evening, when they spoke to each other, it was not for God to search for the lost man, but to communicate their mutual love. Only the angels, the luminous stars, and the moon light witnessed their moments of intimacy, and of the perfect love between Adam, Eve and Jehovah God their Creator. This was so, until the day when the serpent approached Eve.

THE SERPENT OF EDEN

S ATAN CAME WITH another plan for man, using the serpent as his instrument. In the Spanish Bible, Reina Valera Chapter 3:13, Eve told God it was "La serpiente" that deceived her. The definite article "*La*" before a noun in the Spanish language, indicates that the noun is a feminine gender. However, there are nouns that do not change gender when the definite article "*La*" is placed before them. The serpent falls under that category. Whether it's a male or a female serpent, it is called "*la serpiente.*" God speaks all languages. I believe He inspired the grammarians to write all the rules that pertains to the proper verbalization of all languages. It's not by coincidence that this animal falls under the category of the nouns that do not change gender and was assigned the definite article "*La*" in the Spanish language. That indicates more than just the proper grammar of a language. In the Garden of Eden, that serpent was indeed a female. *La serpiente* was none other than the evil spirit known as—Jezebel; Satan himself, under the disguise of a female entity.

The Bible identifies the Jezebel spirit later in the Scriptures, having possessed the daughter of Ethbaal, king of the Sidonians. His name means "priest with Satan"; he was in the service of Astarte, which is another name for Jezebel. His daughter, who was the wife of Ahab, king of Israel, was named Jezebel after the spirit.

The Jezebel spirit is also known in the Scriptures under several other names, "the queen of heaven" (Jeremiah 7:18; 44:19), "Ashtoreth" (1 Kings

11: 5, 33, 2 Kings 11:13), "the goddess Diana" (Acts 19: 24–27, 34–35), and "Jezebel" (Revelation 2:20)

⋏ ⋏ ⋏

Throughout the ages, the Jezebel spirit remained a mysterious figure. *She is not a powerful, fallen female angel.* There were no angels of the feminine gender. She did not create herself. Nevertheless, her worshippers spoke of her as a powerful goddess who is worshiped all over the world. The Canaanites, the Babylonians and the Assyrians worshiped her under the names Ishtar, Astarte or Ashtoreth. The book of Acts mentions her under the name "Diana." There was a silversmith named Demetrius and others who fabricated silver shrines in her honor.

Let's read more about this industry and this goddess: *"For a certain man named Demetrius, a silversmith, which made silver shrines for Diana, brought no small gain unto the craftsmen; Whom he called together with the workmen of like occupation, and said, Sirs, you know that by this craft we have our wealth. Moreover you see and hear, that not alone at Ephesus, but almost throughout all Asia, this Paul has persuaded and turned away much people, saying that they be no gods, which are made with hands: So that not only this our craft is in danger to be set at nought; **but also that the temple of the great goddess Diana should be despised, and her magnificence should be destroyed, whom all Asia and the world worship.**" (Acts 19: 24–27)* "So mightily grew the word of God and prevailed." *(Acts 19: 20)* This teaching of Paul prevailed, and according to them it had, persuaded and diverted crowds of people away from the workers. Their main concern was that "the temple of the great goddess Diana may be despised and her magnificence destroyed, **"whom all Asia and the world worship"** She is indeed, honored, and worshiped worldwide.

In the voodoo religion, she is worshiped under the name Erzulie. Demetrius used the talent that God gave him to serve the devil. He let Satan corrupt his talent because the manufacturing of these abominations brought him considerable gain. He chose money at the cost of his soul. He preferred to honor Diana rather than God.

The Jezebel spirit appears in the book of Kings with the same determination she had in the Garden of Eden that is to destroy the servants of God. *"Was it not told my lord what I did **when Jezebel slew the prophets of the LORD,** how I hid an hundred men of the LORD's prophets by fifty in a cave, and fed them with bread and water? (1Kings 18: 13)* The one mentioned in this verse is the wife of Ahab, king of Israel, who killed the prophets of the Lord. She was possessed with the same spirit that tempted Eve in the Garden of Eden, before she was born.

The Scriptures tell of the story of the vineyard of Naboth, which was in Jezreel. Jezebel's husband, King Ahab, coveted the vineyard of Naboth and wanted him to give it to him in exchange for another vineyard, which Ahab claimed was better than Naboth's, or he would give money to Naboth for it. (1Kings 21: 2 – 6) Naboth refused to let him have it. He told Ahab that it was the inheritance of his fathers that he wasn't selling it. Ahab, disappointed by this refusal, became very sad. The saddest day for Satan is when a Christian stand on his faith in Jesus, and His sacrifice on the cross refuses to sell out, and refuses to make any kind of deal with him, no matter how lucrative it may seem.

When Jezebel learned that Naboth had refused to give his vineyard to her husband, she took all measures in her power, even to the point of lying about him, to have him murdered, so that her husband could take possession of his vineyard. She used ruse, by writing letters in the name of Ahab and she used his seal to authenticate the letters in which she accused Naboth of blaspheming God and the king. Jezebel also solicited the people and authorities of the city to fulfill her decrees, which were to stone him to death for this big crime. There happened to be two malicious men of her caliber, who carried out her request, approved by the authorities. They led Naboth out of the city and stoned him to death.

Some Christians have compromised their walk with the Lord in exchange for the unclean things of this world with a prosperity label on it, supposedly to be the better things the enemy has offered them. The gospel of Jesus Christ is our inheritance; some preachers have compromised it with the Jezebel spirit, which Ahab worshiped under the name of Ashtoreth. These preachers have chosen money and fame over their precious inheritance. They have betrayed the Lord. Naboth chose death rather than to betray his forefathers by given his inheritance to a devil worshiper. He didn't care about the title that was before Ahab's name, and he wasn't worrying about the consequences of his refusal, which cost him his life. That's the cost of loyalty!

Jesus mentioned Jezebel in the book of Revelation his letter to the church of Thyatira: *"And unto the angel of the church in Thyatira write; These things said the Son of God, who has His eyes like unto a flame of fire, and His feet are like fine brass; I know your works, and charity, and service, and faith, and your patience, and your works; and the last to be more than the first. Notwithstanding **I have a few things against you, because you suffer that woman Jezebel, which calls herself a prophetess, to teach and to seduce My servants to commit fornication, and to eat things sacrificed unto idols.** And I gave her space to repent of her fornication; and she repented not. Behold, I will cast her into a bed, and them that commit adultery with her into great tribulation, except they repent of their deeds. And I will kill her children with death; and all the churches shall know that I am He which searches the reins and hearts: and I will give unto every one of you according to your works. **But unto you I say, and unto the rest in Thyatira, as many as have not this doctrine, and which have not known the depths of Satan,** as they speak; I will put upon you none other burden."* (Revelation 2: 18- 24)

▲ ▲ ▲

There were no problems in the church itself. Jesus underlined its good works, which increased. It had faith, love, and was constant, until the day that it let Satan penetrate its doors through the woman Jezebel.

In His letter to the **church of Pergamos,** Jesus said: *"I know your works, and where you dwell, where Satan's throne is. And you hold fast to My name, and did not deny My faith even in the days of Antipas was my faithful martyr, who was killed among you where Satan dwells. **But I have a few things against you, because you have there, those who hold the doctrine of Balaam, who*** *taught Balak to put a stumbling block before the children of Israel, to eat things sacrificed to idols, and to commit sexual immorality"* (Revelation 2:13- 14)

Jesus reproached this church for letting people teach false doctrines in the church. ***The doctrine of Balaam taught the people to eat things sacrificed to idols and to commit sexual immorality.*** Whether it be in Pergamos or in Thyatira, through the doctrine of Balaam or Jezebel, the teachings are identical because it is one spirit, Satan operating under different names. Let's continue with the Church of Thyatira. This deviation from the word of God was the beginning of Catholicism. The woman Jezebel came with her own laws, and it was under the influence of this prophetess, possessed by Satan that everything changed for the worst. The Jezebel of the church of Thyatira was not the wife of Ahab mentioned in the book of Kings, but these women were possessed by the same spirit, which has been operating since the Garden of Eden.

It was the Jezebel spirit who influenced the leaders of the church to introduce these changes and these abominations into the church of Jesus Christ. The church leaders diverted the eyes of the people away from Jesus, far from the foundation of the apostles. Introducing works, as means of people's salvation and went as far as making the church attendees believe that once they were affiliated with the church and they had received the church sacraments their entrance into heaven was guaranteed. The word of God declares, *"For by grace are you saved through faith; and that not of yourselves: it is the gift of God. Not of works, lest any man should boast."* (Ephesians 2: 8–9)

Salvation is found only in Jesus Christ. Church membership or any man—invented sacraments inspired by an evil spirit do not guarantee anyone, entrance to heaven, but only faith in Jesus Christ and His finished work on the cross. You must confess your sins to God and obtain forgiveness for your sins, by the shed blood of Jesus, which cleanses the stain of sin. Jesus said, *"Verily, verily, I say unto you, He who believes on Me has everlasting life."* (John 6:47) He is the only one who gives eternal life. It was in the divine plan of God, before the foundation of the world, to redeem man, to reconcile man to Himself, and to eradicate this venom of sin, which became the Motive of his actions.

The Jezebel spirit, through the church leaders introduced the cult of the dead into the Church. She influenced them to give two dates of remembrance to the dead in the calendar to honor them; November 1ˢᵗ All Saints' Day and November 2ⁿᵈ All Souls' Day. This is an abomination; this practice is forbidden in the word of God. Ecclesiastes says to us concerning the dead, *"For the living know that they shall die: but the dead know not anything, neither have they any more a reward; for the memory of them is forgotten. Also their love, and their hatred, and their envy, is now perished; neither have they any more a portion forever in anything that is done under the sun. (Ecclesiastes 9: 5–6)* The dead cannot help anyone according to the word of God, they know nothing.

If you are a member of the Catholic Church, perhaps you pray, to the saints to come to your help when you have a problem. You prostrate yourself before them, with your candles in hand, to ask them for favors. Those saints to whom you pray are ordinary people who lived on this earth and who died. This practice of praying to the dead, the cult of the dead is the product of religion. Those men and women, if they were born again, are asleep in Jesus. We have already seen in Ecclesiastes that they can't help anyone.

⋏   ⋏   ⋏

The church took it upon itself to put laws in place, thus changing the word of God and making a doctrine out of what it believed was good for the faithful. No church is qualified to canonize another man into sainthood. Besides, to become a saint in the Catholic Church after you die, your family has to pay a substantial amount of money to the church. We are talking about thousands of dollars. Therefore, the majority of poor people whose family cannot pay such a huge amount of money, will never achieve that status. However, when you put your faith in Jesus Christ and ask Him to come into your heart, He forgives your sins, His blood cleanses you of all unrighteousness. He justifies you by giving you His righteousness. Then this title of "saint" is afforded to you on earth, while you are living, and the title remains yours throughout eternity. Most importantly, it's free! Jesus paid the price for all who would believe in Him to become saints in His kingdom. In the kingdom of God, the title of "saint" is not just reserved for a privilege few, but for all the children of God, rich or poor.

There are a few verses in the New Testament in the epistles of the apostle Paul, where he used the word "*saint*" to greet the believers who were alive. Let us see some verses, "*Salute Philologus, and Julia, Nereus, and his sister, and Olympas, and all the saints which are with them*" *(Romans 16:15)*

"*Paul and Timothy, the servants of Jesus Christ, to all the saints in Christ Jesus which are at Philippi, with the bishops and deacons. (Philippians 1:1)*

"*Salute every saint in Christ Jesus. The brethren which are with me greet you.*" *(Philippians 4:21)*

Every person who is born again is a saint; not because of their own perfection, but their position in Christ qualifies them for that title. Any other method used by the church to declare a dead man or woman Saint is man-made. It's the product of religion, and it's inspired by Satan under the disguise of the Jezebel spirit. No man is qualified to declare another "*saint*" after his death, because at least two people would have had to testify to having received a miracle from this dead person.

The word of God is true, not what man or religion declares. We have just read in Ecclesiastes concerning the dead, "they will have never again any part in all what is made under the sun." If someone tells you, he has received a miracle of healing or of any kind from a dead person, it was performed by a demonic spirit. According to the word of God, it is impossible.

Physical death is the final chapter in all men's life. The dead in Christ will rise from the dead. They will come back to life again. All those who believe in Jesus are not dead, they sleep in Jesus. They are living beings that are awaiting the sound of the trumpet to rise. The Bible says, "*For if we believe that Jesus died and rose again, even so them also which sleep in Jesus will God bring with Him. For the LORD Himself shall descend from heaven with a shout, with the voice of the archangel, and with the trump of God: and the dead in Christ shall rise first.*" *(1 Thessalonians 4:14, 16)*

Jesus declared, *"Now that the dead are raised, even Moses showed at the bush, when he called the LORD the God of Abraham, and the God of Isaac, and the God of Jacob.* **For He is not the God of the dead, but of the living: for all live unto Him.***" (Luke 20:37 - 38)*

Let us see another verse, which will help you understand this truth further. These are the words of Jesus spoken to Martha, Lazarus's sister, when He went to raise him from the dead after four days in the tomb. Jesus said to her, *"I am the resurrection, and the life:* **he who believes in Me, though he were dead, yet shall he live: And whosoever lives and believes in Me shall never die.** *Do you believe this? (John 11: 25- 26)*

From the Scriptures, we know that God is not the God of the dead but of the living. At the time of physical death, the child of God sleeps in Jesus. Physical death is just a way for him to get rid of his earthly body so he can receive his glorified body at the resurrection. It is Satan, who operates under the disguise of the Jezebel spirit, who is the god of the dead—the god of all those who reject Christ. Those who do not have Jesus Christ in their lives are dead, spiritually speaking. The work of regeneration which the Holy Spirit operates in the life of the believer, has never taken place in their lives.

▲   ▲   ▲

I believe a minister of the gospel has to be cautious, about telling dreams he or she may have had concerning a dead person they knew when that person was living. That can encourage practices which are associated with the "cult of the dead." After all, it is supposedly someone who knows the word of God that is telling them of his encounter with his deceased relatives, friends or any other in his dream. Therefore, there is no problem if the people he or she is ministering to have their encounters with the dead in their dreams and also hold on to any lies that a demon spirit might have told them that is contrary to the word of God.

I believe it doesn't matter how real a dream portraying a deceased person may seem, or how good it may have made you feel, the fact is God will not violate His word. He forbids interaction of any kind with the dead. He is not the God of the dead but of the living. Once a person has crossed over to eternity, whether he or she is in hell or with the Lord, that person cannot come into the land of the living as they please in any way shape or fashion to speak or interact with the living.

This story in Luke of the rich man and Lazarus clearly shows it's not God's way to send a dead person to speak with the living. While they were living, Lazarus was a poor beggar. He sat at the rich man's gate, then they both died. Lazarus was carried to Abraham's bosom by the angels, and the rich man was buried and went to Hades, which means hell. There, he was tormented and he was thirsty. He was begging Abraham for water. The fact is, Abraham could have sent him an ocean of purified water, and it would not have satisfied him. The physical need may have been met, but he would still be tormented, he would still be longing to be where Lazarus was. Until the thirst in his soul was quenched, nothing he desired would have satisfied him. His fate was sealed. The thirst in his soul and the torment will remain for eternity.

The thirst in the soul of man must be quenched here on earth by accepting Jesus Christ as his Lord and Savior to obtain the forgiveness of his sins. Once he died all he can do is beg for water and be in torment eternally. Let's look at some verses of that story: *"There was a certain rich man, which was clothed in purple and fine linen, and fared sumptuously every day: And there was a certain beggar named Lazarus, which was laid at his gate, full of sores. And it came to pass, that the beggar died, and was carried by the angels into Abraham's bosom: the rich man also died, and was buried. And in hell he lift up his eyes, being in torments, and saw Abraham afar off, and Lazarus in his bosom. And he cried and said, Father Abraham, have mercy on me, and **send Lazarus that he may dip the tip of his finger in water, and cool my tongue; for I am tormented in this flame.** Then **he said, I pray you therefore, father, that you would send him to my father's house**: For I have five brethren; that he may testify unto them, lest they also come into this place of torment. Abraham said unto him, they have Moses and the prophets; let them hear them. And he said, No, father Abraham: but **if one went unto them from the dead,** they will repent. And he said unto him, if they hear not Moses and the prophets, neither will they be persuaded, **though one rose from the dead.** (Luke 16: 19-20, 22-24, 27-31)*

The rich man told Abraham: "No, father Abraham; but *if one goes to them from the dead*, they will repent." He wanted to send someone *from the dead* to earth to his family. Abraham, a man of God who understood the ways of God knew that was not possible, answered him "if they do not hear Moses and the prophets, neither will they be persuaded **though *one rise from the dead*.**" Abraham knew that a dead person cannot come to speak with the living in whatever way, in dreams or other. *That person would have to rise from the dead to come into the land of the living.* What Abraham was also saying was that these people may be so hardened that it doesn't matter who preach the gospel to them, they would not change. It was not up to Abraham to grant such a request; it was up to God.

God didn't grant the request of the rich man for the dead to come to the living in the Old Testament. Jesus Himself told us about these two men, and this story is recorded in the New Testament. Therefore, God has not changed His mind about the dead visiting the living, in this situation, or for any other reason in any way, shape or fashion, whether they are in hell or with the Lord. Therefore, next time you see a dead person in your dream whomever it may be, disregard it. Whatever that deceased person has said to you, however incredible it may sound like it's a lie. It may sound like the truth, but if you were to follow up on it, you would discover that it's a lie. Satan does that also in order for you not to see the reality of hell.

▲　▲　▲

The problem with these deceased people that are appearing to the living in their dreams is that one can see people who have never asked God for the forgiveness of their sins, they have rejected Jesus Christ and have deliberately refused God's plan of salvation through the blood of Jesus. When these people die and go to hell, and relatives, and friends may see them all dressed up in nice clothing and looking good, when in reality they are in torment exactly as Jesus described it. If that relative or friend saw the torment of that person, they would run to Jesus Christ to be saved and the devil doesn't want that. He wants you to join that family member, or whomever it might be, in their torment. That's why Satan sends a demon spirit looking very good that may resemble that deceased person you knew, but it's not the person.

The Bible says, *"For the living know that they shall die:* **but the dead know not anything,** *neither have they any more a reward; for the memory of them is forgotten. Also their love, and their hatred, and their envy, is now perished;* **neither have they any more a portion forever in anything that is done under the sun.** *(Ecclesiastes 9:5)* Even if a Christian were to see a saved loved one in his dream he should dismiss that dream. God is not the author of confusion. Once again whether the person is in hell or with the Lord, God would never allow that person in any form or fashion to interact with the living. I must add that the rich man was in hell, not because he was wealthy, but because he wasn't serving God. Often times, God communicates with the living through the Holy Spirit, by means of the living word, never through a dead person.

A true Christian will never celebrate the holiday of the dead. Those who do are influenced by the Jezebel spirit, whether they know it or not, since she is the one who implemented it. In reality, it is the dead who celebrate the dead. The word of God is there to guide all men, to enlighten them, but they prefer darkness rather than the light.

The Catholic Church has, under the influence of the Jezebel spirit, embraced the worship of idols, and carved images, forbidden by God in the fourth commandment. It is written, *"You shall not make unto you any graven image, or any likeness of anything that is in heaven above, or that is in the earth beneath, or that is in the water under the earth. You shall not bow down yourself to them, nor serve them: for I the LORD your God am a jealous God, visiting the iniquity of the fathers upon the children unto the third and fourth generation of them that hate Me; And showing mercy unto thousands of them that love Me, and keep My commandments." (Exodus 20:4 - 6)*

The Lord reiterated this law in Leviticus. He said: *"You shall make you no idols nor graven image, neither rear you up a standing image, neither shall you set up any image of stone in your land, to bow down unto it: for I am the LORD your God." (Leviticus 26:1)*

You say that you love God and yet you worship these idols. Anything you pray to, you also worship. You would not pray to it, if you did not believe it had the power to deliver you. It is an abomination in the eyes of God. Not only does He prohibit it, but He punishes those who give themselves to these practices. It is an insult to the Lord to make carved images of people He has created and then pray to them as if they were God. That is why you do not get answers to your prayers to the point where you lose heart. And some have taken refuge in all kinds of ungodly, evil practices to fulfill their desires. The Jezebel spirit gave preeminence to Mary in the church, whom she says is the mother of Jesus. In reality, it is she who occupies that place. Mary, the mother of Jesus, the Son of the living God has nothing in common with Jezebel.

Through the church leaders the Jezebel spirit, succeeded in making the people of the church believe that Mary is the one who gives all believers' access to her Son Jesus. Listen to the words of Jesus. *"Then said Jesus unto His disciples, if any man will come after Me, let him deny himself, and take up his cross, and follow Me." (Matthew 16:24)* The way to get access to Jesus is through the cross. To get to the cross you must deny yourself. It simply means you must stop being your own god. You must surrender your life totally to Jesus.

I am not talking about the fourteen Stations of the Cross, which is a man-made tradition of praying before fourteen carved images, depicting the crucifixion of Jesus Christ, and leaving Him in the tomb at the last station. I am talking about the finished work of Jesus Christ on the cross. His sacrificial death upon the cross to set free all who would yield their lives to Him. I am talking about our resurrected Savior, who is no longer in the tomb, but is reigning in glory at the right hand of His Father.

Jesus Christ cannot be mixed with fabricated images, whether in print, carved or any other form; He cannot be associated with any form of idol worship, including the rosary. Jesus said to the Samaritan woman, *"But the hour comes, and now is, when **the true worshippers shall worship the Father in spirit and in truth:** for the Father seeks such to worship Him. God is a Spirit: and they that worship Him must worship Him in spirit and in truth. (John 4: 23–24)*

The Jezebel spirit who portrayed herself as Mary has elevated herself to such a high level in the church that prayers, which must be addressed only to God are addressed to her as well. In the rosary, the most adored prayer dedicated to her begins with the creed: *One Our Father, Three Hail Marys' and the Doxology,* which refers to the Trinity and ends with *Salve Regina.* The creed is followed by five decades the *"Our Father,"* is mentioned one time in each decade followed by *ten Hail Marys'* and the *Doxology* which is repeated one time in each decade. It is fair to say that in the rosary, she is placed higher than the Father, the Son and the Holy Spirit. This practice is forbidden by God from the first to the fourth commandments.

It is the Jezebel spirit, who is the queen of heaven not Mary the mother of Jesus **Christ.** The Holy Spirit inspired Jeremiah the prophet to write the following: *"Seest you not what they do in the cities of Judah and in the streets of Jerusalem? The children gather wood, and the fathers kindle the fire, and the women knead their dough,* **to make cakes to the queen of heaven,** *and to pour out drink offerings unto other gods,* **that they may provoke Me to anger."** *(Jeremiah 7: 17–18)* **The queen of heaven provoked God to anger** therefore, there is no way she could be the mother of Jesus Christ, the Son of God.

⟁ ⟁ ⟁

Salomon, inspired by The Holy Spirit, asked a series of questions in the book of Proverbs. The answer to all of them are in the Bible. Jesus later gave us the answer to one of them in the book of John. The questions were, *"Who has ascended into heaven, or descended? Who has gathered the wind in His fists? Who has bound the waters in a garment? Who has established all the ends of the earth? What is His name, and what is His Son's name, if you know?" (Proverbs 30:4)* His name is the MOST-HIGH GOD! And the name of His Son is JESUS!

Jesus' answer to "who has ascended into heaven, or descended" is found in the book of John, *"And no man has ascended up to heaven, but he who came down from heaven, even the Son of man who is in heaven."(John 3:13)*

No other person has ascended to heaven but Jesus. Mary was never taken up to heaven. Mary is awaiting the sound of the trumpet to rise from the dead, along with the multitude who have accepted Jesus as their Lord and Savior, to go meet her Son in the air and to reign with Him eternally. As we have seen, it is Jezebel who is the queen of heaven. Nowhere in the word of God does it say that Mary, the mother of Jesus, was taken up to heaven nor ascended to heaven in the manner in which Jesus did. There is absolutely no verse in the Bible that even comes close to suggesting that. We just read in the book of Jeremiah that the queen of heaven is evil. Again, she is Satan under the disguise of a woman.

So when you pray to the queen of heaven, you are praying to Satan. This doctrine is the fabrication of religion, inspired by Satan who is always seeking the adoration of the children of God. If your religion teaches something that is not in the Bible, then your religion is wrong. The word of God warns against adding or taking away from the Scriptures, in (Revelation *22:18-19*). Some people think that Mary will come to receive them at the gates of heaven when they die. They are expecting to go to heaven, yet they have never made peace with God by the blood of His Son, Jesus. The Bible says: ***"For there is one God and one Mediator between God and men, the Man Christ Jesus."*** *(1 Timothy 2: 5)* The only requirement to go to heaven is repentance towards God for our sins, and accepting Jesus Christ by faith as our Lord and Savior. Jesus said, *"I am the way, the truth, and the life:* ***no man comes unto the Father, but by Me."*** *(John 14:6)*

▲   ▲   ▲

Beloved! Your eternal life is too precious to continue believing and following the devil under the disguise of a female spirit who pretends to be the mother of Jesus, with one thing in mind: to take you to hell. It would be too late for you on the day you discover that you had a relationship with your church and not with Jesus Christ. Membership to your church does not write your name in the Lamb's book of life. No human hand can write your name in that book. And if your name is not written in it, you will then have the same fate as Satan, who infiltrated the church under the name of Jezebel. ***"And whosoever was not found written in the book of life was cast into the lake of fire."*** (Revelation 20:15)

Satan introduced materialism and the love of money into the church. These are some examples of the depths of Satan of which Jesus spoke. He does everything with such craftiness that no man is capable of detecting his deceptions if the Holy Spirit does not help him. There were faithful servants in Thyatira, who refused to follow her. Satan thought he was going to infiltrate the church of Jesus Christ as an undercover agent, but Jesus blew Satan's cover by identifying the woman Jezebel with the words "who have not known the depths of Satan." Jesus was speaking about her craftiness, her false doctrine, her seductions and how Satan infiltrated the church using the woman Jezebel as his instrument.

▲   ▲   ▲

There are some who believe that Jesus was referring to the Jezebel spirit, which possessed the wife of Ahab, king of Israel, not an actual person. I believe that Jesus was speaking of an actual woman, a self-appointed prophetess that established herself in the church of Thyatira, and was corrupting the servants of God. This woman was possessed by Satan, who also possessed Jezebel the wife of Ahab, and that spirit never left the church. The Jezebel spirit is still doing it today in the modern church. There are servants of God to this day who do not know her depths. Besides, no human being can fully know them. The only one who knows Satan's depths perfectly well is Jesus. He can go lower than Satan could go, and Jesus can also go higher than he could reach and control everything between his depths and his heights.

If you think since this letter was written to the church of Thyatira and since it was written two thousand years ago, you are not concerned, you are mistaken. You only have to look at what's going on in the churches, and you will see Jezebel's footprint in the churches. She came against the church of Jesus Christ, not one denomination. Additionally, it is the confusion she has propagated in the church by her false teachings and the dissension she has provoked among the believers that have caused the church to branch into all these denominations that we know of today.

At the beginning of the letter to the church of Thyatira, Jesus is described with His eyes like a flame of fire, looking at all that is taking place. Nothing escapes His sight. His feet were like brass, walking with His judgment against the atrocities that are taking place in His church. An institution that allows the Jezebel spirit, the queen of heaven, to be their queen will pay a very high price for her company. For she is an immoral, corrupt spirit and she surely will pass on her immorality, and her corruptions to her subjects.

We wonder why there are so many scandals of pedophilia, homosexuality and all kinds of other sexual perversions in the church. The church that has rejected Jesus Christ and the preaching of the cross, the church that has rejected the foundation of the apostles of Jesus Christ, the church that has mingled the gospel of God with the teachings of Jezebel, the church which has elevated Jezebel to a place higher than Jesus Christ, will face the judgment of God. The word of God declares: *"For the time is come that **judgment must begin at the house of God**: and if it first begin at us, what shall the end be of them that obey not the gospel of God?" (1 Peter 4:17)*

THE SEDUCTION OF JEZEBEL

WE HAVE SEEN in Scriptures that most of the time it is under the disguise of the Jezebel spirit that the devil attacks the servants of God, and he is always after their destruction. When Satan sends a woman on a mission to seduce a servant of God, mainly to lead him to sexual immorality, he sees standing before him a goddess, perfect in all aspects, beautiful, charming, with a great personality, and whatever else he adores. She is the ideal wife, whom he dreamt to have and he wonders why God had not sent her into his life before he met his wife. If He had, he would have married her. So he ventures into an affair, but he and this woman agree to keep this affair clandestine. In the times in which we are now living, this is not limited to women seducing men. Satan is also sending men to seduce men who are ministers of the gospel, and women to seduce women who are in the ministry, and have a proclivity toward homosexuality, for the sole purpose of destroying them.

The power of the blood of Jesus Christ that was shed on the cross will defeat any kind of proclivity towards any kind of sin. If the one who has such a tendency would seek deliverance from Jesus Christ, His finished work on the cross guarantees their deliverance. If you choose to follow the Jezebel spirit path, be prepared to face the bitter consequences of your choice. The Bible says: *"Fear them not therefore:* **for there is nothing covered, that shall not be revealed; and hid, that shall not be known."** *(Matthew 10:26)*

"But if you will not do so, behold, you have sinned against the LORD: and be sure **your sin will find you out."** *(Numbers 32:23)*

"He discovers deep things out of darkness, and brings out to light the shadow of death." (Job 12: 22)

*"He also shall be my salvation; **for a hypocrite shall not come before Him**." (Job13:16)*

There is no getting away with sins in the Kingdom of God. But there is grace to forgive all sins. After sin is consummated, this servant of God is going to have the painful experience of the seductions of the Jezebel spirit. It is at this moment that he will see Satan through the individual that seduced him. This individual being used by the devil will stop at nothing, to debase the servant of God, and to scandalize him. He did not know that this relationship was going to cost him his ministry. Some have left the ministry, and nothing is ever heard of them again. Some have lost their family, there are even some who have committed suicide. They did not know that this clandestine relationship would cost them their lives.

▲   ▲   ▲

In the book of Ecclesiastes Salomon wrote: *"And I find bitterer than death the woman, whose heart is snares and nets, and her hands as bands: whoso pleases God shall escape from her; but the sinner shall be taken by her." (Ecclesiastes 7:26)* He who pleases God, is he who has put his faith in Jesus Christ. He has been regenerated by the Holy Spirit, and makes it his priority to take up his cross daily and maintain a relationship with Jesus through prayer and the reading of the Word of God. Thus allowing the Holy Spirit to do His progressive work of sanctification in that life. Such a person is protected by God against her guile.

The maidservants of God must be on their guard as well. There are also evil men who infiltrate the church. They appear as ministers of justice, but they have no relationship with Jesus Christ. In truth, they are ministers of Satan who commit all kinds of wicked deeds in the church and who seduce women to deviate them from their faith. Before moving on, I wanted to show you who Jezebel is, the role she played in the fall of man, and her influence in the spiritual and moral decline of the church. We can conclude that Jezebel is not a female spirit, or a goddess who is worshipped all over the world, but instead a shrewd masculine spirit unlike any other. Therefore, Satan is the first transgender entity to infiltrate the human race. He can disguise himself to whoever he wants to, and take the form of anything—even of an animal in order to fulfill his plans.

Disobedience and rebellion towards God never remains unpunished. If I left, the despicable acts of Jezebel, the wife of Ahab, king of Israel used by Satan as an instrument to massacre the prophets of God and unfairly shed the blood of Naboth and do not tell you how God judged her, I would have neglected to show you one of God's greatest attributes, His faithfulness towards His servants. God declares in His word: *"Touch not My anointed, and do My prophets no harm." (Psalms105:15)*

Afterwards, through Elisha, the Lord spoke these words concerning Ahab: *"And the word of the LORD came to Elijah the Tishbite, saying, arise, go down to meet Ahab king of Israel, which is in Samaria: behold, he is in the vineyard of Naboth, whither he is gone down to possess it. And you shall speak unto him, saying, thus says the LORD, Have you killed, and also taken possession? And you shall speak unto him, saying,* **thus says the LORD, in the place where dogs licked the blood of Naboth shall dogs lick your blood, even yours."***(1 Kings 21: 17–19)*

After God had spoken this word about Ahab, he was in a battle with Syria Let's read what took place in that battle: *"And a certain man drew a bow at a venture, and smote the king of Israel between the joints of the harness: wherefore he said unto the driver of his chariot, turn thine hand, and carry me out of the host;* **for I am wounded. And the battle increased that day: and the king was stayed up in his chariot against the Syrians, and died at even***: and the blood ran out of the wound into the midst of the chariot. And one washed the chariot in the pool of Samaria;* **and the dogs licked up his blood***; and they washed his armour; according unto the word of the LORD which He spoke." (1 kings 22: 34-35, 38)*

The word of the Lord concerning Ahab, in regard to Naboth, whom Jezebel (his wife) had killed in order to take possession of Naboth's vineyard, which he coveted, came to pass on that day.

▲ ▲ ▲

Jehu, King of Israel, was chosen by God to carry out His judgment on Jezebel. The word of the Lord that came to Jehu was: *"And you shall smite the house of Ahab your master, that **I may avenge the blood of My servants the prophets, and the blood of all the servants of the LORD, at the hand of Jezebel. And the dogs shall eat Jezebel in the portion of Jezreel, and there shall be none to bury her.** And he opened the door, and fled."* (2 Kings 9: 7, 10)

Jehu did not hesitate to go to Jezreel to execute God's decree concerning Jezebel. Let's read how that wicked queen met her demise. When Jehu arrived there, Jezebel was near a window and there were some men near her. Jehu asked them to throw her down, and they did exactly as they were told, her blood spattered on the wall and on the horses. Then Jehu said, *"...Go see now this cursed woman, and bury her: for she is a king's daughter. **And they went to bury her: but they found no more of her than the skull, and the feet, and the palms of her hands.** Wherefore they came again, and told him. And he said, **This is the word of the LORD, which He spoke by His servant Elijah the Tishbite, saying, In the portion of Jezreel shall dogs eat the flesh of Jezebel: And the carcase of Jezebel shall be as dung upon the face of the field in the portion of Jezreel; so that they shall not say, This is Jezebel."* (2 Kings 9: 33 – 37)

Yes, the dogs ate Jezebel and the dogs licked the blood of Ahab, as God had said. This was the end of this instrument of Satan. God leaves no wicked deed unpunished.

▲ ▲ ▲

God is always searching for His children who have fallen under the seduction of the woman Jezebel spirit. She only has one thing in mind: the destruction of man. That is why one must have compassion for a child of God who have fallen under her seductions. If they have truly repented, and asked God for forgiveness and have forsaken their sin. Yes, they have their responsibility in their fall, but that does not mean we must inflict upon them the knockout punch. We have seen servants who have been in certain situations and, in turn, have taken full responsibility for their actions, and recognized their failure was their own fault. God can restore such a man, or woman, so that they can again become a vessel of honor at the hands of the Lord, and be used by Him with power. The Bible says, "For the gifts and calling of God are without repentance." (Romans 11:29)

If you continue to revisit the past failures of a servant of God, to the point where you can 't receive what God has poured into that vessel, which He has restored. You are going to miss out on the biggest blessing that person could have been to your life. By residing in their past, it is as if you are searching through the garbage of **the Jezebel spirit, who is the mastermind behind their fall.** If you go search through her garbage with the intentions of accusing a man or a woman God has forgiven, and whose sins God no longer sees because they've been washed in the blood of Jesus. Let me tell you, the stench of her ordure will stay on you.

Your tongue will never be able to defile what God has cleansed and sanctified. You will never be able to destroy, with your tongue, the man, or the woman, who walks with God and with whom God walks. If you speak badly about him, or her, with friends, or foes, everywhere you go with the intention of discrediting this servant, and you think that you are going to succeed, you are greatly mistaken. It is Satan who is using you as he is the first slanderer. It is understood that you are doing the work of your father, the devil, and, most of the time, by a motive of jealousy. To your own defeat, you will never succeed. The blood of Jesus is more powerful than the sins committed by a man, or a woman, who has asked Him for forgiveness. That's why it cleanses them perfectly well. The blood of Jesus is more powerful than your tongue. That's why your tongue will be powerless in destroying the servant of the Lord. You can hide behind religion, manipulate situations, lie and bring accusations to carry out the mandates of the forces of darkness against a servant of God.

I assure you that the day will come when those with whom you have been slandering the servant of God, clearly see that you were an instrument in the hands of Satan to destroy, with your tongue, the servant of God and the ministry, which He entrusted to him, or to her.

The anointing of the Holy Spirit in his or her life is His stamp of approval on their ministry. When you try to demean a man or a woman of God by displaying their past, it is actually a great honor to the Lord, Jesus Christ. It shows that the power of His sacrifice on the cross, is what changed the person whom you are doing your best to destroy with your tongue. It is at the cross that the person whom you demean found the grace of God for the forgiveness of his, or her sins, and they are now a vessel of honor in the hand of their Savior. There is no sin which is above the grace of God.

The Temptation of Eve

S ATAN CAME IN the Garden of Eden with the determination to achieve his plan. He will use whoever, and whatever to concretize his wicked plan. He knew that disobedience to God carries enormous consequences with it, and if he succeeded in executing his plan, he would change the destiny of man. Just as it was for him, because of his revolt against God. His destiny had changed—of the immortal creature that he was, to one with a definite end. His days are numbered! He began questioning Eve on the instruction, which God had given to her husband concerning the tree of the knowledge of good and evil, with the intention to confuse her and to puzzle her mind so that he could carry out his murderous plan. And he succeeded.

The dialogue between Eve and the serpent is recorded in the book of Genesis. Let's read it! *"Now the serpent was more subtle than any beast of the field which the LORD God had made. And he said unto the woman, Yea, has God said, **you shall not eat of every tree of the garden?**" (Genesis 3:1)*

> *Let us go over what God said to Adam: "…**Of every tree of the garden thou may freely eat**: But of **the tree of the knowledge of good and evil,** you shall not eat of it: for in the day that you eat thereof you shall surely die." (Genesis 2:16–17)*

Satan distorted the word of God to arrive at his perverted purpose. Can you see how he twisted the word of God to deceive Eve? He did not ask the question as God spoke it to Adam. God said **they could eat of every tree of the garden, except for the tree of the knowledge of good and evil.** Satan, to confuse Eve said to her "Has God indeed said you shall <u>not</u> **eat of every tree** of the garden?

"And the woman said unto the serpent, we may eat of the fruit of the trees of the garden; but of the fruit of the tree which is in the midst of the garden, **God has said, you shall not eat of it, neither shall you touch it, lest you die.**" *(Genesis 3: 2 -3)*

Something else is going on in Eve's mind. She did not answer the serpent according to the order which God had given to them. God never said anything about touching the tree, He said not to eat of it. She added these words herself, "**nor shall you touch it, lest you die.**"

God said, "For **in the day** that you eat thereof **you shall surely die.**"

"*And the serpent said unto the woman, you shall* **Not surely die.** *For God does know that* **in the day you eat thereof,** *then your eyes shall be opened, and you shall be as gods, knowing good and evil.*" *(Genesis 3: 4-5)* Satan used the words "***surely die*** and ***in the day***" the exact words spoken by God in his reply to Eve. But he added one simple deadly word to the word of God "**NOT.**" He told Eve "you will ***NOT surely die.***" In his answer to Eve, he did not use her word to deceive her. He knew God didn't tell her, "nor shall you touch it, lest you die." God didn't leave any doubt about the death sentence it was clear "you shall surely die."

▲   ▲   ▲

The serpent used a portion of the word God had spoken to Adam and distorted it to his advantage. The serpent's question was formulated in a way to confuse Eve and to make her doubt the command of God. He succeeded. The instructions had clearly been given by God to Adam concerning that tree, as well as the consequences if he disobeyed. The way she answered the serpent left the door wide open for him to enter and inject his lethal venom into the human race.

Every erroneous doctrine has some element of truth. The devil is the mastermind behind every false doctrine and his sole purpose is to deceive the people of God, and to lead them astray. That's why it's extremely important to study the word of God like the (brothers) brethren in Berea did they searched the Scriptures to find out if they were taught the word of God right. (Acts 17:10-11) Or else to be under the leadership of a pastor who is rightly dividing the word of truth. (2 Timothy 2:15) The word of truth is "Christ crucified." He is the word; He is the truth. From what we have read, there are no better words to describe the devil then the words Jesus spoke to those who rejected Him and were seeking to kill Him. *"You are of your father the devil, and the lusts of your father you will do. He was a murderer from the beginning, and abode not in the truth, because there is no truth in him. When he speaks a lie, he speaks of his own: for **he is a liar, and the father of it.**" (John 8:44)*

The serpent contradicted the words of God, by saying to Eve "you will *not* surely die." In other words, he told Eve that what God said to them was not true. To seal his plan and to prevent Eve from analyzing what he had just said to her, he immediately gave her an explanation as to why God didn't want them to eat the fruit, in doing so, he left no doubt in Eve's mind and no need to question him. His ultimate goal was to make Adam and Eve eat the fruit of the tree, to disobey God. He knew that if he earned Eve 's trust, Adam would not be suspicious in partaking of the fruit if he received it from his wife.

He finalized his plan by adding these words: "Your eyes will be opened, and you will be like God, knowing good and evil." Eve felt within herself that she had nothing to lose, but rather everything to gain. She had the assurance that she would not die. She believed in the words of the serpent and rejected God's order. She did not trust God, her Creator, any more. Satan had succeeded in making her believe that God was not telling the truth. He gave her the true reason behind God's order. He had succeeded in making Eve believe that he was the one who was telling her the truth, that he was the one who wanted her to be elevated to greatness, that she could rise higher than any dimension God could propel her to. It's by eating the fruit that she would be raised to the rank of God and have the knowledge of good and evil.

After this explanation by Satan, Eve was persuaded that there was nothing wrong with the tree. She made her choice. She followed the way of the serpent. *"And when the woman saw that the tree was good for food, and that it was pleasant to the eyes, and a tree to be desired to make one wise, she took of the fruit thereof, and did eat, and gave also unto her husband with her; and he did eat." (Genesis 3:6)*

So Satan, under the cover of a female serpent, also known as the Jezebel spirit, introduced sin into this perfect and beautiful garden. He polluted the human race with this cancer called **sin**. When Adam and Eve ate the fruit, their disobedience to God affected all of creation. The human race was left to carry the burden of the consequences of sin. Adam and Eve did not comprehend the magnitude of what had just taken place. They recognized that they were naked. *"And the eyes of them both were opened, and they knew that they were naked; and they sewed fig leaves together, and made themselves aprons." (Genesis 3:7)*

Adam and Eve became independent of God. Before they fell in sin, it was God who had provided whatever they needed. After the fall, they sewed their own fig leaves to make themselves aprons. They concocted this ingenious plan to cover their nakedness. They thought this would remedy the situation, or appease their conscience of the guilt from their disobedience. To this day, this is true for the majority of people. When they are facing difficult circumstances, most of the time brought on by their own actions, they try to find the solution or the remedy for the situation on their own. They'll try whatever means, even if they have to lie, instead of going to God to seek His forgiveness for whatever sin they have committed. The reason is pride. They don't want to admit they made a bad choice. If only they would humble themselves and go to God, they would find a Father with arms wide open ready to forgive and to restore them. No man can fix the damages done by sin.

The fig leaves that Adam and Eve made covered their reproductive organs. Symbolizing this was their means to cover and to protect their offspring from the consequences of their disobedience. It was also their way to make peace with God. Since they were no longer naked, they could stand in His presence, as they were accustomed to before their fall. They had seen the nakedness of the physical body and they had tried their best to bring a solution to what their eyes could see. The real problem resides in what the eyes could not see. There was nothing that they could do to resolve what had just taken place— neither for themselves, nor for their descendants. In this physical nakedness, man became an immoral, depraved, confused being without purpose and ability to make the right decisions. Man lost his joy and his peace. When sin is consummated, the soul of man is always affected. It becomes a spiritual matter and it has an eternal impact. It is no longer an affair between man and his carnal desires, but between man and God.

▲　▲　▲

THE GLORY DEPARTED!

The eyes of Adam and Eve did not open with the knowledge of good as the serpent had told to them. They did not yet know that good departed from them and that from this day forward, nothing of what is called "good" would come out of them. They became sullied beings. It was evil that dominated their lives. The glory of God, which had been on them, was their covering, but they lost it. Let us read in Psalms *"For you have made him a little lower than the angels, and has crowned him with glory and honor."* (Psalm 8:5)

The glory of God departed from them once they sinned. God is Holy; His glory could no longer serve as a covering for sinful man. Satan, the biggest enemy of mankind, used man to destroy himself! He knew that Adam and Eve were crowned with God's glory. He was Jealous of their happiness, their great privilege of being in the presence of God, and of the honor, which was bestowed upon them. Adam and his wife, Eve, were stripped of all that is divine as a result of their moral choice, but they were not taken by surprise. They had received the order from God and He told them what would be the consequence if they did not obey.

For the first time of their existence, they were experiencing the reality of their soul plunging into deep darkness. Their biggest nightmare was the bitter experience of hiding far from the face of God. It meant that they deprived themselves of peace, joy, and of the goodness of the Lord. The light of God, which was in them, had gone out. Without this daily guide, man is lost.

It was hell on earth. These words were never spoken in their conversations before their disobedience, but now they were living it. It was chaos. They probably were living in anguish; they had moments of deep sorrow, and remorse. They undoubtedly shed bitter tears. It is the reaction that sin produces when it is gratified. The situation was so confusing that they did not know how to approach God. It was complete despair. The only thing that they could think to do was to hide far from His face. They were in the same garden, but far away from God—far removed from His face. That's the separation that sin produces between God and man. From that day on, there was an abyss between God and the humans that He had created.

Adam and Eve then realized that the serpent had lied to them, and that it was God who had been telling them the truth. The serpent had also disappeared far away from them. They could not find him to explain what had happened. They were probably asking themselves how they could find communion with God, peace, and joy again. The only thing that interested Satan then, and that still interests him now is the fall of man. Mental anguish, anxiety, desolation, tears, remorse, and the loneliness that occurs in an individual's life as a result of sin, does not interest him. He obtained what he wanted! It was the separation of Adam and Eve from their Creator. He takes pleasure in the suffering of man and he works incessantly to push man to disobey God. As soon as he succeeds, he moves on and leaves the victim alone to face the consequences of his actions.

God is holy; it is against His nature to cohabit with sin. He loves all of us; it brings Him sorrow when sin separates Him from His creations. In His love for Adam and Eve, seeing such suffering, such misery, He reached out to them. He was not going to leave them in the hands of Satan. *"And they heard the voice of the LORD God walking in the garden in the cool of the day: and Adam and his wife hid themselves from the presence of the LORD God amongst the trees of the garden. And the LORD God called unto Adam, and said unto him, where are you?"* (Genesis 3:8–9)

It was God who planted the garden in Eden; He knew perfectly well where they were. He questioned Adam on the state of his soul. Physically, they were in the middle of the garden, but spiritually they were lost. *"Adam answered, And he said, I heard Your voice in the garden, and I was afraid, because I was naked; and I hid myself."* (Genesis 3:10)

*He was not just afraid; he was tormented. It is written: "There is no fear in love; but **perfect love casts out fear: because fear has torment. He that fears is not made perfect in love.**" (1 John 4:18)* God's love for them didn't change. From this day forward, man can love God perfectly only through Jesus. He can have perfect peace when his mind is focused on God. *"You will keep him in perfect peace, whose mind is stayed on You: because he trusts in You. "(Isaiah 26:3)*

Adam heard the voice of God at the place where he sinned. To this day, God comes to us where we are in our sinfulness to save us. The feeling of hopelessness overwhelmed Adam and fear gripped him. He was afraid of the future, afraid of the consequences of his disobedience, afraid of the many questions he had and to which he had no answers. He and his wife were Afraid of the wrath of God and of his rejection. They were afraid of not being able to communicate with Him anymore.

Adam told God, "I was naked." The nakedness of the soul is worse than physical nakedness. You can sew fig leaves to cover physical nakedness. But only God can provide a covering for the nakedness of the soul. Everything that they had enjoyed, everything that they had possessed, belonged to God. Satan had nothing to give to them, except to condemn them day and night, because they had disobeyed the instruction God had given to them. However, God was not going to leave them in this state of despair.

▲　▲　▲

He came to them. In their state of sinfulness, they were unable to go to Him. Adam and Eve hid in the garden. The sinner always hides behind something. Whether it be alcohol, drugs, immorality, vices, material possessions or their success. We've seen great politicians, doctors, lawyers, musicians and many others fall in disgrace because of sin. Their success was what they hid behind until the day when this cancer called sin, which gnawed at them was exposed, and this was their downfall.

Man is always afraid of the consequences of his actions. He always sees the consequences after he has made his choice, despite knowing that the path he chose was not right. Later, he faces the reality of the high price that he has to pay for his poor choice. In Adam and Eve's disastrous situation, the only thing that was in their favor, it is that Adam could hear the voice of God calling him, and he answered. In any situation, no matter how horrific it is, if you can hear the voice of God calling you and you answer Him, this is the end and the beginning of everything. "... *Today, after so long a time; as it is said, today if you will hear His voice, harden not your hearts." (Hebrews 4:7)* Wherever you are in your earthly pilgrimage, if you hear God's voice calling you, answer Him.

THE PLAN OF REDEMPTION

THE INTERROGATION CONTINUES. Let's read God's reply to Adam in these verses in Genesis.

"And he said, who told you that you were naked? Have you eaten of the tree, whereof I commanded you that you should not eat? And the man said, the woman whom you gave to be with me, she gave me of the tree, and I did eat." (Genesis 3:11–12) This has been the problem with man since creation. He is always looking for someone else to blame for catastrophes of his own making. He never likes to take responsibility.

I would like to draw your attention to Adam's answer. He pointed the finger at Eve as being the one who was responsible for his disobedience. Adam knew that it was the serpent who had seduced his wife, when that happened, he was in the garden. However, at no time did the serpent have any dialogue with Adam, so, he could not tell God that it was the serpent who seduced him. If Adam had made such a statement, the serpent would have defended himself and told God that he never had any conversation with Adam. He would have been right and Adam would have passed as a liar.

Satan knew very well that after he had achieved his plan, God would question Adam because he was the one to whom the order had been given, and he was to pass it on to his wife. The responsibility of the garden was entrusted to Adam. The main character in the Garden of Eden was Adam. He was the target of Satan. Even though the enemy used the serpent to deceive Eve, he never told her to give the fruit to her husband. In fact, he did not even mention Adam's name to Eve in their conversation. He left the decision to Eve to give it to her husband. He wanted Eve to carry the sole responsibility for the fall of her husband.

To save his own skin, he seduced Eve to substantiate his defense. So, the blame could fall on her, since Adam could not point the finger at the serpent. Satan thought that by using the serpent as his instrument, he would be free of any consequences that would follow. Thereby, leaving the burden on Eve as the one who was responsible for the disobedience of her husband to God's order. And also since what he does best is accuse us before God, continually, it would be easier for him to accuse Eve before God, as the one who was responsible for giving the fruit to her husband. It is written in the Bible: *"And I heard a loud voice saying in heaven, now is come salvation, and strength, and the kingdom of our God, and the power of his Christ: for **the accuser of our brethren is cast down, which accused them before our God day and night**." (Revelation 12:10)*

Adam and Eve could not see Satan the instigator of their fall. God told Adam to watch over the garden. Therefore, it was his responsibility to watch for any intruders. However, Satan is a shrewd spirit that is beyond comparison with any other being created by God. He came with a strategy that no human being could discern. Only obedience to the word of God can spare a man from falling into Satan's traps.

What Satan has perhaps forgotten, or that he didn't know, is that God is omnipresent, omniscient, and omnipotent. He is everywhere, He knows everything, and He is Almighty. Satan did not know that man's fall would be his eternal defeat.

⋏ ⋏ ⋏

The interrogation continues.

"And the LORD God said unto the woman, what is this that you have done? And the woman said, the serpent beguiled me, and I did eat." (Genesis 3:13) Eve's answer to God pointed the finger to the serpent, to tell God that the serpent was responsible for her action. Although Satan was the author of Adam and Eve's fall, in reality, they were liable for their actions. God told Adam what would happen to him, if he did not obey His order.

The judgment of God that the devil had tried to avoid by using the serpent to deceive the woman, actually fell upon him. That is why he was the first one to receive his sentence in this judgment. God knew Satan's motives.

He was jealous of God's relationship with the man He created. It was a form of retaliation against God. He used the serpent to deceive Eve in order to inject his venom into the human race. *"And the LORD God said unto the serpent, because you have done this, you are cursed above all cattle, and above every beast of the field; upon your belly shall you go, and dust shall you eat all the days of your life." (Genesis 3:14)* God reduced the serpent to nothingness. It will forever remain the animal that is the most detested of all creations.

The following words were directly addressed to Satan. *"And I will put enmity between you and the woman, and between your seed and her seed; He shall bruise your head, and you shall bruise His heel." (Genesis 3:15)* That was to take place on the cross. God had a plan of redemption for the human race. The cross was introduced as the means to reverse the damage Satan inflicted upon the human race. It is the seed of the woman who shall bruise the head of the serpent. The seed of the woman is masculine; it is a "He." The seed of the woman is Jesus Christ, who was to be born to Mary.

Although the Catholic Church presents a statue of Mary with a serpent under her foot. God never assigned this mission to her. This is the fabrication of religion. It comes from the imagination of men. This image is inspired by Satan, who wants to undermine what has been said here—that Jesus, the seed of the woman, would destroy him at the cross. If Mary could have bruised the head of the serpent, that is to say, destroy his power, Jesus would not have needed to come to the world, go to the cross and shed his blood, for the remission of sins. God would have let Mary fulfill this mission. She was a virgin and the conception of Jesus was immaculate, coming from the Holy Spirit. This verse clearly explains it *"But while he thought on these things, behold, the angel of the Lord appeared unto him in a dream, saying, Joseph, you son of David, fear not to take unto you Mary your wife: **for that which is conceived in her is of the Holy Spirit**." (Matthew 1: 20)*

Even so, Mary inherited the sin nature due to her natural birth. The Bible declares, *"For all have sinned, and come short of the glory of God." (Romans 3:23)* The father and the mother of Mary had physical relations, a condition required between a man and his wife for the conception of a child. David wrote of this nature in Psalm 51, he said, *"Behold, I was shape in iniquity; and in sin did my mother conceive me." (Psalm 51:5)* He was not referring to the sexual act. He was saying that from conception the human being has inherited the sin nature. This is a nature in man that predisposes him to sin. It's a nature that is always rebelling against God and does the opposite of what He commands.

David was conceived by a mother who had the sin nature so it was passed on to him in the womb. Psalm 58 also speaks about the sin nature, inherited from conception. *"The wicked are estranged from the womb; they go astray as soon as they are born, speaking lies." (Psalm 58:3)* It is for this reason that we all need a savior.

Let us read together the salutation of the angel Gabriel, when he went to Mary to announce that she would give birth to Jesus. *"And in the sixth month the angel Gabriel was sent from God unto a city of Galilee, named Nazareth, to a virgin espoused to a man whose name was Joseph, of the house of David; and the virgin's name was Mary. And the angel came in unto her, and said, Hail, **you that are highly favored**, the LORD is with you: blessed are you among women." (Luke 1: 26–28)*

Mary found favor in the eyes of the Lord to fulfill this holy assignment. No one deserves the favor of God. But out of His goodness, He freely gives it to man. Here are the words which came from Mary's mouth after the angel Gabriel spoke to her: *"And Mary said, my soul does magnify the LORD, and my spirit has rejoiced in **God my Savior**. For He has regarded the low estate of His handmaiden: for, behold, from henceforth all generations shall call me blessed." (Luke 1:46–48)*

She called God "her Savior," therefore, proving that she felt the necessity of having a Savior. She was referring to her Son Jesus to whom she was going to give earthly life. He is the only Savior of man. And He was going to give eternal life to her in return. Because she was also in need of a Savior, she could not possibly be the Redeemer, nor Co-Redeemer, and in Catholic terminology Co-Redemptrix, of the human race. We must respect her and we must love her, but we should not worship her, or pray to her.

During Mary's earthly life, a woman wanted to praise her, listen to how Jesus responded to that. *"And it came to pass, as He spoke these things, a certain woman of the company lifted up her voice, and said unto Him, blessed is the womb that bare You, and the paps which You have sucked. **But He said, yea rather,***

blessed are they that hear the word of God, and keep it." (Luke 11: 27–28)
She was praising the womb that bore Jesus and the breast that nourished Him.

Jesus was saying to that woman, and to the rest of us that praise is due to God alone. It is not a question of exalting Mary to please Jesus, but rather to hear the word of God and to apply it in our daily life. The word of God forbids making carved images of Mary and praying to her. A true child of God would not participate in such activity.

Jesus is God. When He appeared to John on the island of Patmos, He identified Himself as follows: *"I am Alpha and Omega, the beginning and the ending, says the LORD, which is, and which was, and which is to come, the Almighty." (Revelation 1:8)* He has no beginning nor end. Creation begins with Him and ends with Him. This means that He created everything. Therefore, since He is God, He could not have a mother. Mary was born of her parents, then she died. The Scriptures speak of her as the mother of Jesus. *"These all continued with one accord in prayer and supplication, with the women, and* **Mary the mother of Jesus**, *and with his brethren." (Acts 1:14)*

When the Scriptures speak of her as the mother of Jesus, they are referring to the human nature of Jesus, His incarnation in Mary's womb as the Son of man, the Son of David. This is what the angel Gabriel said to Mary: *"And, behold, you shall conceive in your womb, and bring forth a Son, and shall call His name Jesus. He shall be great,* **and shall be called the Son of the Highest:** *and* **the LORD God shall give unto Him the throne of His father David"** *(Luke 1:31–32)*

Mary was a descendant of David. Therefore, Mary is the mother of Jesus, the Son of Man. The Son of David. Again, this is referring to the human nature of Jesus. He is the Son of God. He has never ceased to be God. However, in His incarnation, He took the human nature to fulfill His mission on the earth as Man. That's why, when speaking of His human nature, He is referred to as "the Son of Man, the Son of David." He is a descendant of David. Note that the angel told Mary, "You will conceive in your womb and **bring forth a Son.**" He did not say you will give birth to a Son. The Son she was to bring forth had always been. He is the Alpha and the Omega He has no beginning nor end. Jesus is the *only one* who came into this world and did not inherit the sin nature. His birth was supernatural! That's why He alone was qualified to crush the head of the serpent.

▲   ▲   ▲

Mary did not follow the earthly ministry of Jesus. The following passage of Scripture clearly shows this: *"While He yet talked to the people, behold, His mother and His brethren stood outside, desiring to speak with Him. Then one said unto Him, Behold, Your mother and your brethren stand outside, desiring to speak with You. But He answered and said unto him that told Him, who is My mother? And who are My brethren? And He stretched forth His hand toward His disciples, and said, behold My mother and My brethren! For whosoever shall do the will of My Father which is in heaven, the same is My brother, and sister, and mother." (Matthew 12:46–50)*

Jesus' mission was to bring back the lost human race to his Father from His own mother to the unknown person at the far end of the earth. His mother and His brothers were standing outside of the place He was ministering and they wanted Him to come outside to speak to them. They had a choice to make; stay outside or go in where Jesus was. He was always with them, but they did not believe in Him, that's probably why they were outside. There is nothing outside that interested Jesus that He would leave the work of His Father to go to them. It was up to them to come to Him and learn from Him.

To this day, there are a lot that are on the outside because they do not believe in Jesus. They want those who have made the choice to leave the world, and enter the kingdom of God (by putting their faith in Jesus and believing in His finished work on the cross to save their soul) to come on the outside to take part in the pleasures of this world. But there can never be fellowship between light and darkness.

However, things changed for His mother and His brothers. They became believers. They were no longer on the outside. On the day of Pentecost, Mary and the brothers of Jesus were among the disciples who were praying in the upper room, awaiting the promise of Holy Spirit He made. We read in the book of Acts: *"These all continued with one accord in prayer and supplication, with the women, **and Mary the mother of Jesus, and with his brethren**. And when the day of Pentecost was fully come, they were all with one accord in one place. And suddenly there came a sound from heaven as of a rushing mighty wind, and it filled all the house where they were sitting. And there appeared unto them cloven tongues like as of fire, and it sat upon each of them. **And they were all filled with the Holy Spirit, and began to speak with other tongues, as the Spirit gave them utterance."** (Acts 1:14, 2:1–4)*

Mary's Son saved her! He saved His brothers! What a glorious ending! It is well understood by now that the seed of the woman is Jesus. When God said to Satan, "you will bruise His heel" in Genesis 3:15, He was speaking of Jesus, the seed of the woman. God wasn't implying that Satan had so much power that he would hurt Jesus in this confrontation. It was in the plan of God, from the foundation of the world that Jesus would shed His blood on the cross for the remission of sins. It is by this sacrifice that He would redeem mankind. It is written in Hebrews: *"And almost all things are by the law purged with blood; and without shedding of blood is no remission." (Hebrews 9:22)*

▲　▲　▲

As we have seen previously, Satan injected the venom of sin into the human race in the Garden of Eden using a female serpent also known as the Jezebel spirit. Satan disguised himself as a female entity to bring down the human race. Jesus Christ, the seed of a female, the woman Mary, redeemed the human race by crushing "La serpiente" Satan's head on Calvary's cross. Jesus shed His blood to give eternal life to whoever believes in Him. It's a choice every man has to make. You can come where Jesus is, and receive eternal life, or you can stay on the outside, in this world that has nothing good to offer, and is under the control of the wicked one. If you choose to stay on the outside, it will cost you your eternal life.

THE VERDICT

THE SENTENCE OF Adam and Eve is pronounced.

The inequality between the man and the woman was the plan of the Jezebel spirit. It was never what God intended. To avoid any confusion, God gave the order to Adam, who had to transmit it to his wife. God would have confirmed that the instruction given to her by her husband, concerning the tree of the knowledge of good and evil, came from Him. God always does everything to perfection. He had not created one extremely strong, and the other one so weak, that she would be an easy prey in the hands of Satan. God did not give preference to Adam. Eve was not less important that God chose to give His order to Adam and not to her. It was not in the plan of God that one would have dominion over the other. This was God's original plan for them. *"And God blessed them, and God said unto them, be fruitful, and multiply, and replenish the earth, and subdue it: and have dominion over the fish of the sea, and over the fowl of the air, and over every living thing that moves upon the earth." (Genesis 1:28)*

God is omniscient. He knew what was going to happen. I think that He gave the order to Adam to transmit it to Eve, not only to avoid the "he said, she said" scenario, but also that each one would take responsibility for their action. There were no notes to compare. There was one order, given to Adam, and it was confirmed by God when he transmitted it to his wife. There was no inequality in the garden. It was the Jezebel spirit that hates men who destabilized the relationship of the couple. Keep in mind that the Jezebel spirit is Satan himself. The venom that the Jezebel spirit injected into Eve, was that she would dominate over Adam. From this day forward, Adam would be submitted to Eve and she would do what she wanted, when she wanted, where she wanted, and she did not have to be accountable to her husband. Satan was aiming at the family structure. He knew that the husband, who is under the authority of Jesus Christ, is the guardian of the home. If he can confuse him, or displace him, then he can enter that home and destroy anything he can get his hands on: The marriage, the children, the finances, etc. Everything is up for grabs once the father is absent.

A man doesn't have to leave his home to be an absent father. He can reside at the home and be oblivious to what's going on in his house, especially when the wife wants to take charge. To maintain the peace within the home, he takes the back seat and lets her rule. The result is almost always a disaster. On the other hand, it could be that he delegates the leadership of the home to his wife by his own volition. In some cases, the result remains the same: disaster.

It was Eve who had made her decision alone. She had not even asked her husband if she could eat of the fruit. She ate it, then passed it to her husband to consume. In all of that Adam lost his identity. He was confused. He betrayed his Creator and he did not know who he was anymore. Until today, thousands upon thousands of his children do not know who they are. That is why they end up incarcerated in prison. Or, you may see them roaming the streets with apathy. They are involved in all kinds of debauchery that ruin their lives. God addressed this problem in Eve's sentence for her disobedience.

> *"Unto the woman He said, I will greatly multiply your sorrow and your conception; in sorrow you shall bring forth children;* **and your desire shall be to your husband, and he shall rule over you."** *(Genesis 3:16)*

The Lord always has the last word. He overturned the counsel of Satan, by pronouncing these words on the woman, "your desire shall be for your husband, and he shall rule over you." God entrusted the dominion in their relationship to Adam. Dominion, not to beat her, demoralize her, revile her, or trample her underfoot, but to help her make the right choices. Her husband was to become her role model, who before doing anything, would seek God's approval in prayer.

The dominion was given to Adam to bring order to the family structure and to put the husband back in his rightful place. God wanted Eve to learn submission, and to be accountable to her husband. Through this order, the plan of the Jezebel spirit in which she gave dominion to the woman over the man would be ruined. Some men think that women are inferior to them because of the words spoken by God in this sentence. The Lord did not denigrate Eve in doing so. He placed her under her husband's protection. From that day on, the man became responsible for the spiritual direction of his household, which includes his wife, and his children.

From that day on, every woman who wants to dominate over her husband, and who refuses to allow him to exercise his leadership role in the home, is under the influence of the Jezebel spirit. The woman whose life is led by the Holy Spirit will be a helpmate to her husband. She will not be passive, but she will fulfill her duties next to him as God intended. The woman who is being led by the Holy Spirit, will recognize the importance of these words spoken by God. She will try her best to give way to her husband so that he can exercise such a noble role in the eyes of the Lord.

> *"And unto Adam He said, because you have hearkened unto the voice of your wife, and has eaten of the tree, of which I commanded you, saying, you shall not eat of it: cursed is the ground for your sake; in sorrow shall you eat of it all the days of your life; Thorns also and thistles shall it bring forth to you; and you shall eat the herb of the field; In the sweat of your face shall you eat bread, till you return unto the ground; for out of it were you taken: for dust you are, and unto dust shall you return." (Genesis 3:17–19)*

"In the day" that Adam and Eve ate the fruit of the forbidden tree they died spiritually. They could no longer stand in God's presence. They hid from Him. Spiritual death is the separation of the soul from God. However, the physical death sentence became effective later. Physical death is the separation of the soul from the physical body. *"And all the days that Adam lived were nine hundred and thirty years: and he died." (Genesis 5:5)*

⚔ ⚔ ⚔

Adam heeded the voice of his wife and ate from the forbidden tree. There is more to this than the eating of the forbidden fruit. The devil introduced God in this conversation, as the one who was not telling them the truth. The integrity of the Lord was questioned. However, the severity of the sentence proved who God is: The one who is in control of His creation. It also proved that the devil is a liar. The solution to remedy the situation was in God's hands. Before expelling them from the garden, God clothed them. *"Unto Adam also and to his wife did the LORD God make coats of skins, and clothed them." (Genesis 3:21)*

Adam and Eve had become sinners. The sinner will never be able to stand in the presence of a Thrice-Holy God. It is written in the Bible that the seraphim worship God and never ceased to proclaim His Holiness. *"And one cried unto another, and said, Holy, holy, holy, is the LORD of hosts: the whole earth is full of His glory." (Isaiah 6:3)* No, the sinner will never be able to stand in God's presence with what he has fabricated, sewed, or constructed. The fig leaves that Adam and Eve sewed for themselves were of no use.

God would never accept anything made by the hand of the sinner to resolve a spiritual problem. An innocent animal had to shed its blood for God to find coverings for them. ***"For the life of the flesh is in the blood: and I have given it to you upon the altar to make an atonement for your souls: for it is the blood that makes an atonement for the soul. For it is the life of all flesh;*** *the blood of it is for the life thereof: therefore, I said unto the children of Israel, you shall eat the blood of no manner of flesh: for the life of all flesh is the blood thereof: whosoever eat it shall be cut off." (Leviticus 17:11, 14)* This animal sacrifice was pointing to Jesus the Lamb of God who would later shed His blood on the cross to pay the debt of sin, so that man could be clothed in His righteousness. God clothed them with the skin of that animal symbolizing the righteousness of Christ. Then He expelled them from the garden.

THE CHOICE OF THE MAN

A DAM AND EVE inherited the sin nature. It was obvious in Eve's language after they left the garden. *"And Adam knew Eve his wife; and she conceived, and bare Cain, and said, I have gotten a man from the LORD." (Genesis 4:1)*

The words to look at in her statement are "I have"—clearly the focus is on herself. What she is saying here is that she is the one who, by her own ability, has gotten a man. She nevertheless, added, "From the Lord"—meaning that the Lord helped her. Even so, the Lord was in the background. The Bible says: *"Who can bring a clean thing out of an unclean? Not one." (Job 14:4)* This son, whom Eve claimed she had gotten, was the first murderer of the human race. Cain, by motives of jealousy, assassinated his brother, Abel.

Cain was a tiller of the ground and brought fruit as his offering to God. Abel was a shepherd and brought the first-born of his flock and their fat as his offering to God. The Lord accepted Abel's offering, but rejected Cain's. Their parents had undoubtedly told them the story of the Garden of Eden and how God had sacrificed an animal to clothe them. I strongly believe Cain and Abel fully understood the significance of what the Lord had done to provide coverings for their parents. This blood sacrifice is what afforded a temporary forgiveness of sin before the death of Jesus on the cross. Those animal sacrifices were a foreshadowing of the cross where Jesus would die to reconcile man to God. The blood of this innocent animal was their model of what it takes to make it right with God; not fig leaves.

The shed blood of the animal Abel offered to God, made his offering acceptable. Cain did not take that into account. He wanted to give to God the labor of his hands. It is written, ***"But we are all as an unclean thing,*** *and* *all our righteousness's are as filthy rags; and we all do fade as a leaf; and our iniquities, like the wind, have taken us away." (Isaiah to 64: 6)*

Sin has made all men unclean. Therefore, the Lord cannot accept anything from the sinner without the blood of Jesus, which cleanses every man who believes in Him of all unrighteousness. Salvation is a personal matter. Therefore, Abel's offering could not cover Cain. There is no substitution when it comes to the dealings between men and God. He is not interested in the works of our hands. First and foremost, He wants us to have a relationship with Him through the blood of His Son Jesus.

⋏   ⋏   ⋏

Anything man will do for God, or will offer to Him, is looked upon as "filthy rags," if it's not through Jesus Christ, who shed His blood on the cross. They are of no value and don't count for anything. We can say that Eve lost two sons, by the fact that God expulsed Cain far from the face of the earth. Up to this point, she was in total control of her family. I think the furnace of affliction changed her speech, after she went through this tragedy. She didn't express herself as she did when she first came out of the Garden of Eden. Listen to what she said thereafter: *"And Adam knew his wife again; and she bare a son, and called his name Seth:* **For God, said she, has appointed me** *another seed instead of Abel, whom Cain slew." (Genesis 4:25)*

The son she said *"I have gotten a man..."* was Cain, and he was a murderer. After the death of Abel, she conceived again, but this time, she said **"God has appointed me another seed instead of Abel, whom Cain slew."** Adversity had changed her speech from *"I have"* to *"God has."*

She was referring to the promise God made in the Garden of Eden, when He told the serpent the seed of the woman will bruise his head. It was not until she conceived her third son, we hear her name God as the one who is solely responsible of appointing the promised seed. She realized she would have no part in the seed God promised.

The seed would come forth from God and would be placed in the womb of the woman to become flesh, in order to fulfill His mission to save mankind from their sins. Jesus Christ, the seed of the woman, whom God was referring to in Genesis, and who would bruise the head of the serpent, was from the lineage of Seth, Eve's third son (the one she finally recognized was appointed by God). She understood then, what God has appointed is much better than what she can acquire or what she can designate herself. Furthermore, a man born the natural way could not fulfill the promise.

Eve's statement with regard to Cain, still resonates to this day. A lot of people have gotten things themselves that they think the Lord helped them acquire until failure sets in, then, they find out that the Lord was never in it. Their plan was of the flesh, or was inspired by the devil. Adam and Eve chose the lie and rejected the truth. As a result, they lost everything. From the joy that they had, they fell into desolation, and from abundance to lack. They wanted their independence, God gave it to them. However, along with it, from that day on, Adam would have to earn his living himself, by the sweat of his face.

Although Adam and Eve were created in the image of God and according to His likeness, He never called them *son* or *daughter*, or His children. He called them mankind. It is written in Genesis: *"Male and female created He them; and blessed them, and **called their name Adam,** in the day when they were created." (Genesis 5:2)* God called the first man Adam, which means "red earth" when He created him since he was formed with the dust of the earth. The meaning of the name Adam He called both in this verse *in the Hebrew is **mankind.***

Jesus is the only one God declared to be His Son. *"And lo a voice from heaven, saying, **this is my beloved Son,** in whom I am well pleased." (Matthew 3:17)*

If God had called Adam and Eve son and daughter, or His children, He never could have expelled them out of the garden. It is not His nature to expel His children, but He chastises them. If He had called them His children, He never could take away this title from them, even after their fall. The children who would be born of them would also be called children of God. He had been careful to inform the descendants of Adam and Eve that after their fall, the children who would be born of them would be born in their likeness after their image. It is extremely important that we understand what's being said here. *"And Adam lived an hundred and thirty years, **and begat a son in his own likeness, and after his image;** and called his name Seth." (Genesis 5:3)*

This verse clearly explains that the children of Adam and Eve are not sons and daughters of God but rather His creatures. They are begotten in the image of Adam in his own likeness. The sons and daughters of Adam and Eve are sinners. They have inherited the sin nature from their parents. The children of Adam and Eve are depraved, immoral, corrupt, murderers, jealous, envious, ungodly, malicious, thieves, idolatrous, traitors, drunkards, liars, slanderers, selfish, prideful, rebels, disloyal, avaricious, and ungrateful. How could a Thrice-Holy God live forever with sons and daughters of this nature? This is what Adam and Eve have inherited from Satan and transmitted it to their descendants. It is the sin nature that is wreaking havoc in the world in which we live.

▲   ▲   ▲

It is by the sacrifice of Jesus on the cross that those who accept Him as their Lord and Savior become children of God. *"But as many as received Him, to them gave He power to become the sons of God, even to them that believe on His name." (John 1: 12)* It is the children of Adam and Eve that murder one another. It is the sons of Adam that you see in the news with knives in hand decapitating other human beings just like animals are decapitated. It is the sons and daughters of Adam that assassinate thousands of babies by abortion in the womb of their mother. I heard a pastor say that "these babies feel the pain of the instrument which comes to destroy them in their mother's womb. They try to get far away from it, but they can't do anything. And they have nowhere to take refuge. They are too little to defend themselves." Those babies were destroyed before they had their chance to bring their contribution to earth.

Among the assassinated babies were doctors that will never see an operating room nor bring relief to a sick person through their treatments. There were professors who will never teach— no human life will ever be affected by their inborn greatness. There were pastors, evangelists and missionaries who will never exercise their ministries, as well as presidents and politicians who will never contribute to improving the quality of life for their constituents. Abortion, which is an odious crime, is the inheritance of the disobedience of Adam and Eve. The dollar is the driving force behind this industry. What you feel by reading this passage, I also felt. Pain gripped my heart as I wrote it. It is the sons and daughters of Adam and Eve that are drug traffickers affecting thousands of homes. As a result, many lives are destroyed. There are many young people who are incarcerated and who would never walk the streets as a free man or woman in their lifetime, because of crimes perpetrated by defending their territories.

The sons of Adam and Eve, steal, rape, and rape their own daughters and their own sons. The daughters and the sons of Adam and Eve, engage in prostitution, selling their body for a wage. The sons and daughters of Adam and Eve, practice homosexuality, forbidden by God. The sons and daughters of Adam and Eve, indulge in witchcraft and practice incest. God said to Moses to give the children of Israel His law concerning such practice. The following verses in" Leviticus 18: 6 – 18, 20 are God's warning against practices that are common among the sons and daughters of Adam and Eve.

6 None of you shall approach to any that is near of kin to him, to uncover their nakedness: I am the LORD.
7 The nakedness of your father, or the nakedness of your mother, shall you not uncover: she is your mother; you shall not uncover her nakedness.
8 The nakedness of your father's wife shall you not uncover: it is your father's nakedness.
9 The nakedness of your sister, the daughter of your father, or daughter of your mother, whether she be born at home, or born abroad, even their nakedness you shall not uncover.
10 The nakedness of your son's daughter, or of your daughter's daughter, even their nakedness you shall not uncover: for theirs is your own nakedness.
11 The nakedness of your father's wife's daughter, begotten of your father, she is your sister, you shall not uncover her nakedness.

12 You shall not uncover the nakedness of your father's sister: she is your father's near kinswoman.
13 You shall not uncover the nakedness of your mother's sister: for she is your mother's near kinswoman.
14 You shall not uncover the nakedness of thy father's brother, thou shalt not approach to his wife: she is your aunt.
15 You shall not uncover the nakedness of your daughter in law: she is your son's wife; you shall not uncover her nakedness.
16 You shall not uncover the nakedness of your brother's wife: it is your brother's nakedness.
17 You shall not uncover the nakedness of a woman and her daughter, neither shall you take her son's daughter, or her daughter's daughter, to uncover her nakedness; for they are her near kinswomen: it is wickedness.
18 Neither shall you take a wife to her sister, to vex her, to uncover her nakedness, beside the other in her life time." (Leviticus 18: 6 – 18)
20 "Moreover you shall not lie carnally with your neighbor's wife, to defile yourself with her."
"You shall not lie with mankind, as with womankind: it is abomination." (Leviticus 18:20, 22)

It is the sons and daughters of Adam and Eve who practice bestiality, and this is what God said against this practice: *"Neither shall you lie with any beast to defile yourself therewith: neither shall any woman stand before a beast to lie down thereto: it is confusion. Defile not ye yourselves in any of these things: for in all these the nations are defiled which I cast out before you."* (Leviticus 18: 23 - 24)

▲　▲　▲

Sin has reduced man to a level lower than the animals. It is not the animals that came towards man to mate with him. It is man who went after them to mate with them. Friends, all of these unclean practices you've just read are the products of the sin nature; it is horrible! There are not words, really, in the vocabulary of man to describe it. Do you see why Satan is the biggest enemy of man? It is he who has sullied the human race.

None of what you have just read resembles God. Throughout the ages, the violation of these divine laws has caused many people to shed bitter tears. You may not have practiced any of the sins mentioned above, but it was the sin nature that drove you to do what you did, and you have hidden it in the depths of your being. It is a secret that you want to forget, or bring under the proverbial "Let sleeping dogs lie." However, it is of utmost importance that you take this sin, or this vice, and confess it to the heavenly Father to obtain the forgiveness of your sins through the shed blood of Jesus Christ.

Jesus has issued a decree to man, He told Nicodemus, *"marvel not that I said unto you, you must be born again." (John 3:7) And* He did not leave this open for debate. The sons and daughters of Adam and Eve cannot inherit the Kingdom of God; they are too corrupt. They must be "BORN AGAIN," as Jesus said.

The biggest victory that a man can have is not over his enemies, or his problems during his pilgrimage on this earth, but over the enemy of his soul. This victory is obtained when Jesus Christ becomes his Lord and Savior. God in His infinite wisdom and goodness, knew what awaited the sons and daughters of Adam. He sent His Son Jesus, to deliver us from the grip of the wicked one and from the bondages of sin.

WHERE WERE YOU GOD?

MANY PEOPLE ASK a lot of questions concerning the fall of Adam and Eve. I often hear people ask, "Why did God allow the serpent to tempt Eve? Why didn't He stop him from getting to her?" If He had, we wouldn't have so many problems on the earth! The fall happened because of Eve's final decision. She had made up her mind that eating the fruit of the tree was the way to go, even though God commanded them not to eat it. Knowing the ruse of the enemy they were facing, God didn't leave them to deal with him on their own. They were crowned with God's glory and they were continually in His presence.

One thing we must know about Satan is that he is tenacious. He will continue to come back repeatedly until he weakens his prey or bends his will. God probably brought to Adam and Eve's remembrance numerous times that they were not to touch that tree. Eve probably ignored all the promptings of the Lord that tried to lead her away from that temptation. As He does often for us. It is written in the book of Job, *"For God speaks once, yea twice, yet man perceives it not. In a dream, in a vision of the night, when deep sleep falls upon men, in slumberings upon the bed; then He opens the ears of men, and seals their instruction, that He may withdraw man from his purpose, and hide pride from man. He keeps back his soul from the pit, and his life from perishing by the sword. (Job 33:14–18)*

When we face temptation, the word of God tells us that the Lord makes a way of escape, in order for us not to become a statistic in the hands of the evil one. (1Corinthians 10:13) The way of escape God made for all of us is to keep our mind focus on Jesus and His sacrifice on the cross. The Christian's place of victory, and also where the spirit who is behind the temptation was defeated. God has given us His word to teach us right from wrong, to teach us His will, and to let us know the things in life that are forbidden and that we shouldn't touch.

In addition, God uses people that we don't even know, who have no clue about what's going on in our lives, to talk about a particular issue that He is dealing with us, to bring us to the right path. He also tries to talk to us through the preaching of the word, or leads us to read a passage of Scripture. Or, we can hear that still small voice telling us to stay away from that business deal, that relationship, that friend, that magazine, that website, that job, to stop gambling, etc. When we do what we want to do, we do not take into account the word of God, we completely ignore it. We put a blind fold over our eyes and let whatever word that is coming to us fall on deaf ears. Then we completely shut that still small voice out from saying one more word. That's how determined we can be when we want our way.

There is one thing I am sure of; the Lord did everything He needed to do on His part to avoid this fall. When you look at the enormity of the cost of that fall, there was no reason for Him not to. God's creation was affected in its entirety. He had to become man to die an ignominious death on the cross to redeem His creation. He gave specific instructions to Adam concerning the tree. He, and his wife understood these instructions from God and they understood what the consequence would be if they disobeyed. I believe God allowed the serpent to engage Eve in this dialogue because she and her husband were well equipped to deal with Satan; they had His word.

Jesus' way of escape, when the devil came to tempt Him in the desert, was total submission to the will of His Father and Obedience to the written word of God. His mind was focused on His father. He obeyed what the word said instead of falling for Satan's lie. What Adam and Eve should have done in the Garden of Eden is what the Holy Spirit tells us to do in the New Testament. It works for many who have applied it to their lives. *"Submit yourselves therefore to God. Resist the devil, and he will flee from you." (James 4:7)* "Submit to God," means Adam and Eve's faith should have been exclusively in God, their

Creator. They should have submitted their will to God. They should not have been interested in any other means for obtaining whatever the serpent was offering to them. He offered the fruit to Eve, so that they could be elevated to the rank of God.

We should never accept any other means the devil may try to tempt us with, or any method invented by man to get the things we desire. Whether it be spiritual, material, physical or financial, except through the cross of Christ. The word of God is true. If they had submitted themselves to God and resisted the devil, he would have fled from them.

However, some people are so determined to have their way, they rather submit to the temptation of the devil, than to submit their will to God. That was the problem with man from the Garden of Eden, which still persists to this day. God gives us His word, we know what's forbidden, and we know sin has consequences.

When we start messing around with ungodly things, the Holy Spirit intervenes with the word of God to enlighten us, exhort us, rebuke us, and to bring us back to our senses. He does this so that we will be able to forsake the way of the enemy, but we often ignore God. We do what we want to do, because it feels good. We'd rather "…enjoy the pleasures of sin for a season." (Hebrews11:25) Afterwards, when we have to face the consequences of our actions, we start asking, "Why did God let that happen?" Thank God, He let it happen because, when it comes the will of man, it is God's last recourse. The consequence of that sin is what is going to bring us back home, because the pain is so unbearable. We need the Master's touch to bring healing and restoration. Thank God for Jesus, our Master.

⋏ ⋏ ⋏

People of God, nothing you do, or don't do, will neither diminish nor increase God's love for you. However, you need to know that when you are living in sin day in and day out, God is not happy about that. He loves you, but sins grieve Him; He is never happy about sin. He sent His Son, Jesus, to die on the cross for you and sent the Holy Spirit to help you live a victorious life in Christ. But, when you chose your ungodly lifestyle over the provision God made available to you, do you think He is happy about that? Anyone who tells you otherwise is trying to appease your conscience and make you feel comfortable in your ungodly lifestyle. They are an accomplice of Satan, the enemy of your soul, whose ultimate goal is to take you to hell. God's word to you is: Repent! In 2 Chronicles 7:14, God was speaking to His people. He called their sins "wicked ways" and His word to them was to repent and to turn from those "wicked ways." In our present time, our sins are still "wicked ways" in His sight. The forsaking of sins always brings comfort to the person who is not living right before the Lord. It always feels as though a truckload of dirt has lifted off of his, or her, soul.

Adam and Eve made the choice to eat the fruit of the tree of their own free will, and nothing was going to change that. The question which must be asked is not "Why God did not take His magic wand and hit the serpent in the head to avoid this nightmare?" But rather "Why have they disobeyed God, this Supreme Being who gave them everything?" On the spiritual plan, He crowned them with glory, and on the material plan, He placed at their disposal everything that they needed. The fault of Adam and Eve's fall lies not with God, but with man who wanted to be his own god. And it has not changed to this day.

At the present moment that you are reading this book, I wonder how many thousands of souls are going to perish in Hell, in the lake of fire, which was really prepared for Satan and his fallen angels and not for man. God informed these people in various ways about what would happen to them if they did not seek forgiveness for their sins through the blood of Jesus. They refuse to answer the call of God. They reject His Son Jesus, who alone has the power to spare man of such a destiny. And on the day of the great white throne judgment, when they receive their sentence, they will also say to God "Why did you not prevent the pleasures of this world from enticing me to the point of not answering your call." If you are among those people, I would not have wished it for you. It is not something that we would wish to happen to our worst enemy. If I could, I would ask you then, "Why didn't you answer God when you heard Him calling you?"

Man will do whatever he wants to do until the day he has to deal with the consequences of his actions. On that day, the fear of the Lord will come upon him. You never have to doubt the sincerity of a man with God after he has gone through the furnace of adversity. After he has sinned against God, and he is left to deal with the shame, the remorse, the hurt, the despair and the torment as a result of his sin. If he is a child of God, he will never touch that thing again that caused him so much grief.

Since the Garden of Eden, the pointing of fingers never stopped. Some people have said "they don't want anything to do with the gospel, because of the failures of some ministers of the gospel." People who think like that are in rebellion against God. There will come a day, the Day of Judgment, when they will not be able to stand before God and point their finger at men and women who have failed God, and use then the reason as why they never repented for their sins and accepted Jesus Christ as their Lord and Savior.

They will not be able to give such an excuse to God. The enemy may be pointing at ministers of the gospel who have failed God to discourage you from serving Him. But what he is not telling you is that those ministers who have failed, know God. And God loves them and He promised in His word not to forsake the believers. The Holy Spirit has and will continue to convict them for their sins. Some have repented and will make it right with God, while you are still dwelling on their sins and letting their failures be a stumbling block to the salvation of your soul.

Listen to me! Stop the finger pointing and stop making someone else responsible for your own rebellion toward God. Your excuses won't fly when you stand before God on judgment day. Adam and Eve tried it. Adam thought putting the blame on Eve, and Eve blaming the serpent, could exonerate them. It didn't spare them from God's judgment. However, there was a redemption plan put in place for mankind by God's grace to keep all, who would accept it, out of hell. Focus on the cure for your own sins, which is the blood Jesus Christ shed on Calvary's cross for you. You can be forgiven of all of your sins right now and make it to heaven if you take your eyes off the failures of mortal men and put them on Jesus Christ. He is the one who died on the cross for you, to give you eternal life, not the pastor to whom you are pointing your finger.

THE CROSS

Before the foundation of the world, the cross was in the mind of God. When He created the planet earth, He gave it four directions to which we refer to as the cardinal directions: north, south, east and west. When you draw a line to connect north and south, west and east you're looking at a sign that is similar to a cross, and that's not a coincidence. The Designer of planet earth designed a cross to give it its directions. For any person, any pilot or any captain of a ship to find their way around the world, they must rely on the four cardinal directions. The engineer and the architect must also rely on these directions to draw and execute their construction plans. If it were not for these cardinal directions, which form a sign similar to a cross, it would have been impossible for men to navigate around the world. The cross upon which Jesus the Lamb of God was slain was designed from the foundation of the world to give the inhabitants of earth direction to come back to God.

God is omniscient. He knew that man was going to fall. Therefore, the death of Jesus on the cross was in His plan, before the foundation of the world, to redeem His creation. 1 Peter 1:18 -20 tells us that Christ was foreordained before the foundation of the world, to redeemed mankind. *"Forasmuch as ye know that ye were not redeemed with corruptible things, as silver and gold, from your vain conversation received by tradition from your fathers; But with the precious blood of Christ, as of a lamb without blemish and without spot:* **Who verily was foreordained** *before the foundation of the world, but was manifest in these last times for you."* Also, Revelation 13:8 says that He is the Lamb slain from the foundation of the world. *"And all that dwell upon the earth shall worship him, whose names are not written in the book of life of the Lamb slain from the foundation of the world."* The cross was put in place from the foundation of the world. The plan for the lamb to be slain was also in place from the foundation of the world. Therefore, we can conclude that since the lamb was slain from the foundation of the world to redeem us, then Satan has been a defeated foe from the foundation of the world. Those of us who have made peace with God through the shed blood of Jesus Christ, the Lamb of God, are on the winning side.

One of the greatest inventions of our time is the (Global Positioning System) GPS. It has become an indispensable gadget for most people who rely on it to get from one destination to another. This system could not help us find our way around on earth without the four cardinal directions. It relies solely on them to direct and redirect us when we are lost. The cardinal directions, which form a cross, make it easy for people to go about their everyday lives wherever they are in the world. God wanted the cross to be the landmark of planet earth. In His Omniscience, He foresaw the fall of Adam and Eve and knew that man would lose his way. He chose the cross as the object upon which Jesus would be crucified and through which man would find his way back home to the Father. Man is a fallen creature. He is born lost and to find his way back home to the Father, he needs the cross of Christ. Otherwise, he will be lost forever because nothing else can bring him back home to God.

The cross was designed by God so that through it, man could find his way, not only in the natural, but also in the spiritual. He wanted to tell man that if they didn't rely on these cardinal directions they would never be able to move around, on land, in the air, or on the sea. No man can deny that. It is the same in the spiritual. If you reject the cross of Christ, you will never find your way back to the heavenly Father. He reconciled the world to Himself through the death of His Son Jesus on the cross.

"Now all things are of God, who has reconciled us to Himself through Jesus Christ, and has given us the ministry of reconciliation, that is, that God was in Christ reconciling the world to Himself, not imputing their trespasses to them, and has committed to us the word of reconciliation." (2 Corinthians 5:18-19)

So, when the inhabitants of Earth want to find their way back home to God, they can look at the cross and put their faith in Jesus who was nailed to the cross. That's how important the cross is to God. When He created man, the cross was in His mind.

▲   ▲   ▲

When a man stands up and spreads his arms you can see the shape of a cross.

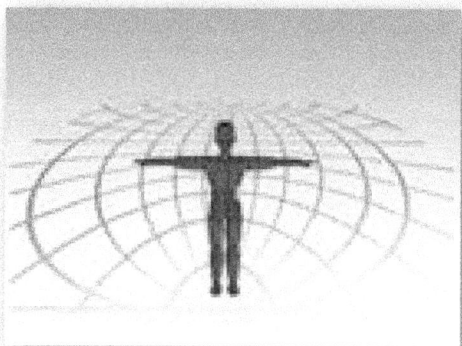

God could have created man with four arms and three legs, and no one would have found it awkward. He created man in the shape that would fit perfectly on a cross. Therefore, when Jesus the Son of God became man and had to die on the cross in order to pay sin's debt. He fitted the cross perfectly. He spread His arms upon it and died to save mankind.

When God commanded Moses to build the tabernacle, He described the furniture layout to be from the court to the Holiest place and it formed a cross. When He dictated to him the position of the twelve tribes of Israel around the tabernacle, their placement, to the North, to the South, to the East and to the West, also formed a cross. I used to be amazed when I looked at the pictures of the arrangement of the furniture in the tabernacle and of the twelve tribes of Israel around it and saw a cross, until the day it dawned on me that whatever is placed under these cardinal directions would always give you the picture of a cross. From the Old Covenant, to the New Covenant, the cross has always been a dominant presence because humanity's redemption depends on the Savior who died on it.

The salvation of the children of Israel depended on the Messiah Jesus Christ, who was to come to die on the cross. We receive our salvation when we put our faith in the Messiah Jesus Christ who came to earth, died on the cross, was resurrected from the dead, ascended to heaven, and is now seated at the right hand of the Father. Although the cross is a precious symbol of Christianity, we have to be careful not to worship those two pieces of wood affixed horizontally and vertically. The enemy is terrified of our Lord and Savior Jesus Christ who crushed his head on the cross. He is terrified of His blood, which ran on it. He is terrified of those who have a close relationship with Jesus Christ. When you read about the power of the cross in this book, it is referring to the power of Jesus Christ, who was nailed to it. There is nothing wrong with having a cross (without the carved image of Jesus) and putting it wherever you want, if you choose to do so. However, when you shift your faith from Jesus and put it in the wood to the point of believing it has the power to protect you, it is idolatry. When you buy a cross with a carved image of Jesus on it and you think it can keep your house safe from evil, it is idolatry. That image is the rendition of the imagination of an artist. It is not Jesus, and it is forbidden by God.

When you are watching a horror movie, and you see the devil running from a wooden or a metal cross, it is just a movie. There is no truth to it. It comes from religion. The devil would like you to believe that the piece of wood has the power. If you put your faith in this wooden piece, he is already a victor. However, when you put your faith in Jesus Christ and His finished work on the cross, you will triumph over every situation that has come from the pit of hell against you. It is the power of Jesus' blood that flowed on the cross which gives you protection and the enemy cannot penetrate it. With that power and protection, you can count on Jesus' word: *"Behold, I give unto you power to tread on serpents and scorpions, and over all the power of the enemy: and nothing shall by any means hurt you."* (Luke 10:19)

There are many people who have no relationship with Jesus Christ, but they have used the cross, the symbol of Christianity, as something they can rely upon for protection. They put it in their cars, in their homes, and around their neck as jewelry, but it is just that—a piece of jewelry. It has no power whatsoever and it can't protect them against anything. They think all they need is a cross for the devil to take flight. ***In the finished work of Jesus on the cross***, (not the wooden beam) ***resides the invisible power of God.*** The invisible power of the cross is the triumph of Jesus Christ over all the forces of hell that came against Him. *"Having spoiled principalities and powers, He made a show of them openly,* *triumphing over them in it. (Colossians 2:15)* The **cross is an invincible weapon** because of **the blood of the Lamb**, Jesus Christ that was shed on the cross. *"And they overcame him by the blood of the Lamb, and by the word of their testimony; and they loved not their lives unto the death." (Revelation 12:11)*

The emphasis is put on the cross because without proper understanding of the purpose of the cross of Christ, man will never be able to understand God's plan for the salvation of his soul. He will not find his way back to God and he will not be able to live a victorious life in Christ. His wellbeing and his joy, everything that affects his life on every level: spiritual, material, emotional, physical and financial, were addressed at the cross. The incurable cancer, called sin, that ravages the soul of man, was eradicated at the cross by Jesus Christ who took away the sin of the world.

⋏　⋏　⋏

When the apostle Paul talked about the cross in his epistles, he was not talking about the symbol of Christianity, the two pieces of wood affixed vertically and horizontally, but of the man Christ Jesus, who defeated Satan at the cross. In his letter to the Corinthians, Paul described the message of the cross or the preaching of the cross as being "Christ the power of God, and the wisdom of God." (1 Corinthians 1:18, 24) That's why it is inexhaustible. The message of the cross or the preaching of the cross is all about Jesus Christ. From His birth to His ascension at the right hand of the Father and even includes His return. If He had not died on the cross, He could not have ascended to heaven victorious over sin, death and hell. If He had not died on the cross, He could not return to take the church with Him (1 Thessalonians 4: 13-18) and after that come back to earth in Glory to reign eternally. (Matthew 24:30) In human terms, we can say the message of the cross is the spinal cord of the gospel. If a person's spinal cord is damaged, he becomes paralyzed. When the message of the cross is omitted from the gospel, it becomes crippled and ineffectual.

It is imperative to know that no one can get saved outside of the sacrifice of Jesus on the cross. After the fall, man became a fragmented being. The purpose of the cross is to restore man— to make him whole again and to reconcile the lost humanity to God. After Adam and Eve disobeyed God, mankind fell into the horrible pit of sin. In Psalm 40, David describes what we can attribute to the condition of the sinful man and the cross of Christ. *"He brought me up also out of a horrible pit, out of the miry clay, and set my feet upon a rock, and established my goings." (Psalm 40:2)* Nothing but the death of Jesus on the cross was designed by God to bring man out of the horrible pit of sin. And there is no pit that is as horrible as the pit of sin. It contains miry clay, which represents the bondages of which man can't free himself. Picture a pit of miry clay: with every step that you would take on your own to come out, the other foot would get you deeper into it. All it does is mar its victims. It is impossible for man to get out of that pit unless he gets help. That's the reason for the cross! It sets man's feet on the solid Rock, which is Jesus Christ. Only His sacrifice on the cross can establish the steps of man. One Christian Hymn says: "All other ground is sinking sand."

I say it to you again, look to Jesus! Your faith must be in Him, not in the two pieces of wood affixed horizontally and vertically, the symbol of Christianity, even though it is very precious to the Christians. When you hear the word *"**cross**,"* let your mind focus on the great victory that Jesus won on the cross over the kingdom of darkness for us. The cross speaks of the limitless love of God for mankind. Jesus suffered the most atrocious and humiliating death anyone could have. He chose to go to the extreme and pay the highest price for the redemption of man.

The debt of sin that Jesus paid for you and for me, by hanging on the cross, was the most lugubrious hours of His earthly ministry. It was the first time that Jesus felt a separation between Him and His Father and it was real to Him. *"And about the ninth hour, Jesus cried out with a loud voice, saying, "Eli, Eli, lama sabachthani?" That is to say, "My God, My God why have you forsaken Me?" (Matthew 27:46)* The human mind could never come up with any words that could explain what He felt at that moment. However, David, inspired by the Holy Spirit, prophesied about Jesus' crucifixion approximately one thousand years before Jesus' death on the cross. He wrote the same words Jesus spoke on the cross *"My God, My God, why have you forsaken Me?" (Matthew*

27:46) in the beginning of Psalm 22:1. These words give us a glimpse of what Jesus was going through that day.

▲　▲　▲

Death by crucifixion was a common practice at the time of Jesus' death. The Bible says, *"Then were there two thieves crucified with him, one on the right hand, and another on the left." (Matthew 27:38)* However, the death of Jesus on the cross cannot be compared to the death of those two thieves, nor any man who had died before him, or after him on a cross, no matter how horrific their death may have been. Jesus had a lot more to deal with. On the day of His crucifixion, there was much more going on than the natural eyes could see, or the human mind could comprehend. He had to face the visible and invisible worlds. The following verses, in Psalm 22, prophetically described the horrors on the day of His crucifixion.

> *"Many bulls have compassed Me: strong bulls of Bashan have beset Me round. They gaped upon Me with their mouths, as a ravening and a roaring lion. I am poured out like water, and all My bones are out of joint: My heart is like wax; it is melted in the midst of My bowels. My strength is dried up like a potsherd; and My tongue cleaves to My jaws; and You have brought me into the dust of death. For dogs have compassed Me: the assembly of the wicked have enclosed Me: they pierced My hands and My feet. I may tell all My bones: they look and stare upon Me. They part My garments among them, and cast lots upon My vesture." (Psalm 22:12-18)*

As for what the human mind could comprehend and the eyes could see, the soldiers arrested Jesus in the garden of Gethsemane and bound Him. When they came to arrest Him *"Then Jesus said unto the chief priests, and captains of the temple, and the elders, which were come to Him, Be you come out, as against a thief, with swords and staves? When I was daily with you in the temple, you* *stretched forth no hands against Me: but **this is your hour, and the power of darkness.**" (Luke 22:52 -53)*

He had to go through a rigorous trial. Pontius Pilate and Herod were enemies; yet on that day, they put their differences aside, and they became friends with the sole purpose of killing Him.

The mockers, the traitors and the liars were in His face spitting on Him, beating, and slapping Him, lying and accusing Him. They flogged Him, and put a crown of thorns on His head. And, worst of all, the religious leaders were among His accusers. Even though His strength dried up, He still had to carry the crossbeam. In addition to that, He had to endure the physical pain of His bones being out of joint. Bear in mind that Jesus was going through this ordeal as a man. His strength dried up, which made it difficult for Him to walk all the way to Calvary with the cross on His shoulders. The soldiers summoned a passerby to come and help Him. *"Now as they led Him away, they laid hold of a certain man, Simon of Cyrenian, who was coming from the country, and on him they laid the cross that he might bear it after Jesus." (Luke 23:26)* Jesus poured Himself out entirely for this cause.

The suffering was so great, the Bible said: *"They gave Him vinegar to drink mingled with gall: and when He had tasted thereof, he would not drink." (Matthew 27: 34)* It was a mixture that was similar to a narcotic. It was given to Him to dull His pain but He refused it. He endured the physical pain, to its fullest, so He could identify with our pains.

He was so thirsty, His tongue clung to His jaws, and when He said "I thirst," this time they gave Him sour wine without the gall to drink. John 19:29. It was a fulfillment of Scripture, for it is written: *"They gave Me also gall for My meat; and in My thirst they gave Me vinegar to drink." (Psalm 69:21)* There is nothing man can offer that can alleviate the suffering of the soul. The only one who could help Jesus in this situation was His Father, to whom He had already cried out. His Father didn't move from His position. Psalm 22:24 says it best, *"For He had not despised nor abhorred the affliction of the afflicted; neither had He hid His face from Him; but when He cried unto Him, He heard."* Jesus was fulfilling His mission, to save His people from their sins and to crush Satan's head. Even though His Father saw what was happening, and heard Him cry out, He was not going to intervene. Jesus had to go through this alone as a man.

The cross represents pain, heartache, loneliness and death. It is also a place of great triumph.

⟁⟁⟁

They divided His garments—

*"Then **the soldiers, when they had crucified Jesus, took His garments, and made four parts, to every soldier a part;** and also His coat: now **the coat was without seam, woven from the top throughout. They said therefore among themselves, let us not rend it, but cast lots for it, whose it shall be:** that the scripture might be fulfilled, which said, they parted My raiment among them, and for My vesture they did cast lots. These things therefore the soldiers did. (John: 19: 23-24)*

It is possible that there were only four soldiers who were left at the cross to finish Jesus' execution. If it were so, even the number of soldiers was designated by God. Regardless of the number of soldiers who were there, the amazing thing is that the soldiers, unaware of what they were doing divided His garments of righteousness into four parts.

This Symbolized, from that day forward Jesus' righteousness was extended to the four corners of the earth. Remember, from the foundation of the world, God gave the earth four directions — north, south, east and west, — which form a picture that resembles a cross when a line is drawn horizontally and vertically to connect them. It was in the mind of God from the foundation of the world, that Jesus' death on the cross would extend His righteousness to people in the four corners of the earth. *John 3:16 declares: "For God so love the world that He gave His only begotten Son, that whosoever believes in Him should not perish but have everlasting life."*

⟁⟁⟁

They didn't divide His coat—
They cast lots for His coat or tunic, but they didn't divide it, like they had done with His garments. The tunic was a beautiful piece of cloth, of high value in their eyes. They gambled for it, but only one soldier took it home with him. ***"The tunic was without seam, woven from the top in one piece."*** That is a perfect picture of salvation. It's perfect, it's whole, and there is nothing to add to it. It is seamless, priceless, and it cannot be divided. You can't tear it because it's too precious. It cost Jesus His life.

Salvation should be desired by everyone, and it's available to anyone who desires it. No one needs to cast lots for it. It's a gift from God! Jesus paid the ransom for us to get it free. The soldiers weren't aware of what they were doing, but what they did had great spiritual truth. Salvation is personal you can't share it with anyone. That's why only one soldier took the tunic (a picture of salvation) home. It is given to whoever wants to receive it. You cannot see how beautiful, how precious and how priceless it is, until you open your heart to receive it. And the only way to receive it is to repent of your sins, and ask Jesus to come into your heart as your Lord and Savior.

▲ ▲ ▲

Moreover, for what the eyes could not see, Jesus had to face Satan himself, and all the forces of hell that came against Him. Jesus called this moment "the hour of the power of darkness" Those strong bulls of Bashan, and dogs spoken of in Psalm 22 were all the demons —the fallen angels of hell —with Satan their chief at the head. Those wicked spirits encircled Jesus; they wanted to devourer Him alive. *"Many bulls have compassed Me: strong bulls of Bashan have beset Me round. They gaped upon Me with their mouths, as a ravening **and a roaring lion**. For dogs have compassed Me: the assembly of the wicked have enclosed Me: they pierced My hands and My feet." (Psalm 22:12-13, 16)*

Satan is described as a raging and ***roaring lion***. Peter wrote in his first epistle, *"Be sober, be vigilant; because your adversary the devil, as **a roaring lion**, walks about, and seeking whom he may devour." (1 Peter 5: 8)*

On that day, at Calvary, the greatest battle for the soul of man was being fought. All this pain and suffering was for me and you— to save our soul! For

Jesus to have suffered as much as He did for the salvation of man, is a matter no man should take lightly.

Afterwards, He gave His life and died on the cross. Jesus endured this atrocious death so that, *"All the ends of the world shall remember and turn unto the LORD: and all the kindreds of the nations shall worship before you."* (Psalm 22:27)

The glorious end to the account of the death of Jesus is that, after three days, He rose from the dead. He came out of the tomb a conqueror— triumphant over Satan and his demonic angelic hosts, death and the grave. Brother Lowry, who has long been with the Lord left us this beautiful song to sing and to celebrate His victory.

> *"Up from the grave He arose,*
> *With a mighty triumph o'er His foes,*
> *He arose a victor from the dark domain,*
> *And He lives forever, with His saints to reign.*
> *He arose! He arose!*
> *Hallelujah! Christ arose!"*
> *Robert Lowry (1874)*

▲ ▲ ▲

I could not leave out this great accomplishment of Jesus' death on the cross. *"And you, being dead in your sins and the uncircumcision of your flesh, has He quickened together with Him, having forgiven you all trespasses; Blotting out the handwriting of ordinances that was against us, which was contrary to us, and took it out of the way, nailing it to his cross."* (Colossians 2:13-14)

No man could keep the perfect law of God given to Moses. They were contrary to man's sinful nature. James wrote, *"For whosoever shall keep the whole law, and yet offend in one point, he is guilty of all."* (James 2:10) Mankind was continuously culpable in the eyes of God because we were always transgressing His law, and this verdict hindered us from having a close relationship with Him. Jesus kept the law in its entirety. He never transgressed any of them. The law was fulfilled in Him and His death nailed the law to the cross.

Those who have accepted Him as their Lord and Savior are no longer guilty in the eyes of God. We find forgiveness for our transgressions of the perfect law of God through His shed blood on the cross. We are no longer hindered. We have access to our Heavenly Father any time of the day, or night, when we call on Him in the name of Jesus. The cross has daily benefits. *"Blessed be the LORD, who daily loads us with benefits, even the God of our salvation. Selah."* *(Psalm 68:19)* It is of His good pleasure to daily load us with benefits that are spiritual, physical, emotional, financial and even protects us from premature death. When we take our cross daily and follow Him. That is when our faith is anchored in Him and we submit ourselves daily to Him.

From the day of the death of God's Son at Calvary and eternally, all that God will do for man will be because of the blood of His Son Jesus shed on Calvary's cross. Jesus paid the ultimate price, in order to bring man back to perfect communion with his Creator. He endured the separation that He felt between Him and His Father so that man could be reconciled to God. Anyone who accepts Jesus as his or her Lord and Savior will never have to go through the separation that sins produce between the unregenerate man and God and experience eternally what Jesus felt on that day.

THE MISSIONARY AND THE CROSS

N O MAN CAN do anything for God if he does not make peace with him by the shed blood of Jesus upon the cross. When God had to send Moses to Egypt to deliver His people from Pharaoh, Moses didn't want to go. He tried to escape this mission by giving excuses to God. One of the reasons he refused to go was because he thought that the children of Israel would not believe that God had sent him. Then God gave him signs, which he had to perform in front of them, which would confirm that He had sent him. These signs were also types and symbols, which addressed the sin nature and the role of the cross in the deliverance of mankind. Moses was a shepherd; he had a rod in his hand. *"And the Lord said unto him, what is that in your hand? And he said, a rod. And he said, Cast it on the ground. And he cast it on the ground, and it became a serpent; and Moses fled from before it." (Exodus 4:2-3)*

In this context, the serpent is a type of the sin nature. Every man is horrified of this nature. It is frightening and it has never produced anything beneficial to man.

"And the LORD said unto Moses, put forth your hand, and take it by the tail. And he put forth his hand, and caught it, and it became a rod in his hand (Exodus 4:4) It was God who pointed out to Moses how to lay his hand on the serpent, that he should take it by the tail. No man is capable of handling sin as he wants. No man has any authority over sin. It has the power to gulp him down alive. The head is always the predominant position— the position of authority. Jesus is the only one who has the power, and the authority to take the serpent by the head. His Father had already entrusted this mission to

Him. The rod is a type of the cross, and the serpent is a type of the sin nature. It is represented in the form of a serpent because it was the serpent that introduced sin into the Garden of Eden, and it entered the human race by Adam's disobedience. When Moses took it by the tail, it became a rod again. The rod and the serpent became one. The serpent could no longer be seen. When the sin nature unites with the cross, it becomes inactive in the believer's life and it cannot prevail any more in that life. When you put your faith in Christ, and your sins are forgiven that's what happens. Your sins unite with the cross; God does not see your sins anymore, but the cross upon which His Son Jesus shed His blood.

> *"And the LORD said furthermore unto him, Put now your hand into your bosom. And he put his hand into his bosom: and when he took it out, behold, his hand was leprous as snow. And He said, put your hand into your bosom again. And he put his hand into his bosom again; and plucked it out of his bosom, and, behold, it was turned again as his other flesh." (Exodus 4:6-7)*

Leprosy is a symbol of sin in the Scriptures. God wanted to show Moses that sin resides in him. He made Moses put his hand back in his bosom. The solution to get rid of our sins is not that simple. Man can see sin in his life, but he will be never able to get rid of it. Moses could not get rid of the sin nature on this earth either. This will happen when we have our glorious body in heaven. Sins affect the soul of man, therefore, it is a spiritual problem. Sin was introduced into the Garden of Eden by an evil spirit, and entered the human race through Adam. It had to be eradicated out of the human race by a Spirit that is Mightier than the one who introduced it. It was introduced by Satan and it was eradicated by the Lord God Almighty who became man and took away the sin of the world by His death on the cross.

God wanted to reveal to Moses what he had in him, so that Moses, and all of the generations later, would read these passages of the Bible and would know that he had a sin nature, just like the rest of us. He found grace in the eyes of the Lord to fulfill this great task and there was nothing good in him that could qualify him for this mission.

God said again to Moses, *"And it shall come to pass, if they will not believe also these two signs, neither hearken unto your voice, that you shall take of the water of the river, and pour it upon the dry land: and the water which you take out of the river shall become blood upon the dry land." (Exodus 4:9)*

It is extremely important that we understand the process Moses had to go through to be prepared for this great task. All the elements that involved the salvation of man were addressed. We have two elements here "blood" and "water" These two elements bring us to the day of Jesus' crucifixion. *"But one of the soldiers with a spear pierced his side, and forthwith came there out blood and water." (John19:34)*

The blood on the earth typified the atoning blood of Jesus, which would be poured on the earth, on the day of His crucifixion to save the inhabitants of the earth from their sins. The water was a symbol of the Holy Spirit. God didn't send Moses to Egypt to perform these signs to impress Pharaoh and his magicians. Moses needed the anointing of the Holy Spirit and the atoning power of the blood as a covering to equip and protect him against the forces of hell that he had to confront. All of these signs were pointing to the cross. When it was time for Moses to return to Egypt for his mission, "…he took the rod of God in his hand." (Exodus 4:20)

It was not the simple rod of a shepherd anymore. It was not Moses' rod anymore, but the rod of God. It was a type of the cross. Without the cross, man is useless to God. All three elements that are involved in the salvation of man were present in this account. The rod typified the cross, the blood of Christ atoned for all sins and the water, which is a symbol of the Holy Spirit who convicts the sinner of sins to bring him to Christ and He also anoints God's servants for service. God cannot use any man if he doesn't address the issue of sin in his life. God prepared Moses for this great mission Himself.

When Moses arrived in Egypt with Aaron, his brother, they had to perform the signs that the Lord had commanded them to do. When Aaron threw the rod down, it transformed into a serpent. Pharaoh then called his magicians who dropped their rods also. Their rods were transformed into serpents as well, but the rod of Aaron swallowed them. As we've already seen, the rod of Moses, which Aaron threw down, was a type of the cross.

▲   ▲   ▲

The cross can defend itself when facing the enemy. It will swallow up all false doctrines. It will expose all false prophets. It will cause all the enemies of God to flee and will triumph over all those who oppose it. It was in the mind of God before the foundation of the world. On it was nailed Adonai, the King of kings, the Lord of lords, the Most- High, the Alpha and the Omega, the Lion of the tribe of Judah, The Almighty God, the Creator of heaven and earth, the Son of the living God, The great I AM, JESUS CHRIST!

Millions upon millions of people across the world can testify of the numerous blessings they have received from it. And for eternity, we will not cease thanking Jesus for His death on the cross to save our souls from the horrors of hell. When the children of Israel were in front of the Red Sea, and Pharaoh's army was in their pursuit, they were gripped by fear. They were screaming, not knowing where to go. *"And the Lord said unto Moses, wherefore do you cry unto Me? Speak unto the children of Israel that they go forward. **But you lift up your rod,** and stretch out your hand over the sea, and divide it: and the children of Israel shall go on dry ground through the midst of the sea." (Exodus 14:15-16)*

Oh what a phenomenon! God told Moses *"**lift up your rod**"* that's the invisible power of the cross, when it's lifted up. Power to divide a sea and let the children of Israel pass through it on dry ground. It is the invisible power that liberates the people of God in their most difficult situations, their most bitter trials, their most painful experiences, their merciless bondages of sins and poverty, and this power heals every disease known to mankind.

Let's look again at what God told Moses concerning the water. *"And it shall come to pass, if they will not believe also these two signs, neither hearken unto your voice, that you shall take of the water of the river, and pour it upon the dry land: and the water which you take out of the river shall become blood upon the dry land." (Exodus 4:9)*

The water that flowed from Jesus' side on the cross is the "living water" He spoke of to the Samaritan woman He met at the well. This story is recorded in the book of John. *"Here comes a woman of Samaria to draw water: Jesus said unto her, give me to drink. Then said the woman of Samaria unto Him, how is it that you, being a Jew, asks drink of me, which am a woman of Samaria? For the Jews have no dealings with the Samaritans. Jesus answered and said unto her, If thou knew the gift of God, and who it is that said to you, give me to drink; you would have asked of Him, and* **He would have given you living water**. *The woman said unto Him, Sir, You have nothing to draw with, and the well is deep: from whence then have you that living water? Jesus answered and said unto her, whosoever drinks of this water shall thirst again: But whosoever drinks of the water that I shall give him shall never thirst; but the water that I shall give him shall be in him a well of water springing up into everlasting life. (John 4: 7, 9-11, 13-14)*

The woman was speaking to the gift of God to the world. In John 3:16 Jesus is the gift of God to the world. Later in that conversation, Jesus revealed to the woman that He is the Messiah. Jesus explained in the book of John that "the living water" that would flow out of the believer is the Holy Spirit. *"In the last day, that great day of the feast, Jesus stood and cried, saying,* **if any man thirst, let him come unto Me, and drink. He who believes on Me, as the scripture has said, out of his belly shall flow rivers of living water. (But this spake He of the Spirit, which they that believe on Him should receive: for the Holy Spirit was not yet given; because that Jesus was not yet glorified.)" (John 7:37-39)**

When a person is born again the regenerating power of the Holy Spirit transforms that life. The living water that will spring up into everlasting life is God, the Holy Spirit, taking up residence in the heart of the believer. "Living Water" is in the heart of that believer, therefore, rivers of living water will flow out of that heart. Paul wrote *"Know you not that you are the temple of God, and that the Spirit of God dwells in you?" (1 Corinthians 3:16)*

Jesus was glorified two thousand years ago. The living water flowed from His pierced side on the cross. The Holy Spirit flows from Jesus. The Bible says He had the Spirit without measure. After Jesus' ascension, the disciples were baptized in that living water on the day of Pentecost when the Holy Spirit descended upon them. This is the only water that will quench the thirst in the soul of man.

▲　▲　▲

God ordered Moses to "pour water on the dry ground which would become blood." You cannot separate the water and the blood. The water became blood. You can't separate the Holy Spirit and the blood of Jesus which flowed on the cross. John said of Jesus *"And I knew Him not: but He that sent me to baptize with water, the same said unto me, **upon whom you shall see the Spirit descending, and remaining on Him,** the same is He which baptizes with the Holy spirit." (John: 1:33)*

Jesus is the one who baptizes with the Holy Spirit. They work in perfect harmony as one. In the Old Testament when a prophet had to perform a task for God, the Holy Spirit would come upon him and once the task was completed, He would leave. But with Jesus, it was different. The Holy Spirit descended upon Him and *He remained.* He never left Him; the two are inseparable. When you reject the cross of Christ, you reject the blood, you also reject the Holy Spirit. When Moses poured the water on the ground, it became blood. Water and Blood, simultaneously flowed from Jesus' side. You can't reject one and keep the other; it doesn't work that way.

When Jesus is no longer preached in the church, when the cross is laid aside, and the believer doesn't seek Him to have a close relationship with Him, that flow of water (the Holy Spirit) will be interrupted. When the river is polluted with the profane things of this world, the result will be spiritual drought. When a mister of the gospel wants the power of the Holy Spirit in his ministry and he rejects the cross of Christ upon which Jesus' blood ran, he opens his ministry to demons to come and operate lying, and deceiving so- called miracles. Once the cross of Jesus Christ upon which His blood ran is laid aside, the Holy Spirit is laid aside as well.

▲　▲　▲

TAKE UP YOUR CROSS

*"And **He said to them all**, if any man will come after Me, let Him deny Himself, and take up his cross daily, and follow Me." (Luke 9:23)* He said it to all, without exception and **his disciples were included**. Mark wrote similarly about this meeting: *"And **when He had called the people unto Him with His disciples also,** He said unto them, whosoever will come after Me, let him deny himself, and take up his cross, and follow Me." (Mark 8:34)*

Jesus is not asking anyone to carry their cross as He did. Many people interpret this verse as saying that it means to carry their burdens, their problems, their sickness, or whatever situations that may be out of their control. If Jesus was telling us to carry our own cross, Isaiah would not have prophesied about Him in these terms: *"He is despised and rejected of men; a man of sorrows, and acquainted with grief: and we hid as it were our faces from Him; He was despised, and we esteemed Him not. Surely He has borne our griefs, and carried our sorrows: yet we did esteem Him stricken, smitten of God, and afflicted. But He was wounded for our transgressions, He was bruised for our iniquities: the chastisement of our peace was upon Him; and with His stripes we are healed. He was oppressed, and He was afflicted, yet He opened not His mouth: He is brought as a lamb to the slaughter, and as a sheep before her shearers is dumb, so He opened not His mouth. Yet it pleased the LORD to bruise Him; He has put Him to grief: when You shall make His soul an offering for sin, He shall see His seed, He shall prolong His days, and the pleasure of the LORD shall prosper in his hand." (Isaiah 53: 3-5, 7, 10)* These few verses selected from chapter 53 of the book of Isaiah, allow us to see what the cross Jesus bore for us was about.

Your illness is not your cross, if you are healed by Jesus' stripes how could your sickness be your cross to bear? If He suffered so much for us on the cross, how could He now ask us to take up oppression, torments, anxiety, rejection, affliction, diseases, grief, sorrow anguish and all the calamities our shoulders and carry them daily to follow him? If that was the case, what would be the purpose of the cross? He bore them on the cross so that we can be free.

It is because of sin that this cross was manifested into the world. Jesus carried it for you so that you can have peace and be free. He could not then ask you to carry your own cross too. When I read these verses of Isaiah, chapter 53, I was forever grateful to Jesus for the great price He paid to give me rest, and it's available to anyone who wants it. The cross that Jesus asks all of us, including His disciples, to take up daily is to submit ourselves, our will to Him daily. This is not an easy task for the man who wants to be his own god.

We must have fellowship with Jesus in prayer and in reading the Bible to help us grow in the knowledge of God every day. We must keep our faith in Him and His finished work on the cross every day. We must trust Him to guide us in our daily activities every day. We must stop making our own decisions, commanding the things we want for our lives ourselves and end up with a wreck, which we then bring to Him to pick up the pieces.

The cross is our road to victory. By following Jesus daily in an attitude of humility, we will be transformed into His image. You may be heading the wrong way in life, but if you make the decision to take up your cross and follow Him, your first step towards another destiny can begin the moment you do. Jesus is not going to force anyone to take up their cross and follow Him. It must be your desire. It is in the interest of every man to follow the one who is the way. Jesus did not say I know the way. He said, *"Jesus said unto him, I am the way, the truth, and the life: no man comes unto the Father, but by Me. (John 14:6)*

He is also the light of the world.

"Then spake Jesus again unto them, saying, I am the light of the world: he that follows Me shall not walk in darkness, but shall have the light of life." (John 8:12)

It is in the interest of every man and every woman to take up their cross and follow the one who is the way, the truth, the life and the light of the world. You will never walk in darkness.

Taking up your cross is the road to success because you will make choices, not in darkness, but in the light. Our trials in life are not our cross. They are part of our pilgrimage on this earth. Had it not been for the trials we faced, we would not have seen God's intervention in every single one of them, when we trusted Him. They allow us to know God in a way we would otherwise not have. We've often heard that each one of us has a cross to carry. If your trials draw you closer to God by seeking Him daily in prayer, then you can then call them your cross. The cross brings the Christian closer to his Savior Jesus Christ.

Taking up your cross is not a sentence or punishment but rather your deliverance. It is the way that leads to Jesus. Do not forget that the cross is the place where the enemy of your soul was forever defeated by the guardian of your soul— Jesus Christ! You must not be afraid of the cross. It is the victory of the Christian.

THE PROPHECIES OF THE NEW YEAR

THE OFFICE OF Prophet is listed in the fivefold ministry gifts "And He gave some, apostles; and some, prophets; and some, evangelists; and some, pastors and teachers; for the perfecting of the saints, for the work of the ministry, for the edifying of the body of Christ." (Ephesians 4:11-12) The message of the prophet is mainly to call the people of God back to holiness and righteousness. He also announces futuristic events. The major problem the church is facing today is that there are a lot of self-appointed prophets and prophetesses that are prophesying lies to the people of God.

At the beginning of every New Year, we would see a couple of prophets and prophetesses on some Christian television networks prophesying to the people of God on what He is saying to them concerning that year. Most of the time, it was about financial prosperity—that they were going to be promoted to a new level in their lives. When prophesied to a pastor, it would be that God said, "His ministry was going to explode, there was going to be a greater anointing on him, or he was going to see things without precedence in his ministry." Most of the prophecies were based on futuristic events that would occur in their lives corresponding to the digits of that year. For example, in the year 2015, the prophecies were based on the number *five*, which is the number of *grace*. And then they would tell the people that they had to give an offering corresponding to the digits of the year as a seed to get into the blessings of that year. They would ask the people to give two thousand fifteen dollars, two hundred fifteen dollars, so forth and so on. By sowing these seeds, the people were promised a huge harvest within the year. It's going to be the same for the year 2016. They will ask for two thousand sixteen dollars, two hundred sixteen dollars, one hundred sixteen dollars, etc. The amount can be higher or lower, as long as what the people are giving has a six at the end, they are in for the blessings.

In the coming year 2017, the prophecies will be based on the number seven It is the number of completion and divine perfection. We see in the Bible that God has used the number seven many times to express His divine intervention, completeness and perfection.

The deceitful prophets, prophetesses, and pastors will use the number seven to amass a fortune by giving the people great prophecies and promises based on the number seven, using Scriptures in the Bible that they have distorted to ask the people to plant seed (money) to partake of the extraordinary harvest that is coming from heaven in the year 2017.

Most of the Scriptures that mention the number seven that they will distort reveal God's creative power, completeness, faithfulness, perfection, divine intervention in the lives of His children. These Scriptures are written to allow us to see the Mighty God whom we serve so in times of trials we can reflect on them to strengthen our faith. Let's look at a couple of verses in the Bible which mention the number seven. There are much more but just to give you an example I chose these two. One speaks of God completing His creation and the other is His divine intervention to give His people the victory by bringing down the wall of Jericho. They have absolutely nothing to do with giving money to the ministry of a man or a woman. So are all the other scriptures that mention the number seven.

*"**And on the seventh day God ended His work** which He had made; and **He rested on the seventh day** from all his work which he had made. **And God blessed the seventh day,** and sanctified it: because that in it he had rested from all his work which God created and made." (Genesis 2:2-3)*

*"But it came to pass **on the seventh day** that they rose early, about the dawning of the day, and marched around the city seven times in the same manner. On that day only they marched around the city seven times. **And**

*the seventh time it happened, when the priests blew the trumpets that Joshua said to the people: "Shout, for the Lord has given you the city! So the people shouted when the priests blew the trumpets. **And it happened when the people heard the sound of the trumpet, and the people shouted with a great shout, that the wall fell down flat.** Then the people went up into the city, every man straight before him, and they took the city." (Joshua 6:15-16, 20)"*

A servant of Jesus Christ will never ask you to give any money corresponding to any number. They always let the Holy Spirit put in your heart the amount to give to His work. The men and women who will come up with the number seven (7) in the year 2017 and every year thereafter to steal your money are employees of the Jezebel spirit. They may have a godly appearance, but in reality; they are not servants of Jesus Christ.

They will sound so amazing that the people that are fooled will give them a lot of money. Those deceitful prophets, prophetesses or pastors will get richer with the money they have gotten from those who are planting seeds corresponding to the number of the year. Unfortunately, there will be no harvest and no windfall from heaven for those who have given their money not to God, but to the servants of a lying spirit.

Keep in mind! God will not give a harvest based on the lies of those deceitful pastors, prophets and prophetesses or others that are employed by the Jezebel spirit to rob His people. And this sad situation will be so *every year thereafter*.

This has been going on for years. Dear friends, giving money corresponding to the number of the year is witchcraft; this is sorcery. Everything God has to say to His children concerning a New Year is in the Bible. A child of God who takes up his cross daily, and follows Jesus, the light of the world, would not need to wait for the first day of the year, to hear a man or a woman who has no relationship with Jesus and who only knows Him by name, to come and prophesy lies to him.

If there are things that you would like to know about your life from God, let God speak to you directly to avoid a demon spirit coming to speak to you. It is written in Jeremiah *"Call unto Me, and I will answer you, and show you great and mighty things, which you know not." (Jeremiah 33:3)* Jesus has reconciled us with our heavenly Father by His blood. We can invoke Him in prayer, in the name of Jesus, and He will answer us as He said. We read in Psalm: *"O you who hears prayer, unto You shall all flesh come. By terrible things in righteousness will you answer us, O God of our salvation; who are the confidence of all the ends of the earth, and of them that are afar off upon the sea You visit the earth, and water it: You greatly enrich it with the river of God, which is full of water: You prepare them corn, when you have so provided for it. You crown the year with Your goodness; and your paths drop fatness. (Psalm 65: 2, 5, 9, 11)* The year is crowned with God's goodness, for His children. His paths drop fatness meaning overflowing abundance, for His children. You don't need to pay these men and women to lie to you concerning the New Year.

When a word of prophecy is given to you, it should be confirming something the Lord already spoke to you about. That's why it is extremely important for the believer to maintain his or her faith in Jesus and His sacrifice on the cross. And have a close relationship with the Lord through prayer and the reading of the Word of God. In order to personally hear from God, the things He is revealing to you concerning your future. So when a word of prophecy comes to confirm what you already know it brings extreme joy to you, and the assurance that you are moving in the right direction.

Many people have encountered great difficulties. Families have been destroyed and many ministries and churches have closed their doors because the person or the pastor to whom the word of prophecy was given acted on a word given to them by a self-elected prophet who has not heard from the Lord at all. And does not have a relationship with Him. Most of the time, these lies are perpetrated to take a couple of dollars from you. Another reason they perpetrate these lies in the name of prophecy is pride. They do it for self-elevation, in search of notoriety.

We are children of God and He loves us. He will perform wonders to grant us our requests. He will deliver us from the snare of the enemy, diseases, premature death, financial hardships, poverty and many other things. When you participate in these lies, and you give money that corresponds with the digits of the New Year, for whatever reason they ask you to give it, you offend God.

▲　▲　▲

Those prophets and prophetesses have the audacity to say that it is God who tells them to ask His people for that amount of money. Their seductive speeches are inspired by the Jezebel spirit. It is with the money you give that she enriches those who make the deceitful prophecies. It is also with your money that the Jezebel spirit reward the pastors that invite those false prophets and prophetesses as guest speakers on their television programs or their church to raise funds. And when the year has passed, you are still exactly where you were on the first day of the year.

Then they come back again, the following year, with the same lies. You didn't receive the blessings of God that they've mentioned the previous year, because God cannot associate Himself with the lies of the Jezebel spirit. By giving them money, you have participated in their lies and have forfeited the blessings that were coming to you. You have put your blessings on hold. If the Lord released the blessings to you, you would give credit to these false prophets and prophetesses believing that they had indeed, heard from God, because everything they said came to pass. If so, you would think what the false prophets and prophetesses of Jezebel had said to you was true. Then Satan would be glorified. Do not participate in these witchcraft practices that do not glorify God, then you will see His wonders all year long.

In the past, I thought what they were saying was true. I gave money in order to receive the blessings— all the good things that they said God was going to do for His children that year. These prophecies were never fulfilled. The word of God warns us against these false prophets in the book of Deuteronomy *"And if you say in your heart, how shall we know the word which the LORD has not spoken? When a prophet speaks in the name of the Lord, **if the thing follow not, nor come to pass, that is the thing which the LORD has not spoken,** but the prophet has spoken it presumptuously: you shall not be afraid of him. "* (Deuteronomy 18:21-22)

The prophet which prophesies of peace, **when the word of the prophet shall come to pass,** *then* **shall the prophet be known, that the LORD has truly sent him.**" *(Jeremiah 28: 9)*

According to what we have just read, we see that when the word has not come to pass, it does not come from the Lord. Let's read what the Lord told Jeremiah concerning these false prophets. *"I have heard what the prophets said, that prophesy lies in My name, saying, I have dreamed, I have dreamed. How long shall this be in the heart of the prophets that prophesy lies? Yea, they are prophets of the deceit of their own heart; which think to cause My people to forget My name by their dreams which they tell every man to his neighbor, as their fathers have forgotten My name for Baal."* *(Jeremiah 23: 25-27)*

In Jeremiah's time, these reprimands were for the prophets of Israel. Some of the prophets of the modern church are no different than those of the past. They've been seduced by the same demonic spirit, and they lie in the name of God. The objective is the same: to make the people of God forget His name. The Lord sees these men as extravagant, and full of folly. *"And I have seen folly in the prophets of Samaria; they prophesied in Baal, and caused My people Israel to err. I have seen also in the prophets of Jerusalem a horrible thing: they commit adultery, and walk in lies: they strengthen also the hands of evildoers, that none does return from his wickedness; they are all of them unto Me as Sodom, and the inhabitants thereof as Gomorrah."* *(Jeremiah 23: 13-14)*

After the people have given their last dollar, expecting the great things promised to them by these men and women who told them that they had heard from God, they end up finding themselves worse off than they were at the beginning of the year. As a result, a lot of these people have abandoned the church, and have indeed forgotten the name of God, because of these men and women's lies. They think that the blame "falls on God for not delivering what He promised."

Let's continue to read more verses in the book of Jeremiah concerning these false prophets. *"I have not sent these prophets, yet they ran: I have not spoken to them, yet they prophesied. But if they had stood in My counsel, and had caused My people to hear My words, then they should have turned them from their evil way, and from the evil of their doings. (Jeremiah 23:21-22)*

▲   ▲   ▲

Darkness covers the nations. Violence is everywhere. Homosexual marriages, debauchery, and perversion of all kinds are the agenda of the day and they are also in the church. I wonder why God never tells these prophets and prophetesses to tell His people to turn away from "their evil way and from their evil doings" since the same moral degradation of Jeremiah's time is prevalent today among God's people. The word they always hear from God is, "this year you are going to pass to another dimension; everybody is going to have their home, their cars, etc. God is about to do this or that…" God *is constantly "about to do,"* but the things they tell you God is about to do never come to pass. While you are waiting for the manifestation of the last thing that they said God was about to do, they come up with something else, without you seeing the fulfillment of the previous prophecy.

Let's go on with what the Lord said about them. Hear the word of the Lord against these prophets. *"Behold, I am against the prophets, says the LORD, who use their tongues, and say, He says. Behold, I am against them who prophesy false dreams, says the LORD, and do tell them, and cause My people to err by their lies, and by their lightness; yet I sent them not, nor commanded them: therefore, they shall not profit this people at all, says the LORD." (Jeremiah 23:31-32)*

People of God, the danger of listening to these false prophets is that God said, "They cause His people to err by their lies and be their recklessness." We also learn from the above verses that they are misleading the people of God with their false prophecies. They are not sent by God, and these deceitful prophets shall not profit the people of God at all. No matter how much money you give them. That's the reason also none of what they prophesied ever come to pass. These false prophets never address the topic of sin so that they can avoid offending the people. Some don't do it in order to maintain their popularity on some Christian television stations.

"The evil ways" that the Lord spoke about to Jeremiah still prevail among His people in our times. These ungodly ways are not advantageous to the people of God. Whatever their nature might be, they can become obstacles that prevent them from receiving the blessings of God. The prophet to whom the Lord speaks will never hesitate to address the topic of sin in order to bring the people of God on the right path, to the ways of God. The lies that are being purported in the name of God, and the financial abuses that are taking place in the church today, are a worldwide crisis.

Even though it started with the preachers in America, it has become a worldwide crisis. Usually, whatever America does, the rest of the world follows, whether it be in the natural or the spiritual. When a preacher in America is preaching prosperity and he is telling the people that in order to obtain wealth, they have to sow financial seeds (i.e., the more they sow the greater the blessings.)

If a pastor from another country is not firmly rooted in Christ and established in his faith (Colossians 2:7) he'll look at the wealth of that American pastor as evidence that the prosperity message works. He'll apply whatever method the American pastor teaches to acquire that wealth. When the pastor preaches about prosperity to his congregation, he'll tell the people that "they have to sow a large amount of financial seeds in order to receive a great financial harvest." And that method is the same all over the world: It's a distortion of Scripture to rob the people of God. This is not an issue with one preacher; this is a worldwide crisis.

I, personally, have heard and have experienced these lies. I have sown money into these lies. I'll share a few with you. There are times when ministers take a passage of the Bible and ask you to put money down on the passage they just read. I heard a preacher on a Christian television preach on Psalm 68:15. She asked the people to sow a seed of sixty-eight dollars and fifteen cents to receive the deliverance she was going to preach about, from a word she said she received from God. There are others who would tell you, "The anointing of prosperity is on me," then they would begin enumerating the blessings that they've received, such as money, cars, clothes, jewelry, etc. All that is said to motivate the people of God to give money.

After giving you a list of their material possessions, they add, "I have just heard the voice of God who said, 'Such and such a number of people have to sow a seed,' and then they would call out the number of people they say God told them would have to sow a seed. The seed would be whatever amount they came up with at that moment. Most of the time, it would be in the range of twenty dollars to several thousands of dollars. This specific amount would have to be sown in order for the people to receive the same blessings that were on the minister's life. Jesus was not the source of these blessings. In all that verbiage, His name was never mentioned!

They preached it was what this person had done, the seed he had himself sown that provided the blessings for them. Now, the people would have to sow into *his* anointing to get similar blessings. The minister had become the one from whom all blessings flow, not "Christ crucified." There was one minister that I remember, who said, "God said He is going to give you a house in ninety days, if you give one thousand dollars" Who would not want a house in ninety days? But if the Lord really said that to him, he would be the first one to sow that thousand dollars to get a house in ninety days, and he would come back after the ninety days to tell us about it.

▲   ▲   ▲

I attended a meeting of one of those preachers and at the time of the offering, he was proclaiming a great financial miracle that God was going to operate for those who gave one thousand dollars. I had gone to the front because I very much needed what he was saying God was going to do. Then he gave the next order for those who, by faith, wanted to double the sum to two thousand dollars, to come to him on the platform. I was among those who went up to where he was. All of us who had agreed to double the amount had the privilege of touching the hem of his jacket.

He told us our harvest was guaranteed by doing that. He also said that those people who had pledged to give the two thousand dollars could give whatever amount they had and then send the balance afterwards. He assured us that the harvest was going to come. All I had in my bag was twenty dollars, and I put it

in the offering. I went back home that night, with great joy in my heart, thinking that God was going to send a miraculous harvest to pay the one thousand
nine hundred and eighty dollars, which I promised to give to His work, then I
would use the rest to pay my rent, which I had difficulty paying.

I waited every day for the harvest the preacher said God was going to give
to His people. In spite of my prayers, I received nothing. The only letter that
I received, was from him telling me that I owed one thousand nine hundred
and eighty dollars to God, which I must pay. Every time he sent those letters
in the mail, I put them in the garbage can. The Lord began to open my eyes
afterwards. I knew what the preacher had said was not of God because it
didn't come to pass.

Many people have left the faith because of these kinds of abuses perpetrated by those men and women who claim to be servants of God, and who are
not. Those workers of iniquity have been seduced by the Jezebel spirit. They
pretend to raise money for the furtherance of the work of God. How could
they think that God would inspire them to lie to His people, to take their
money for the furtherance of His work? It is Satan who is the father of lies. He
is behind these lies. The worst part about it is that they know they are lying.

When the Jezebel spirit inspires a minister of the gospel to lie to the people
of God, when they don't receive what the servant promised and are in financial distress, Jezebel then accuses God for not wanting to help His people. Or,
she will make the believers lose faith in the word of God when they discover
"confession doesn't bring possession." However, faith in Jesus Christ and His
finished work on the cross always does. When the people are in dire situations, and have done what the Lord asked of them in terms of sowing seeds
and confessing the word. When there is no response from God, some fooled
people have even questioned the existence of God. That's how serious these
lies are. They are crimes against the precious souls of the people of God.

In the past, I have also given money corresponding to the New Year, a
Psalm or a passage of Scripture when they asked for it, because I thought
that it was the way of getting the blessings of God that they were preaching
and teaching about. I did not understand that it was witchcraft, that it is a
practice invented by Satan under the disguise of Jezebel to rob the people of

God. These servants of Jezebel are so corrupt; their conscience is seared and they could not care less about the misery of others, as long as they get the multiplied millions of dollars that they are after. All that they see is the dollar! It's up to you to refuse to eat the rotten meats of Jezebel, which are her false teachings delivered from their mouths.

⚔   ⚔   ⚔

Please, note that I am not at all telling you not to give money to the work of the Lord. It is a sacred work and it is important to give money to support it. However, it is extremely important for you to stop funding the ministries that Satan has infiltrated to deceive the people of God. We receive from God because Jesus has paid a great price on the cross to give us access to His blessings. When Jesus is excluded from the preaching of the word of God, when the cross is never mentioned, there only remains manipulation of the word to raise money. When those men and women tell you that they have an anointing on their lives for whatever, and if you join their ministry and plant your seed in their good soil (i.e., their ministry, or their church) you can partake of their anointing, or you will be blessed because of the anointing that's on their lives; they are lying.

Even if a minister of the gospel was greatly anointed, you would not be blessed because you followed his ministry or became a member of his church, but rather because you are rightly related to God through His Son, Jesus. If God leads you to become a member of that church, it simply means that it is a work that He approves of and you would be a blessing to it, He would in turn bless all aspects of your life because you obeyed God.

I have heard pastors testify that they had also given a significant amount of money and had thereafter received a big harvest. It can happen, but if the sacrifice of Jesus Christ on the cross, by which we receive the blessings of God and which guarantees our blessings is never mentioned as the source of this harvest, but rather the seed and only the seed (money) you are listening to the seductions of the Jezebel spirit, which lures you into giving money. In this case, these pastors were seduced by that spirit. Since they promulgate her false teachings, these lies are going to work for them. But it will never work for you, who are children of God, because God does not operate in lies. It is not the intention of Satan to bless you but to steal your money and to reduce your finances to naught by using the name of Jesus.

The name of Jesus becomes a camouflage at the end of every prayer to raise money. As I have already said, it is Satan who invented these false teachings, lies and manipulation to rob the people of God. It is his way of accusing God before His people, and to make them forget His name. When they lose their houses and their cars, when they cannot pay their bills, and some have even gone back to activities that are forbidden by God in order to obtain the money to meet their needs. After sowing so much seeds (money) for a big harvest, they wonder why God did not help them get out of the hellish situation that they were going through. I want you to see for yourselves why you are in the situation that you are in. God is not responsible. It is all the opposite; He wants to help you. He wants to bless you. It will happen when you come out from among those false prophets and prophetesses.

THE YEAR OF JUBILEE

*"Cry aloud, spare not, lift up your voice like a trumpet, and show
my people their transgression, and the house of Jacob their sins."*

(ISAIAH 58:1)

STARTING ON THE Day of Atonement in 2015 and continuing into 2016, several pastors claimed this year to be a "year of Jubilee." This teaching is one example, of many, where pastors are not preaching Jesus Christ and the cross, but are prophesying lies to make themselves richer. Let me say this before I continue. It doesn't matter in what year you are reading this book; it could be the year 2065, and every year thereafter, you need to know about the false teachings concerning "Jubilee." The enemy will always come up with "Jubilee" since it was a law God gave to Moses on Mount Sinai, which is recorded in Leviticus chapter 25. It was practiced in the Old Testament. Satan will continue to distort that passage of Scripture to rob the people of God and then blame God for not helping His people financially.

The purpose of exposing the teachings of these men is to allow them to reexamine themselves and see how far they have steered from the simplicity of the Gospel, which is "Christ crucified." The Believers need to be on guard so that when it comes to these teachings about "Jubilee" they don't go broke giving money that they cannot afford, even going into debt, to satisfy the demands of a God these men are portraying. One that, seemingly, wants a huge sum of money from His people or would settle for whatever the poorest of the poor can give before He can give them a great harvest.

During the week of October 8, 2015, Pastor Benny Hinn aired two programs he taped with Pastor Coy Barker that can be found on Pastor Benny's YouTube channel under the title "The Jubilee trumpet has sounded!" The beginning of the year they claimed to be a Jubilee year. Pastor Benny also aired two programs on his telecast "This is your day" during the week of February 8, 2016, that he taped with Bishop Clarence McClendon, which can also be found on Pastor Benny's You Tube channel, under the title "New Generation" if he has not removed them. I will begin with some of the things Pastor Barker said on the program Pastor Benny Hinn taped with him. I will comment on their Jubilee teaching as we move forward.

Pastor Coy Barker: God took me to a scripture I read many times Paul's writing, 1Corinthians 14:8, the trumpet must sound a certain sound. It's a jubilee year they would sound a certain sound.

Comment--The verse that Pastor Barker quoted to explain the sound of Jubilee that he is heralding, has nothing to do with Jubilee. These verses are about interpretation of tongues. Let's read what is written beginning with verses 6 through 8 in 1 Corinthians 14. *"Now, brethren, if I come unto you speaking with tongues, what shall I profit you, except I shall speak to you either by revelation, or by knowledge, or by prophesying, or by doctrine? And even things without life giving sound, whether pipe or harp, except they give a distinction in the sounds, how shall it be known what is piped or harped?" (1 Corinthians 14: 6-7) "For if the trumpet give an uncertain sound, who shall prepare himself to the battle?"(1Corinthians14: 8)* Verse 8, is the one Pastor Barker quoted to validate his Jubilee teaching. In essence, Paul was instructing the proper usage of tongues. He made a comparison between speaking in tongues and musical instruments, showing the believers that when speaking in tongues is not done in order, all that is heard is cacophony. It makes the same sound as an instrument that is out of tune.

⚑ ⚑ ⚑

Pastor Benny: It's the 70th Jubilee since Joshua entered the promise land and the 40th since the Lord ascended. This Jubilee is like none other.

Comment—Pastor Benny Hinn just gave numbers, that don't mean anything. Since Jesus' death on the cross and His resurrection from the dead every year is a Jubilee year. All that matters to the believers is that— Jesus our Jubilee— went to the cross, died and resurrected from the dead two thousand years ago and is now seated at the right hand of the Father, making intercessions for us as our High Priest.

▲   ▲   ▲

Pastor Barker: See what the Lord spoke to me about you. (Pastor Benny) There is a certain sound that you're giving. When I hear his voice (speaking of Benny Hinn), I hear a certain sound and it's the sound of Jubilee. This is what the Lord said to me. The Spirit of God came all over me and said: "his voice (Benny Hinn's) has become the trumpet that is sounding." Let me tell you something, they had a choice. We come as the messenger (pointing to himself and Benny Hinn) who is the trumpet of God speaking into your lives with a certain sound but at that moment, you have to step into position. Will you hear that sound? Will you respond to that sound? And will you take what God has to bless you with? Because I am telling you there is an overflow coming into your life.

Comment—Pastor Coy Barker's word from the Lord to Pastor Benny Hinn is confusing. I have never seen in the Bible where the Holy Spirit gives a man word for another man, and for the messenger to alter the word of the Lord by including himself in it. That's exactly what Pastor Barker did. *Let's review what He said to Pastor Benny: "See what the Lord spoke to me about you. There is a certain sound that you're giving. When I hear his voice (speaking of Benny Hinn), I hear a certain sound and it's the sound of Jubilee. The Spirit of God came all over me and said: 'his voice (Benny Hinn's) has become the trumpet that is sounding."* Then Pastor Barker added: *"We come as the messenger (pointing to himself and Benny Hinn) who is the trumpet of God speaking into your lives with a certain sound."* Didn't he say that the Spirit of God came all over him, to give him a word for Benny? So how did it change into *"we come as the messenger (pointing to himself and Benny Hinn) who is the trumpet of God speaking into* *your lives with a certain sound?"* It is clear that the Spirit of God never said that to him. He made it up. His Jubilee teaching is false anyway. The Spirit of God would not take part in lies and deception.

▲   ▲   ▲

Pastor Benny: I am here to tell you under this anointing, no lack in your life. If the whole world collapses no lack in your life. Take my word for it. Pastor Barker responded, "That's that certain trumpet.

Comment—Let me tell you this: if you take Pastor Benny's word there will be lack in your life. Pastor Benny's anointing cannot stop lack in your life. It's a false promise. Only Jesus Christ can make that declaration because of His finished work on the cross. If you want to have an overflow in your life, you need to put your faith in Jesus Christ and His finished work on the cross, not in Benny's anointing. It's not a "certain trumpet" but a false trumpet.

▲   ▲   ▲

Pastor Barker: (speaking to the viewers) what's about to happen, is that all your struggles of your past are breaking off of you, because the sound of the trumpet is saying "Jubilee." Go back in Leviticus study what Jubilee means to you. What has been happening in these last few weeks and months God has given the sound of Jubilee.

Comment—People of God! Your struggles will break off of you because of Jesus' sacrifice on the Cross, not because the sound of the trumpet is saying "Jubilee." This is a false promise.   I did go back to Leviticus to study Jubilee. It means: Jesus Christ, the redeemer of mankind. The law concerning the Jubilee year was given to Moses by God on Mount Sinai. The trumpet of Jubilee was sounding for Jesus until He was manifested among us. Now, we have our Jubilee dwelling in our hearts until eternity. Let's read what is written in the Bible about Jubilee. *"And you shall number seven Sabbaths of years unto you, seven times seven years; and the space of the seven Sabbaths of years* *shall be unto you forty and nine years. **Then shall you cause the trumpet of the jubilee to sound on the tenth day of the seventh month, in the Day of Atonement shall you make the trumpet sound throughout all your land. And you shall hallow the fiftieth year, and proclaim liberty throughout all the land unto all the inhabitants thereof: it shall be a jubilee unto you;** and you shall return every man unto his possession, and you shall return every man unto his family. A jubilee shall that fiftieth year be unto you: you shall not sow, neither reap that which grows of itself in it, nor gather the grapes in it of thy vine undressed. For it is the jubilee; it shall be holy unto you: you shall eat the increase thereof out of the field. In the year of this jubilee you shall return every man unto his possession. (Leviticus 25: 8-13)*

The Day of Atonement, (Yom Kippur) is a Jewish high holiday, the most solemn in the Judaic calendar. In the Old Testament, it was the one day out of the year set apart by God for the High Priest to go into the Holy of Holies where he would sprinkle the blood of an animal on the mercy seat to atone for his sins and the sins of Israel. Only the High Priest was permitted to enter The Holy of Holies. It was separated by a veil from the Holy place. Even though the Jews still observed the Day of Atonement, there is no Temple in Jerusalem for them to go to. There is no High Priest to perform the ceremonies of the Day of the Atonement of the Old Covenant

On the day of Jesus' crucifixion, when He died, the veil of the temple that separated the Holy of Holies from the Holy place was torn in two from top to bottom. On that day, Jesus, our High Priest, atoned for the sins of humanity with His own blood. From that day forward, anyone who asks God for the forgiveness of their sins and puts their faith in Jesus has access to the throne of God. We read in Hebrews: *"Having therefore, brethren, boldness to enter into the holiest by the blood of Jesus" (Hebrews 10:19)*

The shed blood of Jesus on the cross fulfilled what the Day of Atonement represented. When Jesus said, "It is finished" there was nothing left undone. Since the trumpet of Jubilee sounded on the Day of Atonement every fiftieth year, Jubilee, therefore, was fulfilled as well. Jubilee represented everything that Jesus' death on the cross would provide for mankind. His blood atoned for all sins of the "past, present and future generations," once and for all. Jubilee was fulfilled in Jesus Christ.

One remarkable thing about Jubilee in the Old Covenant is that lands were sold to whoever wanted to buy them. However, it wasn't the buyer's property permanently. When the trumpet of Jubilee sounded, the purchased land had to be returned to its original owner. When the trumpet sounded, every fiftieth year, all slaves were free, all captives were released, all debts were cancelled, all properties were returned to their original owner (restoration), and everyone returned to their family. Everyone had a new beginning.

The day you accepted Jesus as your Lord and Savior, that trumpet sounded for you. That year of Jubilee will never come to an end because Jesus is the Christian's jubilee. We were sold to Satan due to Adam and Eve's fall. However, when Jesus the one to whom Jubilee was pointing died on the cross. His blood redeemed those who believe in Him. Therefore, Satan had to release those over whom he had rightful ownership. We were returned to our original Owner, our Creator the Almighty God. Jesus is the only one who can give liberty from the bondages of sin to man. That was His mission. The debt of our sins is cancelled.

On the day you gave your heart to Christ, you became a new creation. You had a new beginning. Just like the people had a new beginning in the year of Jubilee. This verse became your position in Christ: *"Therefore, if any man be in Christ, he is a new creature: old things have passed away; behold, all things have become new." (2 Corinthians 5:17)*

We are now sons and daughters, co-heirs of the kingdom of God, through Jesus Christ. Restoration has taken place. We have returned to God, our Creator, who has become our Father by adoption through Jesus. Because of His death on the cross, everything man lost due to the fall of Adam, and Eve has been restored to us. Through the cross of Christ, we can find restoration for every area in our lives. This includes family, health, finances, etc... We will experience restoration in its fullness when we receive our glorious body. Furthermore, He is the only eternal possession the believer has. When we die, we leave everything behind. He is the only one who will be in eternity with us. That's what Jubilee is all about! That's what Jesus our manifested Jubilee has done for us.

▲　▲　▲

Pastor Barker: This morning, I had never seen this, let's go to Leviticus 25:21. *"Then I will command My blessing upon you in the sixth year, and it shall bring forth fruit for three years." (Leviticus 25:21)* God just said this to me: 'I am going to give Pastor Benny's partners a triple harvest. I have never heard that preached on, I've never heard that spoken on. When I read that the Holy Spirit said to you, (the viewers) you that respond, you that hear His voice, you that get involved, don't just sit there when this anointing is flowing. You get involved in this anointing, you began to respond to this anointing. I said "Lord, what is triple harvest?" He said, "They're going to have three years of wages, of income, of profit, at one moment." God is going to break that spirit off of you. They're going to make an investment and in a moment, God is going to give them three years of investments. A harvest that is equal out to what they make in three years."

Comment— God can do anything. We all know that. However, these kinds of outrageous promises based on distorted Scriptures will never bring a harvest. Who wouldn't want to make a financial investment and receive a triple harvest in a moment? In Pastor Barker's words "A harvest that is equal out to what they make in three years." The people who are hearing these men and do not know the Scriptures or who are new believers, believe what they are hearing since these men are quoting Scriptures from the Bible. They give them their last dollar because they are in great financial distress and they really need these triple harvest blessings. Unfortunately, they will not even get one harvest out of these lies, let alone "a triple."

In the Old Testament, there was a weekly Sabbath, a 7th year Sabbath, and a fiftieth year Jubilee Sabbath. Every 7th year the people of God were not to work that year. It was a sabbatical year. They ate of the increase God gave them on the sixth year.

God promised His people to give them a triple harvest in the sixth year preceding Jubilee to sustain them in the seventh sabbatical year, and in the sabbatical year of Jubilee, which fell in succession. The year after Jubilee, they had to return to their land to sow. God provided for them for that year as well while they were awaiting the harvest, up until the ninth year. *"And you shall sow the eighth year, and eat yet of old fruit until the ninth year; until her fruits come in you shall eat of the old store" (Leviticus 25:22)*

God promised them a triple harvest to reveal to them that He is Jehovah-Jireh, their provider. They knew that they were going to be out of work they were worrying about the cares of tomorrow.

The triple harvest that Pastor Coy Barker is talking about will not come to you as a result of the year of Jubilee that he is proclaiming. The Jubilee of the Old Covenant was a shadow of Jesus our provider, **our perfect rest**. The triple harvest of Jubilee in the Old Covenant was a shadow of the overflow that the believer experiences when he put his faith in Jesus and rest in Him.

In fact, the triple harvest of the Christian is God the Father, God the Son and God the Holy Spirit. The triple harvest verse Pastor Barker quoted, speaks of trusting God, and not to worry about tomorrow. To focus on having a closer relationship with God, being obedient to Him, and loving Him. He will take care of you. Jesus told us also in Matthew 6:34 not to worry about tomorrow. God was telling His people not to worry about tomorrow concerning their needs. They were His people. He was their provider. All they had to do was to obey Him, to believe Him, and rest in Him. That has nothing to do with money. It's not necessary to give God money for the triple harvest blessings. God sets the condition on how to receive it. It's not predicated on what you do. Therefore, it's not necessary to give money to receive it. Please! Please! Read the following verses. Listen to what God said about the triple harvest blessings.

"Wherefore you shall do my statutes, and keep my judgments, and do them; and you shall dwell in the land in safety. And the land shall yield her fruit, and you shall eat your fill, and dwell therein in safety. ***And if you shall say, what shall we eat the seventh year? Behold, we shall not sow, nor gather in our increase: Then I will command my blessing upon you in the sixth year, and it shall bring forth fruit for three years"*** (Leviticus 25: 18-21)

Jesus our Jubilee has kept all of God's commandments and statutes. For no human being can keep them perfectly. Because of this fact, when we put our faith in Jesus and His sacrifice on the cross and rest in Him, we receive not just "the triple harvest" but ***all*** the blessings of God through Jesus. Abundance of provision can be found in Jesus Christ. It's not limited to money, but it includes everything man needs for his well-being. One just needs to trust Him to provide for them as the need arises. You would experience the overflow if you stop giving your money to these men. God cannot bless lies and manipulation. Coy Barker is the pastor of a church. I found it strange that "The triple harvest blessings" word, he claimed God gave to him was given for Benny Hinn's partners, not the congregants in his church. Read again what he said God told him. *"God just said this to me: "I am going to give Pastor Benny's partners a triple harvest."* 'They're going to make an investment and in a moment, God is going to give them three years of investments." God would never make such a statement. Knowing that the "triple harvest" He promised His people were not words spoken to make a money deal with man, but rather to teach man to trust Him, and to be obedient to Him. It was God's stipulation in order to receive His "the triple harvest" blessings. *At the end of Pastor Benny's program "This is Your Day," he was selling a book that Pastor Barker wrote.*

Let me say this before I go on: Since many false teachers claimed this year, 2016, is a Jubilee year, they will again come up with their erroneous teachings in seven years to tell the people of God it's a sabbatical year. That God will give them a great harvest if they plant seed money in their ministry. This will be done in order for these deceitful teachers to get their windfall. These deceptive practices will continue every seventh year until it's time to proclaim Jubilee again. Many who will read this book will not fall for the lies. "Make no mistake" they will incessantly ask the children of God to sow seed money in their ministry or church. However, those times are particularly special occasions when they get the most out of the people of God by quoting Scriptures they have distorted.

▲   ▲   ▲

Pastor Barker: There is an anointing on me. I recognize it; it's supernatural for your finances. The very reason Pastor Benny and I are here right now, is to help you get free from debt and the garbage of yesterday, sickness and sins, rejection.

Comment—That's blasphemy! That's arrogance! These words are inspired by the Jezebel spirit, and they are straight from the pit of hell. These words spoken by Pastor Barker reject Jesus Christ, reject His shed blood on the cross. They place Pastor Barker and Pastor Benny as the ones by their anointing that can give the people a breakthrough in their finances. They are the ones, who can get the people "free from debt, get rid of their garbage of yesterday, sickness, sins, and rejection."

▲ ▲ ▲

Pastor Benny: I am feeling it on you.

Comment— Pastor Benny began to scream in a loud voice.

Pastor Benny: Oppression, and depression are coming to an end.

Comment—Once again, Pastor Benny can't set you free. He can't bring oppression and depression to an end, even if he screamed from the top of his lungs. Only Jesus can do it through His shed blood on the cross. Pastor Benny went on to say that the Lord showed him seven things that were about to take place.

▲ ▲ ▲

Pastor Benny: We're about to see angelic visitation. God is about to show His mighty arm.

Comment— God already showed His mighty arm when He resurrected His Son Jesus glorious and triumphant, after three days from the dead. No angelic visitation can be compared to that.

▲ ▲ ▲

Pastor Barker: I just announced this to our church. "I said there is a visitation like you've never seen angelic visitation. Just a few days ago, I stood on our pulpit and said to the people, "there is such an anointing that is going to be released angels are going to appear everywhere.

Comment—I would like to ask Pastor Benny and Pastor Barker angels are going to appear everywhere to do what? Everything God does always has a reason. God assigned angels to every believer to walk with us in our earthly pilgrimage to protect us from danger. *"For He shall give His angels charge over you, to keep you in all your ways." (Psalm 91:11)* God uses angels to minister to us. "And of the angels He says, who makes His angels spirits, and His ministers a flame of fire. Are they not all ministering spirits, sent forth to minister for them who shall be heirs of salvation?" (Hebrews 1:7, 14)

When angels appeared to humans in the Old and the New Testament, they always came with a specific message from God. Let's look at a few examples. *"And there came two angels to Sodom at even; and Lot sat in the gate of Sodom: and Lot seeing them rose up to meet them; and he bowed himself with his face toward the ground. And the men said unto Lot, Have you here any besides? Son in law, and your sons, and your daughters, and whatsoever you have in the city, bring them out of this place:* **For we will destroy this place, because the cry of them is waxen great before the face of the LORD;** *and the LORD has sent us to destroy it." (Genesis 19:1, 12-13)* These angels were on a mission for God **to destroy the city of Sodom** for their sins.

In the New Testament in Luke 1:26-37, the angel Gabriel was sent by God to Mary **to announce to her** that she was going to conceive and bring forth a Son. She was to name Him Jesus.

When Jesus was born, there were shepherds in the fields keeping watch over their flocks, when an angel appeared to them **to announce the birth of Jesus** in Luke 2:8-15.

After Jesus had gone through a series of temptations and triumphed over them, the Bible says, *"Then the devil left Him, and behold,* **angels came and ministered to Him." (Matthew 4:11)**

Paul was sailing on a ship with several people and they met a raging storm. **God sent an angel to tell Paul that he and the crew of the ship he was sailing on, would not perish.** This is recorded in the book of Acts, *"And when neither sun nor stars in many days appeared, and no small tempest lay on us, all hope that we should be saved was then taken away. But after long abstinence Paul stood forth in the midst of them, and said, Sirs, ye should have hearkened unto me, and not have loosed from Crete, and to have gained this harm and loss. And now I exhort you to be of good cheer: for there shall be no loss of any man's life among you, but of the ship.* **For there stood by me this night**

THE YEAR OF JUBILEE

the angel of God, whose I am, and whom I serve, **Saying, Fear not, Paul; you must be brought before Caesar:** *and, lo, God has given you all them that sail with you." (Acts 27: 20-24)*

As you can see Pastor Benny Hinn and Pastor Barker's statements about angelic visitation on the earth are not from God. The angels of God always came on specific assignments for Him. These men didn't tell us why the angels were coming. The angelic visitation they proclaimed is not scriptural. There are no verses in the Bible that speak of angelic visitation from God on the earth because of the release of a mighty anointing from Him.

There are fallen angels that cannot be numbered and Lucifer (Satan) is their chief. We see their deeds daily on earth through murders, depravity, ungodly lifestyle, greed and I can go on and on. The Bible warns us about them. They will accomplish their evil deeds through men. The believers need to be careful with these kinds of prophecies because Jesus warns us.

It is recorded in the book of Mark, "And Jesus answering to them, began to say: *"take heed that no one deceives you. For false christs and false prophets will rise and show signs and wonders to deceive, if possible, even the elect. But take heed; see, I have told you all things beforehand." (Mark 13:5-22-23)* Among these false christs and false prophets who will rise, will be some well-known ministers who have lost their way.

▲   ▲   ▲

Pastor Benny: I had a vision last week, I am telling you before God almighty "I saw young people laying hands on people coming out of addiction, to gambling, drugs and alcohol.

Comment—He also mentioned other things he saw in the vision. But what he said about the youths caught my attention. I know that no one can lay hands on another human being and set him free from addiction to gambling, drugs, and alcohol. If man could do that, Jesus didn't have to come to die on the cross. These powerful chains of addiction of Satan can only be broken by Jesus Christ when one surrenders his or her life to Him. I am not saying Benny Hinn didn't have a vision, but it wasn't from God.

ᴧ   ᴧ   ᴧ

Pastor Barker: It's not by chance or circumstances that you are viewing right now. Pastor Benny and I are connected by the Holy Spirit to bring you into a supernatural flow of your finances. Some of you have been stressed and worried, and anxious and God said, "Don't worry anymore."

Comment— I do not hesitate one minute from saying that this is a lie from the pit of hell. If the Holy Spirit said that to Pastor Barker where does that leave Jesus? Where does that leave His sacrifice on the cross? Friends, the only one who can bring you into a supernatural flow of your finances is Jesus Christ and Him alone, not Pastor Coy Baker, not Pastor Benny Hinn. Only Jesus can bring you into a supernatural flow of your finances," because of what He has accomplished on the cross. The Holy Spirit has already connected every believer to Jesus, the day they made Him their Lord and Savior, to bring them to a supernatural overflow in every area of their lives. The Holy Spirit didn't appoint these men to do a work that Jesus has already accomplished on the cross.

ᴧ   ᴧ   ᴧ

Pastor Benny: "Therefore, you shall not oppress one another, but you shall fear your God; for I am the LORD your God." (Leviticus 25:17)

Comment--- That verse means "no one should take advantage of or prey on another person." That's exactly what he is doing to the people of God with these erroneous teachings, which are causing them to err.

ᴧ   ᴧ   ᴧ

Pastor Barker: Seven is a key number in your Bible. God said, "to those who would **understand the power of seven,** God said he has trusted you be able to make a seed commitment into this ministry (Benny Hinn's) of seven hundred dollars representing your Jubilee. God said to me those who would turn to their phone." Your phone call is going to change your season. Your phone call is going to change everything about you.

Comment—As we have seen, in the Bible, seven is the number of completeness and perfection. It's been exploited by Pastor Barker and Pastor Benny for financial gain. That's why I warned you about the year 2017. Deceitful men and women are going to come after you with the same lies of Jubilee, to get your money. Even though you have not received the great harvest of Jubilee, they promised you for your seven hundred dollars seed. The distortion of Scriptures, the lies and the deception are all about money. Friends, your phone call will never "change everything about you." Neither any money given corresponding to number seven nor any other number. However, your faith being exclusively in Jesus Christ and His finished work on the cross will. And, when He does, it's always with pleasure that the believer blesses His work financially as a sign of gratitude for what He has done for them. Wake up People of God! You will not be debt free and have no more lack because you gave seven hundred dollars to Benny Hinn's ministry, and because of "the power of seven." Is God now in the betting business? He will never bless what's given to Him with a gambling mindset. You should give to the genuine work of God the amount of money the Holy Spirit put in your heart to give. He will always bless you, and give you increase for the money you have given to His work by faith and obedience to Him. But never an amount corresponding to any number in the Bible, or a year. This is witchcraft, this is sorcery.

▲   ▲   ▲

Pastor Benny: There is a mighty promise here the land shall yield her fruit you shall eat your fill. (Leviticus 25:19) We are going to believe God with for the first time in your life everything will be fruitful no more drought you shall eat your fill no more lack no more debt.

Comment—To those who have been following Benny Hinn's ministry and have been sowing seeds (money) for years. Listen again to what this man is saying: "we are going to believe God with you for *the first time in your life; everything will be fruitful. No more drought, you shall eat your fill, no more lack, no more debt.*" The saddest part is that the people are bewitched. They can't even analyze what's coming out of Pastor Benny's mouth. After taking the people's money for years and given them outrageous promises, these people should have already experienced everything he is saying they are going to experience for the first time in their lives.

▲   ▲   ▲

Then Pastor Benny: When you give and obey the Lord like Pastor Coy is talking about, you just simply guarantee your tomorrow.

Comment—This is worth repeating. This is a lie from the pit of hell. It is with sadness to see how Pastor Benny has been deceived. Money sowed into Benny Hinn's ministry based on lies, deception and manipulation cannot guarantee your tomorrow. The blood of Jesus guarantees your tomorrow.

▲   ▲   ▲

Pastor Barker: I get e-mails, I get letters from your partners telling me because of making investment in the kingdom of God through this ministry (Benny's), they have already experienced it.

Comment— Pastor Benny did not respond to that claim. I don't understand why Benny Hinn's partners would send those particular letters and e-mails to Pastor Barker to tell him how blessed they were through Benny Hinn's ministry and not to pastor Benny. Pastor Benny and Pastor Barker said it's all connected to faith. Yes, everything in the kingdom of God is connected to faith in Jesus Christ and His sacrifice on the cross, not on distorted Scriptures, lies, manipulations, and the deceptions these pastors, and others like them, are perpetrating.

▲ ▲ ▲

Pastor Barker: Here is what the Lord took me back to today John chapter 10 always focus one verse 10. *"The thief comes not, but for to steal, and to kill, and to destroy: I am come that they might have life, and that they might have it more abundantly."* (John10:10) God took me back to verse one through nine (John 10:1-9) He was emphasizing something so He could speak verse 10 into existence in their lives and here is basically what He said "you will not follow the voice of a stranger **when you follow the voice of a God voice** you're going to enter a season of overflow."

Comment— The Only God voice we know of in the Bible that we should follow is the voice of Jesus Christ. Jesus said, *"My sheep hear My voice, and I know them, and they follow Me." (John 10:27)* Jesus is the only voice that can bring you to a season of overflow through the cross. That's the only way. John 10:10 has been in existence in the believers' lives since two thousand years because of the cross. The believers need to receive by faith the abundant life that Jesus came to give and they will see its manifestation in all aspects of their lives. If you are a child of God, you don't need to put one cent behind that scripture to benefit from it. Yes, the Spirit of Christ can speak to us through people, but never through a preacher who is quoting Scriptures that he has distorted to mislead the people of God with erroneous teachings to take their money.

▲ ▲ ▲

Pastor Barker: You must take a step of faith, that step of faith, give Him (God) that seven hundred dollars. Seven is such a powerful number, from the beginning to the end. I hear the Holy Ghost so clear right now. Some of you are saying I can't do it. No you can do it, you've got to use your faith. God's calling you to step across the line in your faith. You're the one we're talking to. You're the one that needs the miracle that needs the breakout. It's your due season. Hear the voice of God and hear the trumpet of God sounding right now. You should be running to the phone right now, saying, 'here is my seven hundred dollars. I have to have to have a supernatural miracle. I am going to use my faith' I promised you if you'll take the credit card right now go beyond the norm and watch God.

Comment— People of God! One cannot mix faith in God with the power of the number seven. It's either you give because of your faith in Jesus Christ and His finished work on the cross. Or you believe in the power of seven, since according to Pastor Barker "Seven is such a powerful number." And I repeat, this is sorcery. It's through these convincing appeals that the seductive powers that are behind these men's teachings have seduced the people who are listening to them to give them whatever amount they ask for, even if it is their rent, mortgage, food or utility money.

The Jubilee year teaching is tailored to amass a fortune by telling the people of God that this is a year of debt cancellation. Making them believe that if they sowed financial seeds, they could become debt free. Beloved, stop putting these huge sums of money on your credit cards to finance the lies of Bishop McClendon, Pastor Coy Barker, Pastor Benny Hinn, and others like them. They will leave you further in debt, not debt free. I believe God can bless you financially to pay off your debt. However, it would be wiser to pray and ask the Lord for help in budgeting and to help you live within your means, rather than further submerging in debt brought on most of the times by irresponsible spending habits. And then end up financing these preachers who are promulgating this false Jubilee teaching or "the financial seed sowing" teaching that will supposedly get you out of debt.

▲　▲　▲

Pastor Barker: One girl in Los Angeles area that had been told she couldn't get a raise, she got double what she was making because she heeded the instruction.

Comment—Out of the millions of viewers that were listening and sending money, among all the letters he received the greatest miracle he can recall is a girl getting a raise? The girl might have been praying to God for a raise and God granted her that request. Anything God does for His children must never be belittled because it could be the first step towards a greater miracle. However, we have never heard of any spectacular financial miracles coming from these men's ministries. Because these teachings are based on distorted Scriptures, manipulation, lies and deception and God will not honor them.

▲   ▲   ▲

Pastor Barker: Pastor Benny and I are here for you. To pull you across the line, get you healed, get you delivered, get oppression of off your life, break the spirit of lack off of your life, so you can enjoy.

Comment--- Again, these words are blasphemy and arrogance! These words are from the pit of hell. In essence, they have annihilated Jesus Christ and His sacrifice on the cross. It's Pastor Coy Barker and Pastor Benny Hinn that have replaced Jesus with claims that they could do for the people what Jesus died to provide to every man woman, boy or girl who would confess Him as their Lord and Savior.

There are a lot of new believers who come to know Jesus daily. When they hear these men, they're going to think that God is really speaking to them because they are quoting Scriptures that they have distorted left and right to corroborate their claims. And they have the audacity to tell the people of God that "the Holy Spirit said," and "God said" some mature Christians can spot the lies, but the new believer cannot.

These kinds of preachers are the reason many are abandoning the faith. When they see that what they were expecting from God by sowing these huge sums of money, sometimes using their credit card like Pastor Coy Barker instructed them, didn't happen and all they are left with, is more debts. They become discouraged and confused about the word of God. They think that the word is not delivering what it promised, instead of seeing that they were scammed by these men and others like them. They need to know that these teachings are not from the Holy Spirit.

JUBILEE: THE TRUTH REVEALED

Now, LET'S LOOK at some of the things that Bishop Clarence McClendon said concerning the year of Jubilee.

Bishop McClendon: You are the carrier of the torch and the keeper of the flame. (Pastor Benny) This season is shifting, and the next phase of your ministry assignment is going to be a realm of impartation of the healing grace of Jesus Christ to another generation of men and women.

Comment---There are no Scriptures in the Bible to back up Bishop McClendon's "healing grace impartation" claim. This is the sole duty of the Holy Spirit, who imparts the anointing that was upon Jesus to the person that He has chosen and prepared for service. It is the sole duty of the Holy Spirit to bestow the gift of healing upon an individual. Pastor Benny doesn't know every person that God has chosen and prepared for service. Therefore, Pastor Benny cannot impart "healing grace" to the next generation in any way shape or fashion. He cannot impart his anointing to anyone by laying hands on them. Pastor Benny Hinn has been offering the anointing of the Holy Spirit to people that he doesn't even know for years. I am glad that the anointing doesn't belong to him because if it did, too many witches and warlocks would be walking in that anointing. He would have imparted his "healing grace," and anointing to a lot of witches and warlocks.

Bishop McClendon should tell Pastor Benny to teach the next generation that is on its way to hell with all the depravity, corruption, and confusion that is going on in the world, to repent from their sins and to turn their hearts to the Lord. The next generation is confused (except for the ones who are devoted to preach the whole counsel of God to bring men, women and children to a greater knowledge of Jesus Christ and have rooted their preaching on the foundation that is Jesus Christ, the cross and the power of His blood. Some individuals in the new generation that Bishop McClendon is talking about, don't even know if they are a boy or a girl, a man or a woman. God wants men and women who will take a stand and tell the next generation that the immorality, the perversion, and the depravity that are taking place in our society are wrong.

If Pastor Benny doesn't repent and go back to his first love to preaching Jesus Christ, and the cross, not just mention the cross as a cover up for his deceptive and erroneous teachings. Especially when it comes to asking the people of God for money. He might not find anyone to impart his "healing grace" to. "The impartation of the healing grace of Jesus Christ to another generation of men and women" that Bishop McClendon is talking about will not flow in corrupt vessels.

At one time, I was a partner with Benny Hinn's ministry before the Holy Spirit opened my eyes. I was looking at the display of the Power of the Holy Spirit operating through him. It didn't matter if he knew you or not, one could be a Satanist, if he were in his crusade, he would be among those he was offering his anointing to. Any Satanist who wore a suit and appeared as if he is a minister of the gospel, and any witch who wore a two- piece suit, and appeared as if she were a minister of the gospel could go on the platform to receive the anointing Benny Hinn was telling everyone "you want my anointing, you want my anointing, take it, take it."

I have no doubt that his actions have grieved the Holy Spirit. Because Pastor Hinn is out of place, offering the Holy Spirit's anointing to people the Holy Spirit has not Himself designated. He would never ask Benny Hinn to impart the anointing that is upon him to anyone. In the Old Testament, up until the present time, the Holy Spirit is the one who anoints people for service, He has never delegated that mission to any man.

In the Old Testament the prophet would anoint with oil the man the Holy Spirit had pointed to Him. Besides, the anointing he was and is still offering to impart to people doesn't belong to him. People came from all over the world in pursuit of this anointing he was offering to all. I wanted the anointing in order to do the work of the Lord. Therefore, I was among those who would run to go to the podium when he called forth for the ministers who wanted the anointing he was going to impart to them. By the grace of God, I understood afterwards that he could not give (impart) his anointing to anyone by laying his hands on them, blowing on them or hitting them with his jacket. Not even his mother, his children, son- in-laws, to anyone in his own family because the anointing does not belong to him; it belongs to the Holy Spirit. It is the undertaking of the Holy Spirit to give it to the man or to the woman whom He has prepared to exercise the ministry which he entrusted to them. Pastor Benny has mishandled the anointing of the Holy Spirit. He has played with it like a little child play with a toy. When you mis-handle the anointing of God, in the natural, you are deprived of any logic or reasoning and in the spiritual, you cannot discern the profane from the holy.

▲　▲　▲

Bishop McClendon: The word of the Lord came to me concerning you; I want you to call the man of God. What I've heard Pastor Benny was that this was going to be one of the greatest, most fruitful times in your ministry. But there is something supernatural, something is going to happen in these impar-tation conferences. I want to encourage all of you pastors, all of you men and women of God. There are many of you, I know this by the Spirit. I've been praying like many of you; you have been praying. And you know, there is a dimension in this realm that you've been desiring to come into. Many of us are moving in certain areas in dimension. But there is a dimension, I believe Pastor Benny, God is going to open up in this season, this generation and I know you are an instrumental part of that. I've been hearing in my spirit some very profound things. Apart of the prophetic function in the Body of Christ is a— seeing function. Many times especially in the modern day church, in the 21st century church, when we think of the prophetic, when we think of prophesying we think of speaking, we think of talking, there is an element of that, but the prophet 1Samuel 9 says: 'He that is now called a prophet was before called a seer. The prophetic function really has to do with —seeing into the spirit realm, into the spirit dimension—has to do with the discerning of spirit that doesn't just to do with being able to detect devils and demons, but has to do with understanding spiritual operative, spiritual movement, understanding the things of the Spirit.

Comment— I could not believe this man was saying these things. If I didn't hear him myself, I would have thought that the person who was listening to him didn't hear him right. What do you expect from the "Preacher of L.A."? People of God, this is sorcery. This is divination. Remember! Satan promised Eve to go to a higher dimension in the Garden of Eden and when she followed him, the whole human race was plunged into darkness. There is no such thing in the Bible as *"a seeing function, seeing into the spirit realm, into the spirit dimension."* To look into the spirit realm is divination and this is forbidden by God. I am again repeating one of Bishop McClendon's statements: "But there is a dimension, I believe Pastor Benny, God is going to open up in this season." Why would God "open a dimension in this season" when He has given us the Holy Spirit to guide us into all truth? This falls under the category of divination and God forbids that. Listen to what He told the children of Israel, *"For these nations, which you shall possess, hearkened unto observers of times, and unto diviners: but as for you, the LORD your God has not suffered you so to do." (Deuteronomy 18:14)*

The believers have the Holy Spirit to reveal the things of God to them. God sent us the Holy Spirit to guide us into all truth, to reveal things to come to us. He never said in the Bible that He will open up another "dimension" to the believers.

Jesus said: *"But the Comforter, which is **the Holy Spirit, whom the Father will send in My name, He shall teach you all things,** and bring all things to your remembrance, whatsoever I have said unto you." (John 14:26)*

*"Howbeit when **He, the Spirit of truth, is come, He will guide you into all truth:** for he shall not speak of Himself; but whatsoever He shall hear, that shall He speak: **and He will show you things to come." (John 16:13)***

Therefore, there is no other spirit realm to look into, but the spirit realm of darkness. The teaching of Bishop McClendon is not what Jesus told us before He left the earth. He promised to send the Holy Spirit to guide us into all truth and on the day of Pentecost, Jesus delivered His promise. Jesus sent the Holy Spirit to the church so that we don't go look over the spirit realm for the things of God.

To go look into the spirit realm for any reason, you are crossing the line. If you go into the spirit realm to understand what Bishop McClendon was speaking about in terms of the *"spiritual operative, spiritual movement of God, the things of the Spirit and the discerning of spirit"* you will encounter demon spirits. There are powerful, cunning spirits in the spirit realm that are beyond what any human can discern or comprehend such as *principalities, powers, the rulers of the darkness of this world, and spiritual wickedness in high places. (Ephesians 6:12)* They are the enemies of man. They are always after our destruction. We have to stay within the boundaries of what the Holy Spirit inspired Paul to write in Ephesians 6; 10-18, to take the whole armor of God so that we may be able to withstand in the evil day against these forces of hell.

The Holy Spirit will not protect you from something that He forbids you to do. The word of God is true not what Bishop Clarence McClendon and Pastor Benny Hinn have declared or agreed to.

Discerning of spirits is a gift of the Holy Spirit that He bestows upon a believer as He will. (1Corinthians 12:1-11) It is for the believer to recognize whether he is dealing with the Spirit of God, human spirits or evil spirits. The gift of discerning of spirits is never for the believer to use it to see in the "spirit realm." Paul demonstrated this gift in the book of Acts. *"And it came to pass, as we went to prayer, a certain damsel possessed with a spirit of divination met us, which brought her masters much gain by soothsaying: The same followed Paul and us, and cried, saying, these men are the servants of the Most- High God, which show unto us the way of salvation. And this did she many days. But Paul, being grieved, turned and said to the spirit, I command you in the name of Jesus Christ to come out of her. And he came out the same hour." (Acts16:16-18)*

Even though this girl was saying the right thing about these men, Paul was able to discern she was possessed by an evil spirit and he cast it out of her. She was speaking about God but was not producing the fruit of the Spirit. She was employed by Satan.

As I have said, the teaching of Bishop McClendon falls under the category of divination. We have the Holy Spirit, the spirit of truth to guide us into all truth so that the body of Christ can stay away from the "spirit realm." Listen to the words of Jesus, as previously stated, "Whatever He (the Holy Spirit) hears He will speak; and He will tell you things to come." If a believer seeks the Lord in prayer, the Holy Spirit will convey whatever God has to tell them. Even in the Old Testament, God told His people that anything they wanted to know they should call on Him and He would answer. Let's read this verse, *"Call unto Me, and I will answer you, and show you great and mighty things, which you know not. (Jeremiah 33:3)*

There Bible does not teach "to look into the spirit realm to understand spiritual operative, spiritual movement, and understanding the things of the Spirit, to be elevated to another dimension, and to know the things of God." Pastors, men and women of God that Bishop McClendon was appealing to, you will become a statistic of failure by following his teaching, rather than a testimony for Jesus Christ by following the Holy Spirit, whom Jesus sent to help you and guide you in your ministry.

Pastor Benny Hinn agreed with everything Bishop Clarence McClendon said. If you follow Bishop McClendon's teachings, you will be among the staggering number of pastors that leave the ministry every month and close their churches every year. Any pastor, man or woman of God who follows this teaching will be plunged into darkness. You will open your ministry to demon spirits. The Holy Spirit will not work in such an environment.

Bishop McClendon quoted 1Samuel 9 to corroborate his "seeing into the spirit realm, into the "spirit dimension teaching." The prophet Samuel knew God. He wasn't a lying prophet. Yes, Samuel was called a "seer," but he only saw what God revealed to him. He didn't look into the "spirit realm, into the spirit dimension" to know the things of God. That's why everything he said always came to pass. And, as a result his reputation, was established as an honorable man and a true prophet of God.

Samuel would have never done what Bishop McClendon is saying because he knew it was forbidden by God. When Saul's father, Kish, lost his donkeys, he sent his son, Saul, with a servant to go look for them. When they arrived in the land of Zuph, Saul wanted to return back home because he didn't want his father to worry about him and the servant since it probably took longer than they had anticipated. *And the servant said to Saul "Behold now, there is in this city a man of God, and* ***he is an honorable man; all that he says comes surely to pass****: now let us go there; peradventure he can show us our way that we should go."* (1Samuel 9: 6)

Saul was the king who persecuted David. He had lost his way. This man had crossed the line and God turned His back on him. He was going in battle with the Philistines. As he was going in battle the Bible says: *"And when Saul enquired of the Lord, the Lord answered him not, neither by dreams, nor by Urim, nor by prophets." (1Samuel 28:6)*

People of God, there is a time when God says: "enough is enough." Saul wasn't hearing the voice of God anymore. So, he had to look into "the spirit realm." *Then said Saul unto his servants, seek me a woman that has a familiar spirit that I may go to her, and enquire of her. And his servants said to him, Behold, there is a woman that has a familiar spirit at En Dor." (1Samuel 28:7)*

One thing I want to emphasize is that Saul took one servant with him when he went to look for the donkeys. That servant knew about Samuel and pointed the man of God to Saul. When God was no longer speaking to Saul, his servants (plural), more than one, knew where the medium at En Dor was and they were willing to take him to her. Saul was lost. He couldn't discern that the men surrounding him, who were speaking into his life, were in worse condition than he was. They could not show him the way back to God. In our times, there are many servants who are lost. They can point you to the "spirit realm" to know the things of God, like Bishop McClendon the "Preacher of L.A." is doing. His motives may be different than those of Saul, but there is one spirit realm to look into; it's the realm of darkness, since the Bible does not teach that. It's sad to say there aren't many that can point you to Jesus Christ and His finished work on the cross.

The medium of En Dor hesitated to offer Saul her services, knowing how in the past, Saul had cut off the mediums from the land. *"And Saul swore to her by the LORD, saying, As the Lord lives, there shall no punishment happen to thee for this thing." (1Samuel 28:10)* Even in his lost state, the man swore he was doing the right thing by the Lord. That's what we are seeing today. These men are lost. God is no longer speaking to them, yet, they come with convincing powerful speeches in the name of God to encourage the people of God to go higher into the spirit realm and to go to a higher dimension. No one can take you to a higher dimension than the cross of Christ can. Jesus told His followers, including His disciples, "take up your cross daily and follow me." That's what Bishop McClendon ought to do. Bishop McClendon quoted (1 Chronicles 12:32) more than once to convince the viewers of Pastor Benny Hinn's program that he too, understood the times we are in, and it was Jubilee.

▲ ▲ ▲

Bishop McClendon: Under David's reign, the man of the tribe of Issachar, and the Scripture said they had an understanding of the times. They knew what the covenant people of God were to do.

Comment--- Let's look at this verse *"And of the children of Issachar, which were men that had understanding of the times, to know what Israel ought to do; the heads of them were two hundred; and all their brethren were at their commandment." (1Chronicles 12:32)* Bishop McClendon should have also quoted *(1 Chronicles 12:18)* that says: ***"Then the spirit came upon Amasai, who was chief of the captains,*** *and he said, yours are we, David, and on your side, you son of Jesse: peace, peace be unto thee, and peace be to your helpers;* ***for your God helps you.*** *Then David received them, and made them captains of the band."*

The son of Issachar didn't have an understanding of the times because they were either looking for the things of God in "the spirit realm," or they saw what was going on and formulated with their own intellect what the people ought to do. They had a revelation from the Spirit of God, who allowed them to understand the times and to lead the people according to the revelation

God had given them. It was the Spirit of God who revealed to all the men who joined David's army that He was with David. The times Bishop McClendon is declaring that he understands and is quoting (1 Chronicles 12:32) to validate is the year of Jubilee.

▲ ▲ ▲

Bishop McClendon: As you know Pastor Benny we are in the year 2016, in the Gregorian calendar. But in the Hebrew calendar, it's the year 5775, it's an actual Jubilee year on the Hebrew calendar. We understand in the new covenant that Jesus of Nazareth is our Jubilee; the work is finished. But the scriptures tell us in Hebrews 10:1 and Colossians 4:7 that these things in the Bible, in the Old Covenant, are type and shadow of the things we have in Christ in the anointed one and his anointing. McClendon read Leviticus 25:9-10 to show that Jubilee was a shadow of things to come. Let's take a look at the verses he quoted in the New Testament. *"For the law having a shadow of good things to come, and not the very image of the things, can never with those sacrifices which they offered year by year continually make the comers thereunto perfect." (Hebrews 10:1)*

Comment---The Law was referring to the Law of Moses, which prescribed the animal sacrifices for the temporary covering of sins. Though they were a shadow of Jesus Christ, they could not provide what Jesus Christ would accomplish on the cross. This verse is really speaking about how the sacrifices of the animal could not make those who offered them perfect. They were the shadow of Jesus, the perfect Lamb of God, who would give His life on the cross for the remission of sin. Paul wrote: *"All my state shall Tychicus declare unto you, who is a beloved brother, and a faithful minister and fellow servant in the LORD." (Colossians 4:7)* These verses have nothing to do with the actual Jubilee in the year 2016 for which Bishop McClendon is "sounding the trumpet."

▲ ▲ ▲

The conversation continued on:

Bishop McClendon: What I have come to do is sound the trumpet to you.

Pastor Benny: I am feeling an awesome anointing with you. I am getting blessed.

Bishop McClendon: Pastor there is an anointing on this word, it's because God wants His people to know something has shifted. It's revealing the finished work of Jesus.

Comment— If Jubilee is revealing the finished work of Jesus, then why should McClendon continue to sound the trumpet of Jubilee? Jesus fulfilled Jubilee by His finished work on the cross. Now the believer should rest in that finished work. There is no such thing as "Jubilee" in the New Testament. This passage of Scripture in the Old Testament has been distorted for the sole purpose of amassing money.

▲ ▲ ▲

Bishop McClendon: What I have come to do is sound the trumpet to you today, to declare to you what time it is.

Comment---The only trumpet the New Testament tells us that the believers should be awaiting is the trumpet that will sound when Jesus returns to take the believers with Him. *"For the Lord Himself shall descend from heaven with a shout, with the voice of the archangel, and with the trump of God: and the dead in Christ shall rise first: Then we which are alive and remain shall be caught up together with them in the clouds, to meet the Lord in the air: and so shall we ever be with the Lord." (1Thessalonians 4:16-17)*

▲ ▲ ▲

Bishop McClendon: It is a season of Jubilee. In the spirit and in the natural, and in the supernatural and the earthly realm Jubilee is being declared. It's time for you and me, to embrace it. This is type and shadow but the substance is in Christ.

Comment—Jubilee is no longer a shadow, the shadow, which was pointing to Christ manifested two thousand years ago. Now we have the substance; we have the person, Jesus Christ!

⚑   ⚑   ⚑

Bishop McClendon: I have come to you as a prophet of God, to declare to you that you are moving into a fresh season. *Our High Priest is seated at the right hand of the father making intercession for us and He is declaring for every one of us who would receive this and walk in it by faith, it will be a Jubilee for you.* Remember those two things! To get into the Jubilee, to experience Jubilee you had to consecrate, you had to determine this is going to be different you had to proclaim it. Jubilee was a time debt cancelation; captives went free. After hearing all he had to say about the year of Jubilee, Pastor Benny Hinn replied: "I've never heard such a presentation."

Comment— Jesus atoned for all sins on the cross by the shedding of His blood. The High priest no longer needs to go to the Holy of Holies to atone for his own sins, and the sins of the people. Jesus the spotless Lamb of God has become our High Priest. This is what's written in Hebrews about Him becoming our High Priest "*Seeing then that we have a great High Priest, that is passed into the heavens, Jesus the Son of God, let us hold fast our profession. Wherefore He is able also to save them to the uttermost that come unto God by Him, seeing He ever lives to make intercession for them. (Hebrews 4:14; 7:25)*

"*Who is he who condemns? It is Christ who died, yea rather, that is risen again, who is even at the right hand of God, who also makes intercession for us.*" (Romans 8:34)

Read what the Bible says and read what Bishop McClendon said you will see how he added a lie to that scripture. He stated: "Our High Priest is seated at the right hand of the Father making intercession for us and He is declaring for every one of us who would receive this and walk in it by faith, it will be a Jubilee for you."

The verse he misquoted has to do with Jesus interceding for us. Jesus, our High Priest, at no time said to Bishop McClendon **"for every one of us, who would receive this and walk in it by faith, it will be a Jubilee for you."** Jesus would never make that declaration. Our Jesus of the New Testament is the Jehovah God of the Old Testament. He gave the Law of Jubilee to Moses on Mount Sinai. Therefore, He knows Jubilee was a shadow that was pointing to everything He would accomplish for mankind on the cross. It was Jesus, our High Priest, who removed the shadow when He became flesh and bones and dwelled among us. He is now our eternal Jubilee.

He added: *"**Remember those two things! To get into the Jubilee, to experience Jubilee you had to consecrate, you had to determine this is going to be different you had to proclaim it.**" You have to do these things to get into the Jubilee McClendon is proclaiming. But to experience the real Jubilee Jesus Christ, you just have to believe and rest in Him.*

A new believer who hears Bishop McClendon speaking may be amazed at the things that this man was saying about the year of "Jubilee." Bishop McClendon also quoted Luke 18:4 to validate his claim that 2016 is a "Jubilee" year. Let's look at these verses: *"And He came to Nazareth, where He had been brought up: and, as His custom was, He went into the synagogue on the Sabbath day, and stood up for to read. And there was delivered unto Him the book of the prophet Isaiah. And when He had opened the book, He found the place where it was written, The Spirit of the LORD is upon Me, because He has anointed Me to preach the gospel to the poor; He has sent Me to heal the brokenhearted, to preach deliverance to the captives, and recovering of sight to the blind, to set at liberty them that are bruised, to preach **the acceptable year of the LORD.**" (Luke 4:16-19)*

When Jesus spoke these words, they were for all generations to come. Because He is what Jubilee represented. *"The acceptable year of the Lord,"* was indeed a year of Jubilee. And it was the last one, as it was known in the Old Covenant, for those who have put their faith in Jesus Christ. In the year of Jubilee, all were free, all debts were cancelled, and it was a year of restoration. Jubilee was a foreshadowing of Jesus Christ in whom all is free. He has cancelled the debt of sin that we owed, and He has restored us. Jubilee is done away with, just like the animal sacrifices were done away with when He said, "It is finished" on the cross. He is our eternal Jubilee.

▲   ▲   ▲

Bishop McClendon: The Law of Moses. He said: "The law of Moses, if I had sons and I was in debt, if I died in debt the person I owed could come and take my sons to work off that particular debt, but when Jubilee sounded my sons were emancipated, they were free."

Comment—Bishop McClendon's explanation of the Law of Moses concerning unpaid debt of individuals in the Old Covenant, was pointing to a spiritual truth. Everyone born into the human race owed a debt of sin to God that they could not pay. We were in bondage to sin. In the natural, upon the father's death, if he didn't pay his debt, the children were left to deal with it. The future of those sons could be ruined due to their father's indebtedness. When the trumpet of Jubilee sounded in the Old Covenant, all were free. All debts were canceled. Jubilee was a Temporary break, a foretaste of the freedom and rest that those who believe in Jesus Christ would experience. *Those situations in the Old Covenant that dealt with sins and iniquities, such as the iniquities of the fathers that were passed on to the children when they violated God's law, are all tied together to help you see on a larger scale what Jesus, our Jubilee, has accomplished for mankind on the cross by paying the debt of sin and bearing our iniquities for all eternity.* It is written: *"You shall not bow down yourself to them, nor serve them: for I the LORD Your God am a jealous God, visiting the iniquity of the fathers upon the children unto the third and fourth generation of them that hate Me. (Exodus 20:5)* The children's lives could be ruined because of their father's actions. In the spiritual, up to the fourth generation was affected because of the fathers' iniquities.

Certain sins were passed down in the family line and the children were left to pick up the tab, resulting in what is called a "family curse."

The same way the people felt in the Old Testament when it was Jubilee, is the same way the believer feels the day he accepts Jesus as His Lord and Savior and the Holy Spirit comes to dwell in His heart. The debt of sin is canceled. All family curses are broken. Everyone is responsible for their own sins, the believer experiences freedom from the bondages of sin. Freedom from the iniquities of his fathers that were passed on to him. Jesus bore his iniquities. *"He shall see of the travail of his soul, and shall be satisfied: by His knowledge shall* ***My righteous servant justify many; for He shall bear their iniquities."*** *(Isaiah 53:11) He* receives this freedom because of the decision he made that year to let the Lord of Glory the true Jubilee, come into his life and liberty is proclaimed in that life. His name is forever written in the Lamb's book of life. ***That's what JUBILEE is about!***

> Let's look at these verses also. *"Yet say you, why? Does not the son bear the iniquity of the father? When the son has done that which is lawful and right, and has kept all my statutes, and has done them, he shall surely live. The soul who sins, it shall die. The son shall not bear the iniquity of the father, neither shall the father bear the iniquity of the son: the righteousness of the righteous shall be upon him, and the wickedness of the wicked shall be upon him." (Ezekiel 18:19-20)*

Jesus is the only one who has kept all God's statutes and observed them perfectly. When a person put their faith in Jesus, he has become righteous in the eyes of God. He has done what is right and lawful through Jesus. Therefore, family curses are broken. He is no longer bearing the guilt of his father. Satan has no right to claim him. He now belongs to Jesus, who paid it all on the cross. I hope you have seen that Jubilee was all about what Jesus was coming to accomplish on the cross to set men free. *"If the Son therefore shall make you free, you shall be free indeed." (John 8:36)* It's not because of the Jubilee year that Bishop Clarence McClendon is proclaiming you are going to be free. But because of the one to whom Jubilee was pointing "Jesus Christ and Him crucified."

⋏ ⋏ ⋏

Bishop McClendon: As I was reading this, pastor, the Holy Spirit said something to me so powerful. This is for you my brother; this is for you my sister. The Holy Spirit said to me, "Son, in the Old Covenant, even before Jesus came, I was revealing myself to my people Israel as a God, who regularly sets and resets the button. As a God who designed intervals of time, no matter who you are, what you had done, how long you've been doing it, if you dare to believe (in Jubilee), you could go free in a moment, just like that, you would proclaim liberty." This is the breakthrough.

Comment—The above is what Jesus provided for us by His death on the cross. Anyone, anywhere in the world, at any time can be set free in a moment, by asking God to forgive their sins and putting their faith in Jesus. Let me repeat the words of Bishop McClendon. "No matter who you are, what you had done, how long you've been doing it," Yes, all you need to be free, is a childlike faith in the Lord Jesus Christ.

Pastor Benny: All of them were free at the same time (that is when the trumpet of Jubilee sounded) not one by one.

Bishop McClendon: Now, pastor, you got it, you're in it. This is the breakthrough because of Jubilee, they're all going to be healed. Thousands are going to be at the altar.

Comment— If Bishop McClendon understands that Jesus is our Jubilee so well, then why is he promoting this year as a "Jubilee year"? We are healed, not because of the "Jubilee year," but by the stripes of Jesus our Jubilee. (Isiah 53:5) Thousands will be at the altar, not because of the "Jubilee year," but because of the preachers who are preaching "Christ crucified."

⋏ ⋏ ⋏

Bishop McClendon: He is our Jubilee. Any time a believer in reality, determines to be free, a believer determines to trust in the blood of Jesus, trust in the name of the Lord, freedom and liberty can come. **But, there are times** when God Almighty determines this is a time for liberty, this is a time for breakthrough.

Comment— Notice that after his declaration of how the blood of Jesus can set the believer free, he added another lie. *"But, there are times when God Almighty determines this is a time for liberty, this a time for breakthrough."* So what I am hearing here is that those times when Jesus is not performing as He should, God has to step in to bring liberty and breakthrough to His people. Bishop McClendon's Jubilee teaching is a spiritual cyanide cocktail to the soul. It's a mixture of truth, heresy and blaspheme. Every false doctrine has some element of truth in it. Even when Satan tempted Eve, he used a portion of the word God spoke to Adam to seduce her. A preacher who is mixing truth with heresy and blasphemy is extremely dangerous. He is giving the believers the most potent poison for their soul.

▲ ▲ ▲

Bishop McClendon: God is going to Jubilee us. He is going to Jubilee whole families. I am talking to a mother. You've been praying for your family. Your son, your daughter, I am talking to one. Your daughter is on drug. You've been crying out to God. I have come with a word from God for you. God said: "Stop praying about it…start lifting up your hands and rejoicing that Jubilee has come. Decree it!

Comment— If you were listening to that program, and you have believed Bishop McClendon's teaching, you would become a statistic of Satan. You were listening to a lie. God never told Bishop McClendon to "tell that mother to stop praying for her child because Jubilee is here." Mother, you should continue to pray and put your faith in Jesus Christ and trust in His finished work on Calvary's cross to set your child free. Jubilee (liberty) came two thousand years ago. Put your trust in the finished work of Jesus on Calvary's cross not in Bishop McClendon's and Pastor Benny's Jubilee.

▲　▲　▲

Bishop McClendon: Hear me and hear me very clearly. This was something that God scheduled, He has said to me Pastor Benny, He said: "Son, understand, even in the Old covenant I was so desirous of setting people free, I was so willing to release people no matter what they had done, no matter what errors they had made I was so willing that I set up a time in the calendar, a regular time, where everybody went free and who would hear and who believed." This is the key.

Comment— For God to tell all of this to Bishop McClendon in the year 2016, would mean that people would be forgiven of their sins and would be set free in the Jubilee year that he is proclaiming. If what he said were the case, then why did Jesus come to die on the cross? If God had said such a thing to Bishop McClendon, it would have annihilated Jesus' sacrifice on the cross which was God's plan for man's salvation from the foundation of the world. What he said above is the result of salvation when a believer puts his faith in the Lord Jesus Christ. His death on the cross provides ***every day of the year*** for those who have accepted Him as their Lord and Savior, what Bishop McClendon claimed God told him would happen this Jubilee Year.

Let me say this once more. It doesn't matter in what year you are reading this book. It could be the year 2065, if Jesus tarry. The devil's lies concerning Jubilee will never change. However, when you know the truth he will not steal your money to pay unscrupulous men and women who are teaching you false doctrines.

Imagine how many people would go to hell if they had to wait for Jubilee and for men like Pastor Benny, Bishop McClendon, Pastor Barker and others who have embraced this erroneous Jubilee teaching to sound the trumpet in order for people "to be released no matter what they had done, no matter what errors they had made." A spirit, in the spirit realm Bishop McClendon is looking into probably told him all of this. This was not from the Almighty God, the Creator of heaven and earth. When God set that time in the calendar for Jubilee in the Old Covenant, in order for all men to be free, to rest in peace, for all debts to be canceled and restoration to take place, He had in mind His Son Jesus, who would one day, make every day a Jubilee, for whoever believes in Him.

▲   ▲   ▲

Bishop McClendon: Here is what I am saying, by the word of the Lord. It is time for you, my brother, my sister, to by faith to receive this Jubilee and begin to declare this is going to be a different season than any season in my life. This is a different day then any day. Jesus showed us this if you go to Luke 4:18, in the new covenant how this jubilee operates. Jesus said "the Spirit of the Lord is upon Me. One of the things He talks about the anointing on Him for was to declare the acceptable year of the Lord." 'When he said that every Hebrew knew He was declaring Jubilee and he said today is this Scripture.

Comment— I have already explained this passage of Scripture. All he is doing here is distorting the Scriptures so that he and Pastor Benny can start collecting money.

▲   ▲   ▲

Pastor Benny: This is the time also to sow in the kingdom of God, so God can bless us.

    Bishop McClendon: The Holy Spirit said this to me before we came on, "Benny Hinn's ministry is a great ground for your seed."

    Pastor Benny: God wants to bring them out of debt that's what it is all about. (Jubilee) Jubilee proclaimed liberty throughout all the land. *"And you shall hallow the fiftieth year, and proclaim liberty throughout all the land unto all the inhabitants thereof: it shall be a jubilee unto you; and you shall return every man unto his possession, and you shall return every man unto his family." (Leviticus 25:10)*

▲   ▲   ▲

Comment—This temporary liberty that was proclaimed in the year of Jubilee in the Old Covenant, became an everyday occurrence for those who put their faith in Jesus Christ. On the cross, Jesus, the Lamb who was slain from the foundation of the world, would say these words recorded by John, in which ***all men will find their liberty***. *"When Jesus, therefore, had received the vinegar, He said, **It is finished:** and He bowed His head, and gave up the spirit."* (*John 19:30*) Earlier, Bishop McClendon said the following was the entrance criteria to get into Jubilee: "Remember those two things! To get into the Jubilee, to experience Jubilee you had to consecrate, you had to determine this is going to be different you had to proclaim it." Please note, according to Bishop McClendon, it's what you will do yourself that will determine whether you get into this Jubilee or not. And down below he gave another formula. It's the amount of money you sow into Pastor Benny's ministry.

▲　▲　▲

Bishop McClendon: There is a Jubilee anointing. The Holy Spirit said to me today, "there will be fifty people watching they are to sow a thousand-dollar seed."

Comment— There is no such thing as a Jubilee anointing. These are manipulative words to take the people's money.

▲　▲　▲

Pastor Benny: What if they can't.?
　Bishop McClendon: If they can't, they need to make a vow, a commitment. They can sow fifty, a hundred for a period of time.

Comment-- McClendon decided himself, how they were to pay it. The Holy Spirit is not a liar. If he told Bishop McClendon that fifty people were going to sow a thousand-dollar seed, those people would have had the money to give. Pastor Benny Hinn would have never needed to say "What if they can't?" Pastor Benny would have never questioned what the Holy Spirit told Bishop

McClendon if he believed it. Pastor Benny Hinn was wrong for telling his viewers "it's time to sow." I would like to ask Pastor Benny what happened to the seeds (money) the people have been sowing for years into his ministry? Jubilee was a time of rest for the people so that they could to enjoy the labor of their hands. This Jubilee that Pastor Benny is proclaiming should have been harvest time for those who have sown thousands of dollars into his ministry. The people were not supposed to sow that year. They were to eat the produce of the field of the previous year of their labor.

Let me say this, giving to the work of the Lord should be a continual practice for the child of God, since Jubilee is an everyday occurrence in the life of the believer. We are blessed every day with all kinds of blessings from God. However, we are not talking about the work of the Lord here. These are lies and deception. These men have been promising the body of Christ all sorts of things in return for the money that they sow into their ministries. Now, since they claim it is a Jubilee year, it's time for those who have been given them money to ask for their harvest.

▲ ▲ ▲

Bishop McClendon: There is another level of people 50, I want every person watching me to sow fifty dollars in the soil of this ministry.

Pastor Benny: Then the result will be what?

Bishop McClendon: The result will be supernatural debt cancellation; the result will be the spirit of breakthrough. The result will be an absolute distinction in your family, in your household. You are going to see a favor of God. I am saying this by the Spirit of God.

Comment--- People of God wake up! The Spirit of God didn't say these things to Bishop McClendon. The Spirit of God would never participate in erroneous teachings. Bishop McClendon should not be promising these things in the year he claimed is Jubilee. It should have been your year of harvest for the thousands of dollars you have already sown into Benny Hinn's ministry for years. And it's the same repetition over the years to rake in millions of dollars. Keep in mind my beloved brothers and sisters, it's not the amount of money that you give to Benny Hinn's ministry that will make God give you these things that Bishop McClendon mentioned. However, when your faith is exclusively in Jesus and His finished work on the cross, as the source of all blessings. God will move heaven and earth to bless you, to glorify the sacrifice of His Son on Calvary's cross.

Pastor Benny Hinn and Bishop Clarence McClendon have themselves determined what you must do to get this Jubilee blessing. I hope, you have also clearly seen that the Holy Spirit didn't tell Bishop McClendon to tell the people to sow money into Benny Hinn's soil (ministry) They on their own accord, have declared what the result of you giving them money will be. Friends, the truth is that if you gave them money, you would have sown into a lie. You will never see what they've claimed will happen. Keep in mind the death of Jesus on the cross and His resurrection have fulfilled the Jubilee of the Old Testament that they are proclaiming.

▲ ▲ ▲

On the February 9th 2016 episode, "The Jubilee Trumpet has sounded!" Pastor Benny spoke about a vision he had.

Pastor Benny: Two nights ago I had a vision; really I did. I am laying in my bed I saw the Lord I saw him moving rapidly and I was stunned by it and His robe was flowing like this, (Benny turned in a half circle) I didn't know what it meant. I saw others near Him. They were shaken by his rapid move. I've been thinking it for two days. I thought, is He angry with me? But I don't feel that, of course I feel His gentle love. I still don't know what it means totally."

Bishop McClendon: He escalating the operation. The robe you saw is the glory.

Comment— Bishop McClendon quoted Isaiah 6:1 to explain to Pastor Benny that he saw the glory of the Lord. Let's look at this passage of Scripture.

"In the year that king Uzziah died I saw also the LORD sitting upon a throne, high and lifted up, and His train filled the temple. Above it stood the Seraphim: each one had six wings; with twain he covered his face, and

with twain he covered his feet, and with twain he did fly. And one cried unto another, and said, Holy, holy, holy, is the LORD of hosts: the whole earth is full of his glory." (Isaiah 6:1-3)

Isaiah didn't need anyone to explain to him what he saw. He gives us a clear description of what he saw. He even recognized the angels whom he saw. He said they were "the Seraphim." The Lord clearly explains the vision to Isaiah and allowed him to write it in the Scriptures. In Isaiah's vision the Seraphim, were worshiping the Lord. Benny Hinn saw people with the Lord but he couldn't identify who they were. McClendon didn't explain who they were either. If indeed Benny Hinn saw "the robe of Jesus in a rapid movement" with people he couldn't identify, I believe they are the believers who have been complaining to the Lord about Benny Hinn and his colleagues' false teachings and the financial abuses against the believers. Pastor Benny has been taking millions of dollars from the people of God for years, promising them all kinds of things in return that never come to pass.

The believers have no one else but Jesus to rescue them from these financial abuses. I believe, according to Benny Hinn's vision, the Lord is in rapid movement to come and set His people free from Bishop Clarence McClendon, Pastor Benny Hinn, Pastor Coy Barker and all the others who are abusing His flock financially, teaching them false doctrines and are lying in His name. He is coming to turn over the tables of those merchants in the Temple. He is coming to rescue us in this year of Jubilee that they are all proclaiming to rob the people of God and ultimately turn their heart away from Jesus. Yes, I believe Pastor Benny is about to see the manifestation of that movement.

▲   ▲   ▲

Pastor Benny: While you were talking, I saw the Lord. He said, "Liberty." When he said that everybody was healed, they came out of their wheel chairs, prison doors opened.

Comment— Listen! If Jesus can say "Liberty" and "everybody was healed, they came out of their wheel chairs, prison doors opened," then why did He come to die on the cross to give us that liberty? He was beaten by sinners so that, by His stripes, we can be healed. If that was the case, all Jesus had to say from His throne in heaven is "Liberty" and all that Pastor Benny described would have happened. Jesus could have done that, but He chose to pay the ultimate price to heal us, to open prison doors and to set us free from the bondages of sins. These kinds of declarations from Pastor Benny Hinn clearly show how far he has steered from the cross of Christ.

▲　▲　▲

Bishop McClendon: Now it's time to sow seed. (At the end of the second episode)

Pastor Benny: Is that why Peter asked them to sell their lands.

Bishop McClendon: He understood the season.

Comment—People of God, that's not a haphazard question. It is a calculated question to get the maximum amount of money from the viewers.

Bishop McClendon: (began to pray) I released this Jubilee anointing upon you now take it by faith consecrate it shall be a Jubilee for you if you and proclaim it in your life etc. In the name of Jesus.

Comment— There is no such thing as a "Jubilee anointing" that Bishop McClendon and Pastor Benny Hinn can release on anybody to give them liberty, set them free, to bring them restoration, to give them rest, and to increase their finances. These things are what the sacrifice of Jesus Christ on the cross afforded us. The deceptive practice you have to watch out for is when they tag along "in the name of Jesus." Their whole teaching is wrong. Therefore, adding, "in the name of Jesus" is not going to make it right. His name is just used to put a blindfold over your eyes so that you dig down in your purse and wallet to give them your last dollar. Bishop McClendon delivers his false teachings with powerful, persuasive speeches. He quotes Scriptures, and he defines words in the Hebrew and the Greek languages to corroborate his deceitful teaching. Pastor Benny Hinn is always amazed at everything that he and others have said that are completely false. He is an avid preacher of "sowing seeds (money)," and "wealth transfer."

The powerful, seductive, demonic spirit that is behind this false teaching is the Jezebel spirit, Satan himself. People of God, I want you to notice that they all prophesy lies to each other because they are all seduced by the same spirit.

This deception that is going on in the church, is pandemic. It's a big deal when a renowned preacher, like Bishop McClendon goes to a church overseas to preach to a congregation. It uplifts the host pastor in the eyes of his congregation. No serious pastor overseas who loves the Lord, would share his pulpit with Clarence McClendon the "Preacher of L.A." Some of the believers overseas are subject to the same lies and financial abuses as we are in America. When Bishop McClendon, and others like him, come back to America to tell us about their exploits, the believers see them as someone that the Lord approves. Clarence McClendon "The preacher of L.A." is not a representative of God's kingdom. He has profane the name of Jesus Christ, and has sold the gospel for a spot on the most degrading television series that the worst sinner would not participate in. A Muslim would have never profaned the name of Mohamed like Bishop Clarence McClendon and his colleagues have done.

▲   ▲   ▲

Bishop McClendon: We are going to see the God of A.A. Allen, the God W. Shamback, of Katherine Kuhlman, the God of Dr. Oral Roberts. That God is manifesting in this season and we're in a jubilee year.

Comment---The Names Bishop McClendon has called out, are dead servants of God. I wonder why he didn't say, "the God of Clarence McClendon and the God of Benny Hinn," since he was proclaiming how the Holy Spirit was talking personally to him about the year of Jubilee. These men have left the simplicity of the gospel. This verse is worth repeating. *"But I fear, lest somehow, as the serpent deceived Eve by his craftiness, so your minds may be corrupted from the simplicity that is in Christ." (2 Corinthians 11:3)* They've been deceived by the serpent. They have left the simplicity of the gospel to the point that they don't even know what it means anymore. They've traded the cross of Christ for fame and money.

Bishop McClendon, as well as the other "Preachers of L.A." may not have realized how much they had hurt Christians with this reality television series that had denigrated Christianity and had scandalized the name of Jesus Christ. Even though the show has been cancelled, the damage is done. Bishop McClendon and his colleagues have stooped very low in the name of the mighty dollar and fame. "The preachers of L.A." was not only a show, but also, the mentality of many that are in the ministry. Men like Bishop Clarence McClendon, Pastor Benny Hinn and Pastor Coy Barker and many others have captured the people of God and have kept them in financial bondages for years with their deceptive teachings.

Pastor Benny Hinn, Pastor Coy Baker and Bishop Clarence McClendon are fully aware of the financial struggles people are facing and know exactly what they are doing. The people are drowning in debts. When they hear these claims, they see it as a life line to save them. Then, they send their last seven hundred dollars or their last thousand dollars, only to see that what these men are promising, never comes to pass because these passages of Scriptures are grossly distorted so that they can accumulate a fortune from the people of God. These men have at times spoken about Jesus and the cross. But the Bible says, *"By their fruit you will recognize them"* ... *(Matthew 7:16) Their fruit is deception and lies.*

Friends, for years many people have been given money to these men's ministries on the promises that God told them He was going to do for His people. No one has yet come with a testimony where God has handed them a key to a worry- free financial lifestyle as to fulfill the promises these men have said would happen when the believers sow a substantial amount of money in their ministries.

▲ ▲ ▲

Pastor Benny said one last thing in that episode that I want to mention. He told Bishop McClendon about how ***"Ananias and Sapphira dropped dead*** *for lying to the Holy Spirit,"* (Acts 5:1-10) and Bishop McClendon answered: *"We are going to see that again, the power of God is increasing right now. We are moving into this moment sir."* They have said it with their own mouths and they came in agreement that we are in the season that's going to happen again.

THE POWER OF THE WORD OF GOD

" *IN THE BEGINNING was the word, and the word was with God, and the word was God." (John 1:1)* "*In the beginning*" goes back to the time of the creation of the heaven and the earth in Genesis 1:1. The Word here is not a thought, or just an ordinary word, or part of a sentence; it is a person —Jesus, the living word of God, "He is the Alpha and the Omega," He has no beginning nor an end. (Revelation 1:8) "*In Him was life; and the life was the light of men*" *(John1:4)*

When He became flesh and dwelled among us, God spoke to mankind through His presence. He showed us His love, faithfulness, power to heal the sick, resurrect the dead, and cast out demons. Through Him, God allowed mankind to experience His compassion, His willingness to forgive sins, His generosity, and His power to restore destroyed lives. The holy Scriptures are inspired by God. They are given to us to grow our faith, to know the will of God, to teach us right from wrong, to guide us and to help us live a victorious life in Christ. Additionally, they help us comprehend the sacrifice of Jesus on the cross, its purpose and its benefits, and they help us understand and appreciate the ministry of the Holy Spirit in our daily lives. The Scriptures address every aspect of our Christian walk that affects our relationship with God.

The Bible tells us that the word of God is settled in heaven. "*Forever, O LORD, Your word is settled in heaven.*" *(Psalm 119: 89)* The word came from heaven to earth. That is why, no matter how hard Satan tries to twist God's word to his advantage, it never works. He doesn't have access to it. The Lord went on to make this declaration about His word: "*So shall My word be that goes forth out of My mouth: it shall not return unto Me void, but it shall accomplish that which I please, and it shall prosper in the thing whereto I sent it.*" *(Isaiah 55:11).* No power on earth, or in hell, can resist the word of God. What the word says will happen, will happen. What it says is forbidden remains forever forbidden, and what God blesses through His word remains perpetually blessed.

Among the many verses that describe the power of the word God, I chose the following verses that allow us to see the mighty things the word does for the child of God. *"And take the helmet of salvation, **and the sword of the Spirit, which is the word of God."** (Ephesians 6:17)* The word is the sword of the spirit, which defends us when Satan comes to attack our hearts and our minds with doubts and with fears. When our faith is anchored in Jesus Christ and His finished work on the cross, the word that we speak will strengthen us to stand against his assaults.

God said: ***"Is not My word like as a fire?*** *Says the Lord;* ***and like a hammer that breaks the rock in pieces?*** *(Jeremiah 23:29) Fire* purifies, the word of God can renew the mind. A hammer breaks, the word of God can break down all false teachings, false doctrines, for they are no match to the word of God. And it can break down the stronghold of the enemy in our minds.

> *"For the word of God is quick, and powerful, and sharper than any two-edged sword, piercing even to the dividing asunder of soul and spirit, and of the joints and marrow, and is a discerner of the thoughts and intents of the heart." (Hebrews 4:12)*

David used the sword of Goliath to cut the head of the giant Philistine. In spite of everything, there is no sword on earth that can do in the natural realm, what the word of God can do in the spiritual realm. The soul and spirit of man are inseparable. But only the word of God can pierce through them. Joints and marrow are inseparable, they give us our stability, and control our movements. Only the word of God can penetrate the deepest part of our being and restrain our actions that are not in accordance with the will of God.

ᐱ ᐱ ᐱ

There are many Christians that believe they are in control of the word by what they confess, and the power to make the word work resides in them.

Such thinking has gained prominence in the word of faith doctrine. That shifting has left many with the art of manipulating the word, and as a result many of the things they've confessed, or declared, have never come to pass. The blood of Jesus —the covenant blood— is what gives power to the word. The word corrects us, and edifies us. It allows us to communicate with God and it reveals His will to us.

I am not telling anyone not to confess the word of God. There is nothing else worthy to confess and it plays an important role in the growth of the Christian. God told Joshua to meditate on the word. *"This book of the law shall not depart out of your mouth; but you shall meditate therein day and night, that you may observe to do according to all that is written therein: for then you shall make your way prosperous, and then you shall have good success." (Joshua 1:8)* The book of the law is the Bible. This command applies to all who have put their faith in Jesus Christ and His sacrifice on the cross. God is telling us that His word plays an important role in helping us make the right decisions, when we meditate on it day and night, and apply it to our lives. The result will then be that you will be prosperous and successful in all your ways. However, some men and women distort the word. They interpret it in their own way for their personal gain. They are not doing what God told Joshua. The word of faith then becomes a doctrine that uses Jesus' name. The confession of the word has replaced a relationship with Jesus. Even though in Jesus name is added at the end of the confession, in reality, Jesus is not really Lord. The belief is that what comes out of your mouth has so much power that you are in control of your destiny by what you say. Some people think that they can "make or break" whatever situation they choose by what they confess and that they can even command the angels of God to do whatever pleases them. Some have also said that they can command the angels of God to get them money by using the word, and they'll use Bible verses that they have distorted to corroborate their claim.

▲ ▲ ▲

In the Word of Faith doctrine, the emphasis is put on confession of the word. After all, whatever you confess, you will get. They'll tell you that "confession brings possession," since the power to make things happen is within the individual, not in Jesus Christ and His finished work on the cross. Yes, I know His name is mentioned vaguely at the end of each confession, but the emphasis is never on Him.

The way people are taught to get the things that they desire is to sow seeds towards it and to confess the Word daily until it materializes, since the power to make things happen for you is in what you confess like a robot. So adding Jesus' name at the end of every confession is not of great importance because the power is in your tongue and within you, not in Jesus Christ. The verses most used to convince people that their prosperity, their deliverance and other things that they desire depend on their confessions are: *"A man's belly shall be satisfied with the fruit of his mouth; and with the increase of his lips shall he be filled." and "Death and life are in the power of the tongue: and they that love it shall eat the fruit thereof." (Proverbs 18:20 - 21)*

Yes, death and life are in power of the tongue. However, it is not enough to memorize this particular verse to remind you to watch what comes out of your mouth, so that you don't hinder your prosperity. It is also important to know that, first and foremost, some people need to watch their tongue so as not to gossip and not to slander others. James wrote: *"And the tongue is a fire, a world of iniquity: so is the tongue among our members, that it defiles the whole body, and sets on fire the course of nature; and it is set on fire of hell. But the tongue can no man tame; it is an unruly evil, full of deadly poison." (James 3:6, 8)* The tongue can destroy others and it can edify. You can also destroy yourself by its careless usage. It can cause you great distress. David wrote: *"What man is he that desires life, and loves many days, that he may see good? Keep your tongue from evil, and your lips from speaking guile. Depart from evil, and do good; seek peace, and pursue it." (Psalm 34:12-14)*

⊼ ⊼ ⊼

The priority of your pastor should not be to teach you how to confess the word of God and to endlessly plant seeds, seeds and more seeds, in order to receive material assets. It should be to teach you about the cross, where Christ died to give you victory over every weakness in your life. He should take time to teach you that you have a spiritual problem which no man can tame. Your tongue is actually your obstacle. It is what prevents you from receiving the material blessings that you seek more than God. Your deliverance is in the blood of Jesus that was shed on the cross. The money that you give to your pastor's ministry will never be able to help you. It will enrich your Pastor, and it will help to support his or her superstar image.

If your tongue is full of poison, you can confess the whole Bible around the clock. It will not change a thing. This may be because too many people are crying out to God due to the pain that your tongue has inflicted upon their souls. That is why it is important for you to submit yourself to Jesus and return to the cross to let the Holy Spirit do His work of regeneration in you, to eradicate this venom, which no man, or the amount of money you give to a ministry can eradicate.

It's not good to only confess the Word for the material goods that you are constantly believing the Lord for. It's more beneficial to hide the word in your heart that you might not sin against Him. As a matter of fact, that should be the main reason you are taught to confess the Word with the veracity that you do. *David said, "Thy word have I hid in mine heart that I might not sin against thee" (Psalm119:11)*

Meditating on the word and confessing the word of God inspired by the Holy Spirit, and giving money to His work, are put in place to be beneficial to the people of God. However, this practice has turned into a lucrative business for those who twist Scriptures to teach their own man-fabricated version. When they become your routine and you simply tag on Jesus at the end to obtain the favor of God, you have fallen into a spiral of defeat and deception, without you even realizing it. You've created a problem to which there is no answer. All that you've confessed will never work. That's what deception is all about. God will not share His glory with another. That's why the harvest never comes. The excess of abuses, lies, manipulations, and the distortion of Scriptures to rob the children of God, are creating more heartaches to the body of Christ than benefits.

Let's look at these verses again: *"A man's belly shall be satisfied with the fruit of his mouth; and with the increase of his lips shall he be filled.*

"Death and life are in the power of the tongue: and they that love it shall eat the fruit thereof." (Proverbs 18: 20 - 21)

These verses inspired by the Holy Spirit were written to show to man the power of his tongue. However, since the fall in the Garden of Eden his tongue cannot be trusted. There is nothing good that can come out of his mouth. But when he submits himself to Jesus Christ, the Holy Spirit takes control of his tongue. Then in every situation that he faces, the Holy Spirit reminds him of what the word of God says. The person will confess what the Holy Spirit has put in his or her heart and their belly will be satisfied with the word of God, which the Holy Spirit inspired. That's the only thing that can satisfy man.

God did not give man the responsibility to confess whatever he wants with his mouth to satisfy his belly, without His assistance. Even though he is confessing the word of God, he does not know what he wants. The flesh can want and ask for things that are contrary to the will of God. Man is a fickle being. He may want one thing in the morning, and he would give all that he possesses to obtain it, but when it comes the evening, he changes his mind, and wants nothing to do with it, even if his life depended on it.

The burden, rather, lies with the Holy Spirit, who inspires us the word to confess, according to the will of God. Just as when we pray He doesn't leave us on our own. The Bible says, *"Likewise the Spirit also helps our infirmities: for we know not what we should pray for as we ought: but the Spirit itself makes intercession for us with groanings which cannot be uttered. And He who searches the hearts knows what is the mind of the Spirit, because He makes intercession for the saints according to the will of God." (Romans 8:26-27)* When our eyes are on Jesus (and His sacrifice on the cross) as the source from whom we receive what we confess. Our confessed words will always come to pass because they will always be inspired by the Holy Spirit. And Jesus Christ will be glorified. He is the divine person through whom the word finds its accomplishment. Therefore, my deliverance is not only in what I confess, but also in what I believe.

Many of the prosperity preachers have said: "Your confession is the water which will make your seed (money) grow until it brings forth fruit." When you give money as a seed, and you become like a robot continuously reciting the verses of the Bible that speak about increase, and blessings, your focus becomes your seed and what you are reciting day and night, and you spend a lot of energy memorizing these verses. These activities are like little foxes that will ravage your faith. It is impossible by practicing these rituals every day that you do not end up removing your eyes from Jesus and His sacrifice on the cross, and putting them on your confessions and your seeds instead.

Any confession that excludes "Christ crucified" is manipulation and witchcraft. Many people are discouraged and do not go to church anymore, because they gave a lot of money, they memorized all the verses and confessed the word that correspond to what they were expecting from God, but they did not receive what they were believing Him for. They thought that God did not answer their prayers. Or, even, that He was not interested in their problems, or He was indifferent to their plight. God will never bless what is done with deception, lies and manipulations, orchestrated by Satan to rob His people, while excluding Jesus Christ by whom everything is accomplished in Christianity.

THE BLESSINGS OF ABRAHAM

Lot, Abraham's nephew, his wife and the inhabitants of Sodom were attacked by Chedorlaomer, king of Elam, and a few other kings who were with him. They took their goods and took them into captivity. Abraham and his three hundred eighteen servants went to war to rescue them. The combine armies of the kings were mighty. Yet, Abraham won the war. Abraham could not have won this war without the help of the Lord. He recuperated all the goods and brought back all the people, including his nephew Lot, and his wife.

After he came back victorious over his enemies, Abraham met with two people: Melchizedek, the king of Salem and priest of the Most- High God, and Bera the King of Sodom. The meeting between Abraham and Melchizedek, sheds a light on who is behind the message of greed, with a "prosperity" label on it that is rampant in churches all over the world. In Melchizedek's meeting with Abraham, Melchizedek the priest of God brought bread and wine, symbolizing the broken body and the shed blood of our Lord Jesus Christ. These elements remind us of the last supper of Jesus with His disciples. *"And as they were eating, Jesus took bread, and blessed it, and brake it, and gave it to the disciples, and said, Take, eat; this is my body. And he took the cup, and gave thanks, and gave it to them, saying, Drink ye all of it; for this is my blood of the new testament, which is shed for many for the remission of sins." (Matthew 26:26-28)*

It is to be noted that Melchizedek brought out the elements which are necessary for the salvation of man. This interaction pointed to the cross where Jesus would die to atone for our sins. If blessings are given without the atoning blood of Jesus, it is not from God. This example shows us that the blessings of

God are given only because of His Son's broken body and shed blood on the cross, who has reconciled us to Him.

This is the first recorded event, where Melchizedek, king of Salem and priest of God, brought out bread and wine in his interaction with a man. At that time, Abraham probably did not comprehend the full meaning of these elements. Looking back at that meeting, we see exactly what these elements represented. They were the symbols of the broken body and the shed blood of the Messiah who would later come to die on the cross. These elements are necessary to be in communion with God. It was so with Abraham, and will remain everlastingly so for mankind. It is impossible to receive anything from God when the atoning blood of Jesus is omitted. God is Holy so, the sinner cannot approach Him and He cannot come near the sinner. But the blood of Jesus, which provides the forgiveness of our sins, gives us access to God and God access to us. The interaction between Melchizedek and Abraham continues: *"And he blessed him, and said, Blessed be Abram of the Most- High God, Possessor of heaven and earth: and blessed be the Most- High God, which has delivered your enemies into your hand. And he gave him tithes of all." (Genesis 14:19-20)*

⋏ ⋏ ⋏

Abraham gave the tithe of everything he had to Melchizedek with gratitude for what the Most High God did for him —for the victory that He gave him over his enemies. There was no manipulation in this exchange. Abraham had already won the victory over his enemies and he was in possession of the goods before he gave the tithe. Melchizedek didn't tell Abraham that if he wanted the blessings of the Most- High God, he had to plant seeds (money), and that the more he gave, the more He would pour His blessings on him. Or, that the large sum of money that he gave would make God open the windows of heaven for him. He also did not say that if Abraham's offering meant nothing to him, it would not have any effect on God. It was not what Abraham gave or what he confessed that made God move, but the bread and the wine. Melchizedek blessed Abraham by "the God Most High, possessor of heaven and earth," so that Abraham would know that the only way God blesses is by the bread and the wine or the broken body and the blood of His Son Jesus. Melchizedek did not want the glory that was due to God. He blessed Abraham in a way that left no doubt in Abraham's mind that the blessings were coming from the Most -High God. In this way, Abraham knew that God is moved only by the broken body of His Son and His shed blood. Then Melchizedek blessed the Most- High God for what he had done for Abraham.

There cannot be blessings without Jesus. There cannot be blessings outside of His sacrifice on the cross. There are some preachers who preach this passage of the Bible, and they put the emphasis on the blessings Abraham received and not on the bread and the wine that was pointing to Jesus' broken body and His shed blood on the cross. They want the blessings without the cross, and that's not going to happen! And they twist the passage making it seem that God blessed Abraham because he had given the tithe of everything to Melchizedek. The tithe was given *after* the blood and the wine were presented. Some preachers teach their own methods on how to receive the blessings of God. God cannot receive anything from human hands without the atoning blood that was shed on the cross. The king of Sodom also came to Abraham. Let's read about their interaction. *"And the king of Sodom said unto Abram, **give me the persons, and take the goods to thyself.** And Abram said to the king of Sodom, I have lift up my hand unto the LORD, the Most- High God, the Possessor of heaven and earth, That I will not take from a thread even to a shoe latchet, and that I will not take anything that is yours, lest you should say, I have made Abram rich" (Genesis 14:21-23)*

ᛉ   ᛉ   ᛉ

Abraham refused to give him the "persons," and he also refused the goods (the riches) that the king offered to him in exchange for them. He preferred to be blessed by the LORD God through the bread and the wine, which in our time, would be by the sacrifice of the cross. *"The blessing of the Lord, it makes rich, and He adds no sorrow with it." (Proverbs 10:22)*

The approaches of the two kings were different. Melchizedek king came in the name of "God Most High, possessor of heaven and earth." The king of

Sodom came on his own. The name "God Most High," was never uttered out of his mouth. He did not have any relationship with him. He could not ask for bread and wine. They were of no value to him. What interested him was the "persons," and he was willing to give to Abraham all the goods— great riches —in exchange for them.

What Abraham did for the people of Sodom is a foreshadowing of what Jesus would do later for those who would put their faith in Him. When Adam sinned, Satan had rightful ownership over us. Jesus came down from heaven, paid the debt of sin with His precious blood and delivered from Satan's hands those who have accepted Him as their Lord and Savior. Jesus has not stopped delivering those who desire to have a relationship with Him. Satan has never ceased to cut deals with preachers who compromise the gospel by misleading the people of God, teaching them false doctrines, in exchange for their personal wealth. He is still saying to some preachers, "Give me the persons, and take the goods for yourself."

It was Satan who was behind the king of Sodom's proposal to Abraham. He used different people, whether it be the "woman Jezebel," or the man Bera, the king of Sodom as an instrument to bribe men and women of God, to compromise their walk with God. That spirit has infiltrated the church with his promise to give the goods—the material wealth —in exchange for the people. Satan succeeded in influencing some of the servants of God into excluding Jesus from His gospel and in stopping them from preaching the cross. They've replaced Jesus by sermons that are entirely based on materialism. In many churches the people are taught how to have more money and more material goods, but not a close relationship with Jesus. The name of Jesus is hardly mentioned.

The spirit that possessed the king of Sodom has indeed given luxurious jets, and the lifestyle of the rich and famous to some pastors, in exchange for teaching the people false doctrines and hindering their relationship with Jesus Christ. When you give your money, whether it be one dollar or hundreds and thousands of dollars to these churches and ministries you are funding Satan's agenda Bera, the king of Sodom promised Abraham all the riches for the "persons." He was only interested in the people, so that he could oppress them. He wasn't thinking about the well-being of the individuals when he offered the goods to Abraham in exchange for them. Furthermore, the goods and the riches were intended for Abraham and his family. Isn't this the same thing that is taking place in the churches and ministries where "prosperity" is the core message? The wealth is only for these men and women preachers and their families.

The Lord greatly rewarded Abram for being faithful and for honoring Him. *"After these things the word of the LORD came unto Abram in a vision, saying, Fear not, Abram: I am Your shield, and Your exceeding great reward."* *(Genesis15:1)*

▲ ▲ ▲

The great reward promised to Abraham in this verse, for his refusal to obtain riches from the king of Sodom, was not material wealth, but God Himself, allowing Abraham to have a close relationship with Him and giving him His protection. Abraham didn't have any children yet. The Lord promised him a posterity from which the Messiah Jesus Christ would be born. Many years later his promised son Isaac was born to his wife Sarah.

The Lord then, wanted to test Abraham's faith by asking him to sacrifice his son, Isaac. Abraham accepted His demand and took his son to the place that God had pointed out to him. On Abraham's way there, *"And Abraham took the wood of the burnt offering, and laid it upon Isaac his son; and he took the fire in his hand, and a knife; and they went both of them together." (Genesis 22: 6)* As he was about to slay the child, the angel of the Lord called him from heaven, and stopped him and provided a ram for the sacrifice, in the place of his son. His obedience pleased God, and the Lord said to Abraham, *"That in blessing I will bless you, and in multiplying I will multiply your seed as the stars of the heaven, and as the sand which is upon the sea shore; and your seed shall possess the gate of his enemies. **And in your seed shall all the nations of the Earth be blessed**; because you have obeyed My voice." (Genesis 22:17-18)*

This promise was made to Abraham after he obeyed the Lord. Even though the Lord had asked him to sacrifice Isaac. He did not let him carry out His command. Abraham could not understand why God asked such a thing of him, but he obeyed without understanding. This whole scene was pointing to the cross. Generations later, it is Jesus, the Son of God, who would be given as a sacrifice for the remission of sins. In what's being depicted here, Isaac was a type of Christ, that's why no human hands could kill him. Jesus made this declaration recorded in the book of John, *"Therefore does My Father loves Me, because **I lay down My life**, that I might take it again. **No man takes it from Me, but I lay it down of Myself.** I have power to lay it down, and I have power to take it again. This commandment have I received of My Father."* (John 10:17-18)

The wood Abraham laid on Isaac on their way to the place that God had pointed out to him is symbolic of the crossbeam that was laid on Jesus. Abraham was a type of God the Father. The knife was in Abraham's hand so, he was in control of the knife. Therefore, no one could kill his son. Going back to the day of the crucifixion of Jesus, the soldiers couldn't pierce His side with their spear until He gave up His spirit. No one could kill Him because His Father was in control of the soldier's spear.

In the prophetic Psalm 22:14 depicting Jesus' crucifixion it is written, *"I am poured out like water, and all My bones are out of joint: My heart is like wax; it is melted in the midst of My bowels."* Although it says it felt as though His heart was like wax, and has melted in the midst of His bowels because of the heat of the moment, the fire couldn't consume Him, since the fire was in His Father's hand. There have been times, when I had things before me that looked frightening, I would remember this passage of scripture and I would say, "The knife is in my Father's hand, no one can kill me; the fire is in my Father's hand, it will not consume me." Then I would feel the peace of God and a refreshing wind settling in my soul.

What you've been through in the past could not kill you, nor consume you, because the knife and the fire were in your heavenly Father's hands. What you are going through right now will not kill you, nor consume you, because the knife and the fire are in your heavenly Father's hands, and Satan cannot take them out of His hands. Reassure yourself that God is in control and He is faithful. Hold on to the words, He inspired the Prophet Isaiah to write. *"When you pass through the waters, I will be with you; and through the rivers, they shall not overflow you: when thou walk through the fire, you shall not be burned; neither shall the flame kindle upon you." (Isaiah 43:2)* Therefore, you're coming out of your difficult situation with a great testimony. Just like Daniel came out of the lion's den, and just like Shadrach, Meshach and Abednego came out of the fire unharmed. Their robes were not scorched and there was no smell of fire on them, because the fire was in God the Father's hands. And the greatest, testimony of all, is our Lord and Savior Jesus Christ who resurrected from the dead after three days, with a great triumph over His enemies. Countless Christians can testify to this truth and very soon your testimony will be added to the list. Then, you can say to the Lord, *"O LORD, You are My God; I will exalt you, I will praise Your name; for You have done wonderful things; Your counsels of old are faithfulness and truth." (Isaiah 25:1)*

⋏　⋏　⋏

The apostle Paul explains to us what Abraham's blessing is. It is one of the passages that is the most exploited by the proponents of the prosperity gospel. We see in the Scriptures that God would justify the gentiles by faith. He announced this good news to Abraham: That in his seed all the nations of the earth would be blessed so, that those who believe, are blessed with Abraham the believer. *"Know you therefore that they which are of faith, the same are the children of Abraham. And the scripture, foreseeing that God would justify the heathen through faith, preached before the gospel unto Abraham, saying, in you shall all nations be blessed. So then they which be of faith are blessed with faithful Abraham. That the blessing of Abraham might come on the Gentiles through Jesus Christ; that we might receive the promise of the Spirit through faith." (Galatians 3:7- 9, 14)* The believer receives the promise of the Spirit which is the indwelling of the Holy Spirit in His heart through Jesus.

⋏　⋏　⋏

This passage of Scripture explains it best—that the Gentiles were lost without God. If the Lord had not made this promise to Abraham, the non-Jewish people would be lost forever. Hell would be our final place of dwelling. Let's read another passage of scripture, *"Wherefore remember, that you being in time past Gentiles in the flesh, who are called Uncircumcision by that which is called the Circumcision in the flesh made by hands; That at that time you were without Christ, being aliens from the commonwealth of Israel, and strangers from the covenants of promise, having no hope, and without God in the world: but now in Christ Jesus you who sometimes were far off are made nigh by the blood of Christ. For through Him we both have access by one Spirit unto the Father." (Ephesians 2:11-13, 18)*

When the Lord told Abraham, "In your seed all the nations of the earth shall be blessed, I will bless you," He wasn't talking about earthly riches. The seed of Abraham, in which all the nations of the earth would be blessed, is Jesus. Therefore, the blessing of Abraham is Jesus Christ. We've been justified by faith in Jesus. The problem with the prosperity message is that those who preach it have replaced the true blessing, which is Jesus Christ, with materialism. They tell the people that they can expect to receive wealth from God when they plant their seed (money) in their church or ministry. I have sat in these types of conferences, attended these types of church services. I listened to these types of teachings on Christian television and believed these lies for years, before the Lord opened my eyes to the truth. One can possess houses, cars, and all the material riches of Abraham in multiplied numbers, and still be miserable and empty. They cannot satisfy the soul of man. Abraham was a man who feared God. His priority was never material wealth, but rather being faithful to God. That was obvious in his decision to refuse the riches of the king of Sodom.

The day that you accepted Jesus as your Lord and Savior, you received the blessing God was speaking to Abraham about; you received justification by faith in Jesus Christ, and all the wealth that you would ever need. There is no rejoicing in heaven when you acquire material goods because it's temporal. However, the Bible says, the angels rejoice when a person repents and has received justification by faith through Jesus. *"Likewise, I say unto you, there is joy in the presence of the angels of God over one sinner who repents." (Luke 15:10)* They rejoice when the promise God made to Abram is fulfilled in the life of a person.

Every nation on this earth has millions upon millions of people who have been blessed with salvation because of the promise God made to

Abraham. There is no greater blessing than to be born again into the kingdom of God by the blood of Jesus, to inherit eternal life and to be in communion with God.

When our heavenly Father made this promise to Abraham, He had it in His mind to do one glorious thing for us for which we should be, *"Giving thanks unto the Father, who has made us meet to be partakers of the inheritance of the saints in light.* **Who has delivered us from the power of darkness, and has translated us into the kingdom of his dear Son.** *In whom we have redemption through His blood, even the forgiveness of sins." (Colossians 1:12 -14)*

▲ ▲ ▲

This promise is first and foremost a spiritual promise to save man's soul and to deliver him from his misery. The promise He made to Abraham was fulfilled in Jesus, the Prince of Peace, whom He has given to us to keep our minds in peace amid these tumultuous times. What does materialism have to do with what's being said here? Anyone with common sense would definitely tell you that they would, a million times over, choose peace of mind, which can keep you in good health, over wealth. Peace of mind is given by the Prince of peace, Jesus Christ, the promise and the blessing!

The People of God have given money— a lot of money— as seeds, so that they would receive a harvest similar to the blessings of Abraham. The proponents of the prosperity gospel add in their favorite words to manipulate the people into giving them money. One example is: "God is not a respecter of person. If He did it for Abraham, He can do it for you too." The people of God who are sowing seeds behind the teaching that the blessing God promised Abraham is material wealth, will never see the blessings that they are sowing for because the teaching is wrong and it's a lie. God will never bless a lie that manipulates and distorts His word for personal gain.

Any other means that a preacher introduces to get the blessings of God, other than Jesus Christ and His sacrifice on the cross, does not come from God, but from the flesh, or they are under the influence of the enemy, namely Bera, the king of Sodom who was influenced by Satan or the Jezebel spirit, who are one and the same. This evil spirit's sole purpose is to oppress the believers and rob the people of God of the money God has put in their hands to meet their needs. This is so that they can always be in lack, struggling continuously to meet their needs. Then, finally, when they become so frustrated that they can't take it anymore, they curse God and give up. The only people that are left with the wealth are those who are preaching the lies of the enemy. It's a sin to continue to give your money to these ministries, and churches. You are putting your money behind the lies of the enemy and it will not profit you at all.

⋏   ⋏   ⋏

You cannot bribe God with your seeds, nor manipulate Him with His word. You may be sowing seeds to make things happen for you that you really, really want, but is absolutely not in the will of God for you. There is no amount of money that you can give that's going to make Him change His mind. If He gave you that thing that you are willing to go bankrupt by sowing seeds to get, the heartache, the anguish, the sleepless nights that thing will bring with it would not be worth it. You can be the richest person in the world and no amount of money would be able to get you out of it.

All the promises God made to His children in the Bible will come to pass, because of the ransom Jesus paid with His blood on the cross. This is the sound doctrine. Giving is scriptural. You must give your money to the work of the Lord to help propagate the Gospel of Jesus Christ. If you can discern the lies from the truth, you will be blessed when you give to the work of the Lord. We will talk more about the blessings of obeying God in giving to His work in the next chapter. When it comes to receiving the blessings of God, what you understand makes all the difference.

THE BLESSINGS OF THE TITHE AND OFFERINGS

ABRAHAM WAS THE first person who gave the tithe of all to Melchizedek. Jacob also promised to give God the tithe of everything that he received from Him. (Genesis 28:22) Those men gave the tithe to the Lord before the Mosaic Law was introduced. They gave it to honor God as a sign of gratitude and thanksgiving for His goodness towards them. Our motives for tithing must be the same as those Patriarch to bless and honor God. Some people have said that tithing is part of the Old Testament Law, that the New Testament believer is not required to abide by that Law. Since tithing had been practiced before the law was given to Moses on Mount Sinai, (Leviticus 27:30-34) it's a matter between God and men. It's a form of worshiping and honoring God with what He has placed in our hands and being grateful to Him for what He has done for us.

Our giving is a sign of obedience to His word. The blessings of God always follow obedience to Him. We don't tithe to force God to move His hands to grant us our requests. God attaches great importance to our tithes and offerings to His work. He demands that we bring our tithe to His house where we are fed the word of God. (Malachi 3:8-10), Tithing is the means adopted by God so that there are provisions in His house for the functioning of His work.

▲　▲　▲

The church administrators depend on the tithe to pay the bills, the wages of the employees and other expenses related to the church. Your tithe constitutes ten percent of your salary. In other words, God asks us for ten cents out of every dollar that we earn. The following verses are the promised blessings for those who obey God's command to bring the tithes to the store house, which is the church: *"Bring ye all the tithes into the storehouse, that there may be meat in My house, and prove me now herewith, said the Lord of hosts, if I will not open you the windows of heaven, and pour you out a blessing, that there shall not be room enough to receive it. And I will rebuke the devourer for your sakes, and he shall not destroy the fruits of your ground; neither shall your vine cast her fruit before the time in the field, said the LORD of hosts. And all nations shall call you blessed: for you shall be a delightsome land, said the LORD of hosts."* (Malachi 3:10-12)

Do you think that God would designate these blessings and promises only for the nation Israel, living in Old Testament times? All the blessings that are tied to the tithe are still available for the children of God in our modern times. Today we can obtain the blessings that are tied to tithing is the same way Israel had to get them: by paying the tithe. Are you going to let ten cents on the dollar prevent you from getting these blessings from God? And, for the believers who are under the New Covenant, these promises and blessings are guaranteed, sealed by the blood of Jesus.

The Pharisees wanted nothing to do with Jesus, but they paid the tithe on all their earnings. Jesus said to them, *"But woe unto you, Pharisees! For you tithe mint and rue and all manner of herbs, and pass over judgment and the love of God: these ought you to have done, and not to leave the other undone."* (Luke 11:42) *The* love of God was not in them. However, their tithe was of prime importance to them. No one can love God if he rejects Jesus. We can only love God through Jesus. He is the only one who loves God with all His heart and with all His soul. That is why He accomplished this extraordinary mission for His Father and He was obedient to Him until death. By His remark, Jesus informed them **not to neglect their relationship with Him,** and not to forget all their other duties, which includes **the tithe.** Therefore, the tithe was not only for Israel of the Old Testament. We must be careful not to place the tithe above Jesus. For some the object of their faith is their tithe. Everything that replaces Jesus, or is put above Him, is idolatry, including the tithe.

The tithe is also paid so that we remember, every time we pay it, that it is God who gave us the job for which we get a check. It is He who blesses our enterprises. It is He who gives us health, and strength every day to attend to our occupations. It is also especially, to prevent the enemy from devouring the fruit of our labor. When we go to work, it is God who protects us from the many accidents we could have been involved in, and from all sorts of calamities during the day. It is He who protects our children, our grandchildren, our wives or our husbands. Therefore, the tithe that we give to God, is to thank Him for all that He does for us. In return, He blesses the labor of our hands so that we can continue thriving. The tithe is a bigger blessing for man than it is for the work of God.

The Lord can obtain everything that He needs all by Himself. He can do the impossible without the help of any man. However, none of the blessings and protections that were mentioned can be fulfilled without the hand of the Almighty God. I want to stress that we bless His work with our tithe to express our gratitude for the many blessings that He bestows upon our lives. Like Abraham gave the tithe not because it was the Law but to express gratitude for what the Lord had done for Him.

▲　▲　▲

Our offerings are what we give voluntarily to God, aside from the tithe.

The following verses constitute one of the most beautiful passages in the Bible with regard to giving. A Christian, who fully understands what Paul is saying here, will not think twice when it comes to giving to the work of the Lord. This passage takes away the sting out of giving. Yet, these verses are among the most exploited, the most abused and the most manipulated. However, what they promise will forever remain true.

> **"But this I say, He who sows sparingly shall reap also sparingly; and he who sows bountifully shall reap also bountifully.** *Every man according as he purposes in his heart, so let him give; not grudgingly, or of necessity: for God loves a cheerful giver. And God is able to make*

all grace abound toward you; that you, always having all sufficiency in all things, may abound to every good work: (As it is written, He has dispersed abroad; he has given to the poor: his righteousness remains forever. **Now He who ministers seed to the sower both minister bread for your food, and multiply your seed sown, and increase the fruits of your righteousness);** *being enriched in everything to all bountifulness,* **which causes through us thanksgiving to God. For the administration of this service not only supplies the want of the saints, but is abundant also by many thanksgivings unto God." (2 Corinthians 9:6-12)**

Paul compared our offerings to the labor of a farmer who is sowing and reaping. The sower must sow seeds— and a lot of them— if he wants an abundant harvest. Giving is a matter of the heart. Paul said, "So let each one give as he purposes in his heart, not grudgingly or of necessity; for God loves a cheerful giver." Our reward is compared to the sower who reaps a good harvest after sowing. In return for our giving. In the above verses, Paul spoke about our offerings and the blessings they provide to others. We give on behalf of God. He does not ask us to give our money to His cause, and then leave us in great financial distress. No, He doesn't do that! When we give our tithe and offerings to His work, He multiplies what's left in our hands. What remains will do much more for us than if we kept the whole amount to ourselves, which can escape from our hands like grains of sand.

God is able to make *all grace* abound towards us. *All* means that there's no limit. All our needs will be met spiritually, financially, physically, etc. God does not want His children to live in lack. He wants all our needs to be met while having much more left to do good works. When we are constantly struggling, we cannot help others as we would want to. The seed which God gives to you, that is to say, the money that He gives you, is to increase the "fruits of your righteousness." By continuing blessing His work. God does not give seed to the sower, so that you give it to men and women who have no relationship with Him. By giving the seed, the money God put into your hands, to these wolves, you will lose the seed. There will not be a harvest.

But, when you sow it in the ministries, the television networks, the churches, which advance His cause and put "Christ crucified" in the forefront, "the fruits of your righteousness" will multiply. Do not forget that these "fruits of your righteousness" follow you until eternity.

It is extremely important for you to understand that Paul was talking to born again believers. They could not provide fruit of righteousness if they had not received the righteousness of Christ through His shed blood on the cross. Good works cannot save anyone. However, there will be rewards in heaven for born again believers who have done good works to glorify Jesus. Let me remind you of this verse. *"For by grace are you saved through faith; and that not of yourselves: it is the gift of God: Not of works, lest any man should boast." (Ephesians: 2:8-9)*

The apostle Paul asked for money for the Christians who were in great difficulty— people of the church who were in need. He also gave us a report about the joy that these gathered funds brought to the Christians. The financial assistance not only provided for their needs, it gave them an opportunity to offer thanksgiving to God. They were grateful for this great help they had received and they glorified God for the obedience of their brothers and sisters in Christ. They thanked God for their generosity and recognized that it is because of the Gospel of Christ that they received these funds. When you give your money to help others, you allow them to see the faithfulness of God. You also allow them to experience His love, and this delights His heart.

▲   ▲   ▲

When Paul wrote this passage in 2 Corinthians 9:6-12, he would have never thought that many people would leave the faith because of the abuses, the manipulation and the lies of men who call themselves pastors but in reality, when it comes to money, they are "wolves in sheep's clothing." They know they are lying to the people. They know the people are not getting the great harvest they are promising week after week, for their money but instead the people are living paycheck to paycheck. They can't even save any money to do something good for themselves. Whenever they save a little money, these wolves come up with a word they say they received from God, or they come up with some need for the church. What they call the **need** of the church is really no need at all. It's the preacher's greed and folly and there is no limit for what he may be calling *"the need of the church."* It may be a sixty-five-million-dollar jet.

We know of single mothers, and those who are the most destitute, who out of love for their pastors will give them their last dollar to make their fantasy come true. It's a crime and its gut- wrenching. When you begin mixing this precious gospel with the greed of this world, God takes His wisdom away from you. As a result, you think like a fool and you don't even notice it. You speak like a fool and you don't know it. You act like a fool and you can't see it. The lack of the wisdom of God, will expose you, for who you are— *a fool*— because your thoughts, your speech and your actions will not line up with the word of God. You may quote Scriptures but that will not change the fact that you are— *a fool*— and everyone who has common sense, and who is not bewitched by you, will see it. The only thing you can do about that, is repent.

The Christians of Corinth had sown their seeds (money) for their brothers in Christ in Jerusalem who were in need. It was not for Paul to buy the latest and the most expensive mode of transportation of his time. The book of Acts, chapter 27, gives an account of Paul's voyage to Rome. We see him sailing on board several ships to reach his destination. He used the ordinary mode of transportation of his time to preach "Christ crucified" wherever he went. He was shipwreck three times. You would find this account in Paul's resume as follows: *"Thrice was I beaten with rods, once was I stoned, thrice I suffered shipwreck, a night and a day I have been in the deep."* (2 Corinthians 11:25)

If any preacher needed the most expensive, private boat with his own personal captain, it would be Paul. He could have explained to the believers that he needed this luxurious boat to go preach the gospel of Jesus Christ, but that's not the example he set before us. Sadly, in our times, that's the explanation given to the congregation when they are asked to give money for their pastor to buy the most expensive jet on the market. Paul taught sowing and reaping, but he never used that teaching for self-profit, nor to mislead the Christians and to abuse them financially.

The modern teaching of "Sowing and reaping" goes far beyond the teaching of Paul. It falls into the category of greed, lies, deception, and manipulation for self-gain. The motives of Paul were totally different from those of some pastors in our times who are teaching what Paul taught. Paul used the law of agriculture of— sowing and reaping—first and foremost to show the Corinthians the benefits of sowing into other people's lives to glorify God. Paul was teaching the believers to sow into the lives of those that were in need. The focus was never on self, but rather on others that needed the help. These days the church teaches the people to sow for their own need. That's where the Scripture is twisted. This is where the abuse of that passage lies. It's all about what I can get for myself. Regardless whether it's the will of God or not, if I desperately want it, and I can sow my money to move the hands of God to get it, I am going to sow every penny I've got until I make it happen. In essence, that's what you've been taught. Paul also wanted to encourage the believers to give generously so that they can reap a bountiful harvest. The law of sowing and reaping was his best example to instruct the people to be generous to the work of the Lord. Because God always gives back much more than what you have given. Paul never used the word of God to make promises to manipulate their emotion in order to make them give money that they can't afford, even, if they have to go into debt. He left their reward in the hands of God. He also gave a report of the money collected from those who received it. We know they received the money and they glorified God for it.

⅄   ⅄   ⅄

These days the seeds collected are used to buy private jets, palatial homes, boats and the like while some of the people who are sowing these seeds in these churches are in the same condition as the people for whom Paul was asking money, and in some cases they are even worse off. They are the ones who are faithfully sowing seeds, hoping that one day the harvest promised by their pastor will come their way, so that they can get out of their endless state of lack. I hope that after reading this book, many will be able to experience the blessings of the Lord, after they stop supporting the lies of the Jezebel spirit (by giving their hard-earned money to these ministers) and instead, give their money where Jesus Christ is Lord. Not just in words, but in the preaching and teaching of the unpolluted word of God, that give Jesus and His sacrifice on the cross preeminence in His church.

When it comes to sowing your money. I want you to see for yourself, why you're not getting the things you are sowing after. This passage of Scripture in 2 Corinthians 9:6-12, where Paul taught about sowing and reaping, was distorted by someone who began to teach the corrupt version. Many pastors have embraced the twisted version to collect more money. However, when it is preached in the context in which Paul taught it, its benefits remain eternally true.

The reason I am exposing the financial abuse that is taking place in churches and ministries around the world is not to discourage the Christians from contributing financially to the work of the Lord, but to open their eyes and to advise them to stop funding the lies and manipulation of Satan. Dear brothers and sisters, please, pray and ask the Lord in which church, ministry, or Christian television network He wants you to give your money. He will definitely lead you to the works that honor Him. If you do it for the love of God, it is impossible for you to give your money for the furtherance of His work and to joyfully help brothers and sisters in Christ who are going through difficult times, and the Lord doesn't reward you for your generosity. He will always do much more than you could ever do.

Another passage of Scripture that has been misinterpreted to rob the people of God is found in Genesis. Noah offered burned offerings to the Lord after the flood, to make peace with God through the shed blood of these animals. This was pleasing to God. He then made a covenant with Noah and his sons to never destroy the earth again with a flood. *"And God spoke unto Noah, and to his sons with him, saying, And I, behold, I establish My covenant with you, and with your seed after you. And I will establish My covenant with you, neither shall all flesh be cut off any more by the waters of a flood; neither shall there anymore be a flood to destroy the earth."* (Genesis 9: 8-9, 11) He continued saying: *"While the earth remains, seedtime and harvest, and cold and heat, and summer and winter, and day and night shall not cease."* (Genesis 8:22)

These verses are not about money. These words were spoken by God to establish a covenant not to destroy the earth again with a flood. However, they were turned into a money doctrine ("seedtime and harvest time") to rob the people of God, benefiting only those who preach it. The *seed* is your money, their church or their ministry is the *fertile soil* and the *harvest* is their windfall from the money you have given to them. You didn't give your money to God because what they taught you was a lie. God doesn't need to lie to you to get your money. He is also not going to give you a harvest when you've been lied to by a seductive spirit from hell, who twists His word to steal your money.

Satan does that, knowing that it's not going to work, His desire is to make you question the integrity of the word of God and then tell you, "You might as well give up, because the word doesn't work." When the harvest doesn't come he'll put the blame on God. He'll accuse God of not wanting to help you, in order to discourage you from serving God. He'll do his best to pull you out of the church, oppress you, and finally turn your faith away from Jesus Christ. And God is not responsible for that. If you had taken time to study the Scriptures, the Holy Spirit would have opened your eyes to uncover the lies, the manipulation and the deception behind these teachings.

▲　▲　▲

Sowing and reaping is scriptural, but "**sowing a seed *for a need***" is not. This teaching is from the Jezebel spirit who inspired a minister of the gospel to teach it. And others have embraced it with open arms because it is a multi-million-dollar teaching but only for those who teach it. But, those who are giving to support the lies of Satan are constantly struggling to make ends meet, with no breakthrough in sight. The twisted teaching of "sowing a seed for a need" has for years poisoned the body of Christ. There is no such thing as "sowing a seed for a need in the word of God." The father of that teaching has twisted the Scriptures to make it say so. And some preachers took it, and ran with it because, as stated it's a multi, million-dollar industry.

The sacrifice, on the cross, of our High Priest, Jesus Christ, is sufficient to take care of our needs. When you approach the throne of grace, putting your faith in Jesus Christ, relying solely on His sacrifice of the cross, in your time of need, He will never fail you. Jesus said: "For after all these things do the Gentiles seek: for your heavenly Father knows that you have need of all these things. *"For after all these things the gentiles seek. For **your heavenly Father knows that you need all these things.**" (Matthew 6:32)*

Then, why do the prosperity preachers tell the people of God to "plant a seed for their need?" Our needs are the responsibility of our heavenly Father, just like the needs of little child are the responsibility of her parents. Dear children of God, you don't have to "sow seeds for your need." Our needs are already taken care of by our heavenly Father. Instead, these prosperity preachers should say "sow a seed for a greed." Why do you keep putting money behind something that is freely given to you by Jesus Christ? He alone should get the glory when your needs are met by His grace. The ransom was paid on the cross. That's why any man-invented formula, inspired by Satan, added to this sacred provision, will come back to you void.

◢   ◢   ◢

These verses in Genesis 9: 8-9, 11, are among the most exploited, the most manipulated, and they rake in millions upon millions of dollars. Those who preach the preposterous prosperity gospel, do it with moving, persuasive speeches, promising the believers who listen to them, a big harvest if they give a large sum of money. The prosperity preachers teach that the harvest is always proportional to the quantity of seeds (money) they sow, which is a truth that is grossly manipulated to play on the people's emotions. They say that if the believers want a big house, luxury cars, designer clothes and the like, then they have to sow more money, so that God sees their great faith. In return, He will open the windows of heaven for them and give them a harvest so immense they will not have room to receive it. Then, the people give a lot of money, but the harvest never comes. The harvest will not come for those who sow seeds (money) on the distortion and manipulation of the word of

God. The harvest only comes for the preachers who sow the seeds of lies, manipulation and deceit. The millions of dollars that are collected stay with the preachers, and that's their harvest for doing the job well for Satan.

Many who have given, wait in faith, believing God for the day the windows of heaven will be open for them to receive their harvest. They've sown a lot; therefore, they have the right to wait for their harvest. When they were facing a financial crisis, or whatever they've been sowing for didn't happen, they became discouraged. In the midst of their financial crisis, after they have given so much money, their pastor tells them, to get out of the crisis, they still have to sow more money.

Their seeds became their chains of slavery. Disheartened, some have left the faith. According to them, they did what God said in His word, and they were obedient to their pastor. They gave when he asked them to, and even went beyond what they could really afford to give. However, the fact is, their pastor was manipulating the Scriptures. He seldom mentions the name of Jesus Christ, he has a closer relationship with mammon (material wealth) he never preaches the cross, and he has no relationship with Jesus Christ. Materialism has become the main focus of Christianity, because of the love of money, and the desire of some preachers to live a lifestyle that exceeds luxury. There is no blessing, no harvest, no salvation of souls, when Jesus Christ, and His sacrifice on the cross are rejected.

▲ ▲ ▲

We must be careful not to put every pastor in the same basket. There are men and women of God who are faithful to Jesus Christ. You can write their name all over the following verse, because they apply it in their lives and ministry. *"Study to show yourself approved unto God, a workman who needs not to be ashamed, **rightly dividing the word of truth."** (2 Timothy 2:15)* They are the men and women who will never bow their knees before Baal no matter what he brings before them. They love Jesus Christ with all their heart. They preach His Gospel without compromise, and God knows them. Just like in the Old Testament, they've been preserved by God to do His work. ***"Yet I*** *have left me seven thousand in Israel, all the knees which have not bowed unto Baal, and every mouth which has not kissed him." (1 Kings 19:18)*

Whether you are in North America, the Caribbean, South America, Europe, Africa, or Asia. If you ask God, in prayer, to lead you to His faithful servants, He will do it. And it is in these churches and ministries that you should give your money because these servants of God take the cause of Christ to heart. They are faithful to Him and to His work. Their ultimate goal is to teach you the sound doctrine of Christ, and Satan is terrified of them.

Always remember this great truth, people of God, your tithes must be given to the work of the Lord because God asks for it. It is His way of giving you increase. He multiplies what's left in your hands after you have given the tithe and offering to His work, so that the money you gave becomes a blessing not a loss. The tithe will advance His work. The church that is doing the work of the Lord will not be hindered by finances to spread the gospel. Your offerings will reach countries you probably will never be able to visit in your lifetime. Through the church outreach ministry, a multitude can benefit by what you give, and it will reach those who are in dire need. You must dissociate yourself from the "sheep in wolves' clothing" who are robbing the people of God.

IT'S HARVEST TIME

THERE ARE PASTORS who started their ministries believing and teaching the prosperity gospel, but who have realized that the formula "sowing a seed for a need," doesn't work. They did not receive the harvest from God they were believing Him for to buy a building for their church or ministry. After going into debt to begin their ministry, they could not pay the utility bills and the rent where the ministry was located. People did not come to the services, as they were expecting. Discouraged, they left the ministry. They had seen such a demonstration of wealth by those who preached the prosperity gospel and these men, and women, spoke about the riches of God, as if it were something so easy to get that your seed (money) is what separated you from an enormous harvest.

They made the riches of God seem so easy to get. It was as though God was sitting on His throne and was saying to anyone that came to Him with a large sum of seed money "If you want material goods, or wealth it's all yours." In fact, what the pastors who were just beginning in ministry did not understand was that the wealth they saw, was the money of all those who, just like them, were giving to these men and women. I've heard more than once, how pastors were leaving the ministry by the hundreds. I think one of the reasons for that statistic is because some of them have been deceived by the erroneous teachings of men and women whom they were following who have been in ministry for years and who, apparently, have successful ministries. However, for them, the enormous harvest never came to meet the needs of their ministry.

To the pastors that have left the ministry: This is not the time to quit! It's harvest time! God called you to the ministry for such a time as this. It is the highest calling on planet Earth. Jesus your Lord said: *"Do you not say. 'There are still four months and then comes the harvest'? Behold, I say to you, lift up your eyes and look at the fields, for they are already white for harvest! And he who reaps receives wages, and gathers fruit for eternal life, that both, he who sows and he who reaps may rejoice together. For in this the saying is true: 'One sows and another reaps.' I sent you to reap that for which you have not labored; others have labored, and you have entered into their labors." (John 4:35-38)*

▲   ▲   ▲

I want to accentuate these words spoken by Jesus "I sent you to reap that for which you have not labored..." You were sent by the Lord in the harvest to reap lost souls for His Kingdom. Go back to the ministry! Preach "Christ crucified," preach the blood, preach the cross, glorify Jesus, exalt Him in your ministry; and watch Jesus do what He promised: draw all men to Himself. You will see the difference in your ministry. Reject the false seductive teachings of the Jezebel spirit, who wants to replace Jesus with mammon. And avoid, at all costs, the infiltration of the spirit who possessed Bera, the king of Sodom, (Satan himself) in your ministry or church. This spirit is always after the "persons" in exchange for riches. If you abandon the harvest, you are forfeiting your wages, which are your fruits for eternal life. Your fruits are the souls that are waiting to meet Jesus (the Messiah) like the Samaritan woman. These men, whose ministries you were following, have no relationship with Jesus Christ. You need to grow closer to the Lord and not a superstar pastor. The display of wealth you are looking at is from the Jezebel spirit and Bera, "one and the same." That's their reward for teaching the body of Christ false doctrines. They have compromised the gospel of Jesus Christ with Jezebel and Bera, in exchange for wealth."

I think some of these ministers started well in ministry. Perhaps they let preachers with great names, who were in ministry before them, that have been seduced by the Jezebel spirit infiltrate their ministry with erroneous teachings. They possibly, opened themselves up to these teachings because of the money involved. Perhaps the Holy Spirit had warned them not to go the way of these men, not to embrace their teachings, but they ignored Him. As long as they have breath, it's never too late to go back to the cross. It's never too late to make it right with God. I don't mean mentioning the cross here and there, but truly returning to the preaching of the cross, returning to "Christ crucified."

Some ministers of the gospel would probably say, "There are many other truths to be preached from the Bible. We can't just focus on the cross." To that I would respond, I agree. A preacher must preach the whole counsel of God. He must encourage, rebuke ungodly living, and preach the blessings of God to give the people hope and all the other truths. However, the foundation of the whole counsel of God is: "Jesus Christ and Him crucified." There are no truths that can be preached when THE TRUTH, Jesus Christ, is excluded from the sermons week after week. The cross must be preached, to put the redeeming plan of God in the forefront to usher in the end time harvest of souls, and for the believers to maintain a faithful walk with the Lord. There isn't a book in the Old Testament that doesn't portray Jesus and in the New Testament He became flesh and dwelled among men. Bring Jesus Christ and the cross back into the church, bring Him back into your ministry. Some preachers will not take that chance, for fear if they start preaching the cross, and start addressing sins, then the people might leave, but that's not what Jesus said. He said, ***"And I, if I am lifted up from the earth, will draw all peoples to Myself."*** *(John12:32)* Lift the cross! The decision to go back to preaching Jesus Christ and Him crucified can be the difference in what you'll hear from Jesus *"His Lord said unto him, Well done, good and faithful servant; you have been faithful over a few things, I will make you ruler over many things: enter you into the joy of your Lord. "(Matthew 25:23)* or *"And then will I profess unto them, I never knew you; depart from me, you that work iniquity."* (Matthew 7:23)

▲ ▲ ▲

The questions I would like to ask the pastors who no longer preach Jesus Christ, no longer preach the cross, and no longer preach the covenant blood of Jesus are: When was the last time you preached a sermon about Jesus, and His sacrifice on the cross? How can lost souls be saved in your congregation when you have rejected God's plan of salvation from the foundation of the world which was Jesus' death on the cross? How can you remain faithful, when you have parted ways with the Faithful One, Jesus Christ?

The preaching of the cross shakes the foundation of Hell. It will take away lost souls from the hands of Satan. The devil will do all that he can; he'll give money, power, glory, notoriety, and the fame of this world to a minister of the gospel in exchange for the preaching of the cross. He will do his best to divert a man or a woman from the call of God to serve Him in the ministry. He will put anything she or he would desire at her or his disposal, and let this person think that it is the blessing of God, and that it is He who is giving the increase. God does not reward disobedience, nor rebellion.

The exclusion of Jesus and His finished work on the cross from the Gospel has a negative impact on the earth. It hinders the Holy Spirit. Therefore, sinners cannot be saved and He cannot distribute His gifts to the believers as He would want to, resulting in no anointing and no power of God in these kinds of churches and ministries. The people of God cannot receive the blessings of God that He would want for them.

There will be many pastors who will come to themselves and recognize that they are not preaching the gospel of Jesus Christ. They will see how their messages have done more harm than good. They will turn away from the hellish seductive teachings, inspired by the Jezebel spirit, and will go back to preaching the cross so that the people can receive all the benefits of the cross. But there are others, who are so corrupt, they will cling to the false doctrines inspired by the Jezebel spirit, at the cost of their soul.

The erroneous teachings work well for some preachers because they can reach millions of people on television, on the radio and via the Internet. Many people believed their teachings because they heard them from someone who was on such a large, visible platform. They thought that what they were hearing in the media was the sound doctrine of Christ. Until, some started noticing that none of their prescribed formulas for success, how to become rich, spiritual growth, prosperity and how pastors can expand their churches with man fabricated methods, etc…, didn't work.

There are many self-help books that are written by ministers of the gospel that rarely mention the name of Jesus. This wicked world wants nothing to do with Jesus Christ. So, in order for their books to sell well, Jesus has to be excluded. And yet, Jesus declared: "Without Me you can do nothing." Saved and unsaved people are buying these books to search for answers that were given two thousand years ago at the cross. It is heart- wrenching to see how the children of God rush to buy their latest book, even though, the ones they bought before didn't deliver what they promised. The people of God are blinded by some of these ministers' fame, wealth, and social status. The people even put the books they purchased from these preachers aside because they were useless. These books have helped no one but the people who wrote them. They brought a great financial harvest to them.

The growth of a church is the sole responsibility of the Holy Spirit. As we see in Acts 2:47, "*The LORD added to the church daily those who were being saved.*" If people are not being saved, the church cannot grow because the Lord cannot add unsaved people to it. These people that the Lord added daily to the church were saved because the apostles of Jesus Christ preached about Jesus, His blood, His death on the cross and His resurrection. The Holy Spirit was able to convict the people of sin, which prompted them to give their heart to the Lord.

▲ ▲ ▲

MERCHANTS ON THE ALTAR!

On several occasions, I've seen servants of God use the books they, them-selves, have written to preach the word of God to their congregation. These messages are broadcast on television but, it's something that should never hap-pen. The only book that the servants of God should use to preach from at the pulpit is the Bible. The pulpit is placed on the altar. In the Old Testament, the altar was a type of the cross. It was the meeting place between God, the leader and His people. The Lord spoke to Moses and told him "*And there I will meet with the children of Israel, and the tabernacle shall be sanctified by My glory. **And I will sanctify the tabernacle of the congregation, and the altar:***

I will sanctify also both Aaron and his sons, to minister to Me in the priest's office."
(Exodus 29:43-44)

We understand once a person is born again, they can call on God anywhere at any time. The believers' heart is the best altar that they can address God from. However, in the church the altar is the place where the pastor ministers to God. A place where the hearts the Holy Spirit has touched during the service will go when the pastor gives the altar call to be born again. It is there that the destiny of men, women, young people and children will be changed for eternity. A place where the children of God will receive their deliverance, their healing, the answer to their prayers and guidance from the Lord. No pastor should defile this place.

I have also noticed that a lot pastors do not give any importance to the altar in their church. They seldom give an altar call for the salvation of souls, or ask the people to gather there to pray for them. In some churches it's just a platform. It is probably because many pastors have turned their back on the cross. Some defile it, some never use it. It is the meeting place of God with His people and Satan loathes this place in the churches. That is why, in many churches, he has succeeded in eliminating its use. He has played a role in defiling it, by the promotion of man's written books, which only profits the pastor who has written the book. The pastors who promote their books from the pulpit have no reverence for God, otherwise they would not do it. Such an activity is equivalent to those who were buying and selling in the temple that Jesus drove out in Matthew 21:12.

There is not a book that a man could write that can replace the Bible. There would be no problem if the pastor announced, to the congregation that he had written a book and informed them where the book could be purchased. But, to use it to preach, and to put the Bible aside, is also equivalent to the sons of Aaron who offered profane fire before the Lord in Leviticus 10:1-3. The motive that pushes a servant of God to do this is publicity for their book. The motive for such action is money. Yes, more books sold, more money in your bank account!

It is a great thing to write books. It can encourage Christians in difficult times, or for other reasons. However, it doesn't matter what the degree of one's spirituality is, no man is capable of writing a book that is so well written that the author can preach directly from it and lay the Bible aside. There is absolutely no book a man, or a woman, can write that can replace the Bible. The Bible is inspired of God. It is immutable. This is what keeps the Bible at its most holy place. There is nothing more to add! God did not forget anything. There is nothing that he could have explained better. This keeps all books that man could ever write in their place and at a different level. They are limited!

▲   ▲   ▲

REMEMBER JESUS CHRIST!

In his first epistle to Timothy, Paul wrote: "As I besought you to abide still at Ephesus, when I went into Macedonia that you might charge some that **they teach no other doctrine**." (1Timothy 1:3) Paul asked Timothy to remain at Ephesus, so that he could dissuade the false teachers who were attempting to teach the believers a different doctrine than what Paul taught. In his second epistle, he emphasized the following: *"Remember that Jesus Christ, of the seed of David, was raised from the dead according to my gospel." (2 Timothy 2:8)* Remember! It simply means to never forget. In other words, He told Timothy he was to teach others not to preach any other doctrine than Jesus Christ crucified and raised from the dead.

Paul understood the importance for a minister of the gospel not to stop preaching "Christ crucified," who was raised from the dead. It was a reminder also for Timothy to know that if he swayed from preaching "Christ crucified," he would leave his ministry open for deceiving spirits, and doctrines of demons to take hold of his ministry. Any preaching or teaching that excludes Jesus Christ, His sacrificial death on the cross and His resurrection from the dead can be classified as *"...profane and vain babblings: for they will increase unto more ungodliness." (2 Timothy 2:16)*

▲   ▲   ▲

In the book of Revelation Chapter 2:18-29, Satan infiltrated the church of Thyatira under the mask of a prophetess named Jezebel who was teaching false doctrine and was corrupting the servants of God. The Jezebel spirit's foot print can still be seen in the modern church. Satan has no other objective, then to eradicate the name of Jesus Christ in the church, in order to render the church ineffectual. But this is not possible; Jesus paid the ultimate price for this not to happen. It cost Him His life.

The pastor should preach the whole counsel of God. However, when a pastor makes the deliberate choice to preach what's more appealing to the people rather than to preach Jesus, and the cross, he has betrayed the Lord. The pastor's messages may make the people shout, when they hear the words of motivation (mostly based on materialism), which sound so sweet to the people's ears, but these messages will bring no change in their lives. That's what spiritual adultery is: It is embracing the teachings of the Jezebel spirit and imposing it on the people of God, for whom Jesus died on the cross.

A message that is inspired by Holy Spirit will always bring change to the heart and it will never exclude Jesus Christ from the sermon. When Jesus and His sacrifice on the cross are excluded from the preaching and teaching of the Word, the Holy Spirit cannot work in that congregation. They work in perfect harmony with one another; they are inseparable. When Jesus Christ, is replaced with materialism, money, psychology, manipulation, gimmicks, and the wisdom of man, the Holy Spirit is grieved and hindered. There will be no conviction of sins, which brings repentance towards God and conversion to Jesus Christ. So the people can shout, run up and down in the aisles of the church because they feel so good, but they will remain as they are.

The Holy Spirit, whose mission is to convict man of sin, cannot work in such an environment. Jesus is the Truth and there is no truth to guide the people to, because a lying spirit has replaced the Truth. The ministry of the Holy Spirit is to glorify Jesus. When Jesus is excluded from the messages' week after week, the Holy Spirit has no one to glorify. With His abstention, the pastor has to come up with his own "feel good message" using the word of God he has twisted, and to convey what he knows will make the people shout and dance. It is the Holy Spirit that helps the Christian live a victorious life in Christ. The promises of God, which are eternally true, will never see the light of day in these kinds of churches. The Holy Spirit will not work in any congregation where Jesus is not King and LORD.

Even though the footprint of "the Jezebel spirit" of Thyatira can still be seen in the modern church, the spiritual condition of the modern church is the same as the church in Laodicea, the apostate church. John recorded, in the book of Revelation, *"And unto the angel of the church of the Laodiceans write; These things said the Amen, the faithful and true witness, the beginning of the Creation of God; I know your works, that you are neither cold nor hot: I would you were cold or hot. So then because you are lukewarm, and neither cold nor hot,* **I will spue you out of My mouth.** *Because you say, I am rich, and increased with goods, and have need of nothing; and know not that you are wretched, and miserable, and poor, and blind, and naked. I counsel you to buy of Me gold tried in the fire, that you may be rich; and white raiment, that you may be clothed, and that the shame of your nakedness do not appear; and anoint your eyes with eye salve, that you may see. As many as I love, I rebuke and chasten: be zealous therefore, and repent. Behold, I stand at the door, and knock: if any man hears My voice, and open the door, I will come in to him, and will sup with him, and he with Me. To him who overcomes will I grant to sit with Me in My throne, even as I also overcame, and am sat down with My Father in His Throne. He that has an ear, let him hear what the Spirit says unto the churches."* (Revelation 3:14-22)

▲   ▲   ▲

The spiritual condition of that church made Jesus nauseous. He told the church, "I will *spue* you out of My mouth." That means He wanted to vomit. Have you ever been nauseous? They were lukewarm towards Him and it made Him sick. They knew about Jesus, but they didn't have a relationship with Him. They were preoccupied with materialism. Since the modern church is in the same condition as the Laodicean church, Jesus feels the same way about: "sow a seed for a need" "name it, claim it," "fake it until you get it," "give me my stuff," "the power to make it, is within you," "money cometh," "wealth transfer," and the "deceptive prosperity" kinds of teachings and attitudes. Not forgetting the teaching: "once you are born again, you never have to ask God again for forgiveness, you can go on and sin it's all covered" and all the other "feel good" and "ear tickling" compromising teachings.

The modern church is self-righteous, prideful, blind and arrogant. Some pastors are so arrogant that they no longer dress like men of God to preach the gospel of Jesus Christ. They wear jeans and sneakers behind the pulpit on Sundays. They want to look like "Hip-Hop artists." Or "thugs with pants on the ground" The businessmen of the world have more respect for their secular offices than these so-called pastors have for the offices of the Holy Spirit. You would never see a businessman wear jeans and sneakers to a business appointment. Every time a man or a woman steps behind the pulpit of a church to preach, he or she has a divine appointment with the Lord. He or she should expect the Lord to show up to empower him or her to minister to His people. I've seen a pastor wearing jeans and sneakers ministering in his church at a Christian television station. People of God, listen! If that pastor had an appointment to meet with the President of the United States, or the Queen of England, he would never show up with sneakers and jeans. This man, and others like him, have no respect for God.

These men who want to trash their pulpit have a seductive, evil spirit that is influencing them. That's why the people in their church cannot react and put up with this nonsense. Some congregants think it's Okay, or that their pastor is "cool." Men and women of God, that's not right. These pastors are not setting a good example for your children and grandchildren.

The fact that you wear your best to go to church and teach your children to do the same, shows that you know you are going in the presence of God, who is worthy of you wearing your best for Him. It's a sign of reverence towards Him.

Some of you, who used to dress conservatively because you honor and respect Jesus, whom you were going to fellowship with, have changed your style because of your pastor who feels going in the presence of God is a casual affair. It's not worth dressing up to go in His presence; that's being disrespectful to God. Your pastor has been lied to by Satan, to make him think there is nothing wrong with him wearing jeans and sneakers on Sundays to minister, firstly, to God, and then to His people. This is Satan's ploy to debase the church of Jesus Christ. These pastors are teaching people to "always ask God for His best, because God gives the best," but they don't want to wear their best to come in His presence.

The modern church is full of unsaved people that have not received the white garment of the righteousness of Christ. They think they are saved, but they are not. Among the unsaved are those that came from the Catholic Church. They may think because they go to church every Sunday and shout and dance along with the crowd, they are saved. Just as it was, when they were in the Catholic Church, their salvation was in the church affiliation, rather than Jesus Christ, who can only clothe one in His righteousness by His sacrifice on the cross. This condition exists because the pastors no longer preach the cross, the meeting place between God and men.

The Laodicean church had put Jesus out and had replaced Him with materialism. That's why we see Jesus *outside,* standing at the door knocking. This condition still exists in the modern church. Not every church falls under that category. There are some good churches wherever you are in the world. You just have to pray and ask the Lord to lead you to one. Our human eyes can easily see the church's wealth, especially the private jets that some pastors use for their luxurious and carefree travel. But Jesus said, "You are wretched, miserable, poor, blind and naked."

Going to church on Sundays is a habit for some attendees. The church is no longer a meeting place between God and His children, where, in their encounter, lives can be changed and souls can be saved. It has become a place for social gathering, where they dance to all kinds of music influenced by the world, in the name of worship to Jehovah God, the Thrice-Holy God. When the service is over, they go back home, just as they came. They do not know God. Their relationship with Him is limited to, "Give me, give me, I need, and I need." Their pastor is more interested in material wealth than the well-being of these precious souls, leaving them vulnerable to every wind of doctrine. Those who end up feeling this emptiness in their soul, hop from one church to another and from one religion to another. Some are so disheartened that they end up leaving the faith.

⋏   ⋏   ⋏

Jesus is offering the four things that the church needs to remedy the situation. *"I counsel you to buy from Me gold refined in the fire so you may be rich; and white garments, that you may be clothed, that the shame of your nakedness may not be revealed; and anoint your eyes with eye salve, that you may see. As many as I love, I rebuke and chasten. Therefore, be jealous and repent"* (Revelation 3:18-19)

1-*Refined gold*
Refined gold speaks of humility. Gold is a precious metal. In order for it to be refined, it has to go through the fire to remove its impurities. It is this process that gives it its beauty, and brilliance. Then, the Master Goldsmith can make anything he pleases out of it. The church needs humility —the kind Jesus displayed in His earthly ministry— and it can only be obtained when the Church humbly surrenders itself to the Lordship of Jesus Christ by returning to the cross. When that happens, the church will have true riches that are everlasting.

2-*White garments that you may be clothed...*
The white garments are symbolic of the righteousness of Christ, purity and holiness. Since the church has put Jesus out, it has no covering. It's operating in the flesh, and under the influence of the enemy. With Jesus and the Holy Spirit being absent in the church, its nakedness is exposed. One has to be in deep spiritual slumber for you not to see that the modern church is naked. It can be clothed again in the white garments that Jesus is offering when it returns to the cross.

3-*Anoint your eyes*
Until the church can take a look at itself and see its spiritual condition, there will be no changes. Change will occur when the pastors stop embracing the erroneous doctrine that a minister of the gospel who has been influenced by

the Jezebel spirit comes up with that sounds good. They usually start teaching this false doctrine as if it were their own, while this new teaching, they have embraced is from the pit of hell. They embrace the minister's erroneous teaching probably because of their lack of understanding of Scriptures. And most of all they are blind. They can't see. They can no longer discern what's of God and what's of the enemy. When these pastors go back the cross, the Holy Spirit will return with His anointing balm to open their eyes and allow Jesus to do for them what He did and is still doing for His servants who are faithful to Him. *"Then opened He their understanding that they might understand the scriptures." (Luke 24: 45)*

"And they said one to another, did not our heart burn within us, while He talked with us by the way, and while He opened to us the scriptures?" (Luke 24:32)

In spite of its condition, Jesus has not given up on this church. He is inviting Himself back in. He is standing at the door, He is knocking, and He is also speaking to the church. He is saying, *"Behold, I stand at the door, and knock: if any man hear my voice, and open the door, I will come in to him, and will sup with him, and he with Me."(Revelation 3:20)* He desires to have fellowship with the church. Sadly, the church is too preoccupied with materialism to hear His voice. "If anyone hears my voice" is an individual call. Can someone in the leadership of the church come to its senses and realize that the church has headed the wrong way? That it needs to return to the "preaching of the cross"? Jesus Christ must be at the center of everything, most importantly the sermons, in order to attract lost souls to Him and to maintain a close relationship with Him. That's the only way fellowship can be restored.

It is Satan that has come against the church, but he will not prevail. The church is in a spiritual warfare and the only way it will overcome is by the blood of the Lamb. *"And they overcame him by the blood of the Lamb, and by the word of their testimony; and they loved not their lives unto the death." (Revelation 12:11)* Jesus also said, *"…To him who overcomes will I grant to sit with Me in My throne, even as I also overcame, and am sat down with My Father in His Throne."*

Jesus overcame Satan on the Cross. That's where the church will overcome Satan also. Now, all the church has to do is to return to the cross.

4-*Repent!*

Jesus is asking the church to repent out of love, the great love that sent Him on the cross to die for us. If they refuse to listen to the Lord, they can expect great trials and tribulations, and even sudden ruin.

▲   ▲   ▲

Here is what Paul, under the inspiration of the Holy Spirit, wrote about the church that Jesus is coming back to take with him. He made a comparison with the marital union to explain the union which exists between the church and Christ *"For the husband is the head of the wife, as also Christ is head of the church; and He is the savior of the body. Husbands love your wives, just as Christ also loved the church and gave Himself for her that He might present her to Himself a glorious church, not having spot or wrinkle or any such thing, but that she should be holy and without blemish." (Ephesians 5:23, 25, 27)*

The first miracle Jesus performed is recorded in John 2: 1-11. It was at a wedding in Cana of Galilee, He turned water to wine. I always wondered why the first miracle Jesus performed, recorded by the Holy Spirit, had to do with turning water to wine. The wine is symbolic of Jesus' blood that was shed on Calvary's cross. I believe by turning the water to wine at the wedding Jesus was telling us that the marriage covenant is under the covenant blood of Jesus, just like the church is under His covenant blood. For this reason, the marriage that God approves, and that He is involved with, can never be destroyed by man or Satan.

The blood will never run out of miracles, as long as you remain anchored to Jesus and the cross. All you have to do is call on Him to supply you with whatever you need. He can turn your drought into an overflow. It is Christ, who is the head of the church, not Satan or the Jezebel spirit one in the same. Christ is its savior. He is our High Priest and has paid a great price by shedding his blood on the cross to bring the church forth. By looking at the influence of Satan in the church, I now understand the words of Jesus to Peter, with regard to His church: *"He said unto them, but whom say you that I am? And Simon Peter answered and said, You are the Christ, the Son of the living God."* (Matthew16:15-16) Jesus knew that Satan was going to come against His church. He then said to Peter: *"And I say also unto you, that you are Peter, and upon this rock I will build my church; and the gates of hell shall not prevail against it." (Matthew 16:18)*

Jesus did not say that the church would be built on Peter, the disciple with whom He was speaking. When Jesus said: "… upon this rock will build my church…" He was not talking about the brick and mortar buildings where people go to attend services on Sundays. He was rather talking about living stones who are born again believers, also known as the body of Christ with Jesus being the Head. Jesus is the Rock, the Chief corner stone upon which the church is built. He told Peter you are a stone. Peter means "stone" (a small rock). Jesus also said, "upon this rock" (referring to Peter's revelation that He is the Son of the living God) the church will be built." That is, on the Chief cornerstone, which is Jesus Christ. The following verses speak of Jesus as the Chief cornerstone: *"The stone which the builders refused is become the head stone of the corner." (Psalms 118:22)*

"This is the stone which was set at naught of you builders, which is become the head of the corner. (Acts 4:11)

Peter remembering the word of Jesus to him, telling him that he is a *"stone,"* inspired by the Holy Spirit would later write: *"If so be you have tasted that the* **Lord is gracious. To whom coming, as unto a living stone,** *disallowed indeed of men, but chosen of God, and precious,* **you also, as lively stones,** *are built up a spiritual house, a holy priesthood, to offer up spiritual sacrifices, acceptable to God by Jesus Christ. Wherefore also it is contained in the scripture,* **Behold, I lay in Zion a chief corner stone, elect, precious: and he who believes on Him shall not be confounded."** *(1 Peter 2:3-6)*

Not only Peter, but all believers are lively or living stones, a fragment of the Chief Cornerstone, the **Mighty Living Stone.** "We are being built up a spiritual house, a holy priesthood, to offer up spiritual sacrifices acceptable to

God through Jesus Christ," the Chief Cornerstone. Therefore, the church is not built on Peter a small living stone, although precious in the eyes of the Lord, but on Jesus Christ the Son of the living God. Because of that fact, Satan will never prevail over the church of Jesus Christ.

When the leaders of a church allow the Jezebel spirit to reign in their midst by preaching and teaching false doctrines, that church is left to rely on fads, and gimmicks, which are most of the time taken from the world. In fact, because the Holy Spirit has remained silent, the leaders no longer know what to do. The pastor of that church usually say their fads and gimmicks are their formula, to attract people from the outside. Those fads and gimmicks also keep the members distracted. It's similar to when Adam and Eve sewed fig leaves to cover themselves, after their fall, when the glory of God departed from them.

These activities embraced by the church are just like fig leaves, they're used to blind the people so that they do not see the spiritual drought of the church. They dance, they have a good time, but their feet slip week after week towards the world and gradually away from Jesus Christ and the cross. I believe the children of God should always rejoice in His presence for what He has done in our lives. He is not the God of the dead. I am not against rejoicing in the presence of the Lord when it's genuine, that is, when Jesus Christ reigns in these churches. But, when the rejoicing, (dancing) is done like the fig leaves to hide a spiritual drought and other problems of the church, it's just a façade. That's when it is carnal and it doesn't glorify God.

PROSPERITY RESTORED

"As for You also, by the blood of Your covenant I have sent forth Your prisoners out of the pit wherein no water is. Turn you to the strong hold, you prisoners of hope: even today do I declare that I will render double unto you." (Zechariah 9: 11-12)

IN THE YEAR 2006, I lived in Atlanta, Georgia. I was going through a difficult time and I became so discouraged that I wanted to quit the ministry. It was in this passage of the book of Zachariah that God revealed to my heart that it was only by the blood of Jesus, shed on the cross of Calvary that I would triumph over the situation I was facing and by no other means. Shortly thereafter, a door was opened for me.

In this passage of Scripture in the book of Zachariah a wonderful promise was made to Israel against its enemies. For a great majority of us, these verses speak to our present difficulties. They are very encouraging words. Many times I felt like I was in that waterless pit, but because of this promise I would rejoice, knowing that the power of the blood of Jesus can deliver at any time, in any season, and in any generation.

This promise was pointing to the cross. Because of the covenant blood of Jesus, many will be set free from the waterless pit they fall into. — A pit of despair, heartaches and struggles with no end in sight and from which they cannot come out of themselves. It's a gloomy pit. You can only be a prisoner of hope when you fall into that pit. Knowing, deep in your heart, that you're coming out of it because of the blood Jesus shed on Calvary's cross. When you have hope the light may become dim, but it will never be completely turn off.

Hope will keep it on. The prisoners of hope are those who have put their faith in Jesus Christ and His sacrifice on the cross. God commands the prisoners of hope who are in the waterless pit to return to the "strong hold" which means return to the "fortress." The definition of a fortress in the dictionary is: "Any place of exceptional security." (Dictionary. com Unabridged. Random House, Inc.) Some may have become disheartened because of their dire situation. God is telling those who are disheartened to **return to the cross**. The place of exceptional security. That's where He promised to restore double unto us. It's the place of our victory, where Jesus paid a great price to liberate us from this hellish pit. What a great promise from God!

What I like the most about this promise is that it's a promise the Father made to the Son. It's based on the covenant blood of His Son to bring those who belong to Him out of the waterless, hellish pit we may find ourselves in. Did you get that? Let me repeat it: This promise is a promise made by God the Father, to Jesus Christ, His Son, and it is sealed by the covenant blood of Jesus. If you are a born again, child of God, you will come out of your waterless, hellish pit by the power of God Almighty. This covenant was made two thousand years ago. Child of God! Your deliverance is not in your seed and your confessions, but in the blood of Jesus that was shed on the cross where the covenant was sealed. You are guaranteed "double for your trouble." God, the Father, is saying to each one of us to return to the fortress which is the cross; the meeting place, there He will meet with us to restore "double unto us." It is to your advantage that you accept Jesus Christ as your Lord and Savior. This promise is made to those who belong to Him.

⚔ ⚔ ⚔

I have heard some of the proponents of the prosperity gospel say: "When you give your money to God, if what you give is so little, that it doesn't mean anything to you, it will not mean anything to God either. To make God move in your favor you must give a big offering to show your faith, so that he will answer your prayers." According to Zechariah 9:11-12, the only thing that makes God move is the covenant blood of His Son, Jesus. You must give money to the work of the Lord to enable the gospel to reach lost souls. It can be difficult for the gospel to go forth without your financial assistance. God will always bless your generosity. However, if the reason you give a large sum of money is to get His favor, it will never happen. If God responded to that, He would betray His Son. The sacrifice of Jesus on the cross would have no meaning. The deliverance of man would depend on what he can give to God. Such approach would put the emphasis on what man has given, not what Jesus Christ has done.

The second time God revealed to me that the cross is the answer to man's dilemma was April 2010, at that time I was again facing some difficult times, so much that I could not even pay my rent. The owner of the apartment had taken me to court. I confessed the word, I never stopped giving to the work of the Lord, and I prayed. The Lord spoke to my heart again, as He did back in 2006, this time it was through this passage in Isaiah 10:12-14. The king of Assyria had been used by the Lord to destroy the Northern Kingdom. This was something the Lord had to accomplish because the people's deeds were wicked in His eyes. This king went beyond what the Lord had allowed him to do and he bragged as though it was by his own strength that he had devastated the nations. The Lord resolved to punish him. The passage reads as follows:

*"Wherefore it shall come to pass, that when the LORD has performed His whole work upon mount Zion and on Jerusalem, I will punish the fruit of the stout heart of the king of Assyria, and the glory of his high looks. For he says, by the strength of my hand I have done it, and by my wisdom; for I am prudent: and **I have removed the bounds of the people, and have robbed their treasures, and I have put down the inhabitants like a valiant man: And my hand has found as a nest the riches of the people: and as one gathers eggs that are left, have I gathered all the earth; and there was none that moved the wing, or opened the mouth, or peeped.**" (Isaiah 10:12-14)*

The king of Assyria in this passage is a type of Satan.

When Satan comes against a person, his attacks are subtle. It is his nature to steal. Jesus spoke about him in these terms, *"The thief does not come except to steal, and to kill, and to destroy. I have come that they may have life, and that they may have it more abundantly." (John 10:10)* It is after Satan has stolen, killed and destroyed, one can evaluate the extent of his damages. And after you have evaluated them, you are left dumbstruck. ***Not "a peep" can come out of your mouth,*** as the king of Assyria said. Notwithstanding, Jesus Christ, the Son of God opened His mouth and cried for us on the cross. *"**Jesus, when He had cried again with a loud voice,** yielded up the spirit." (Matthew 27:50)*

He is our voice; He cried to the Father for us, and His voice reached heaven. They were cries of deliverance for mankind. It is the price He paid to deliver us from this tyrant, Satan, who is no longer allowed to steal the blessings of the children of God. Among the things the king of Assyria said, the following really struck a chord in me. *"**My hand has found like a nest the riches of the people. I have removed the boundaries of the people, and have robbed their treasuries.**"* Isn't that what Satan does? He lays his hand on the treasuries of the people, on what belongs to them, and he steals them in order to give them to his servants.

That's the reason many people live in poverty— even extreme poverty — their treasures are in the hands of Satan. The only thing that can change their situation is when they are born again into the kingdom of God. When that happens, God becomes their provider. They may still face some financial difficulties, but God will ***always*** make a way to provide for their financial need. Prosperity was restored at the cross. All those who want prosperity in all aspects of their lives have to come to Jesus Christ and obtain it through His finished work on the cross.

The second time I received the revelation from the Lord. That it was through Jesus' shed blood on the cross, I will come out victorious over any difficult situation I am facing. And that's the only means provided by God, to meet anyone's needs; it went down deep into my soul. My situation had not changed overnight, because I received this revelation from the Lord, but my eyes have never turned away from Jesus and His sacrifice on the cross. This truth will be forever engraved in my heart. Victory is in Jesus Christ and His finished work on the cross!

ᛜ   ᛜ   ᛜ

The fact that God revealed His word to you does not mean that you are not going to encounter difficulties. He is going to test you. At the end of the test, you always discover His awesomeness, and how faithful He is. Whatever the circumstances, do not let your eyes turn away from "Christ Crucified" and resurrected from the dead. Your deliverance is guaranteed through Him!

When you are a child of God, prosperity is not acquired by giving money to any organization, any church, or any ministry on planet earth, nor, by the manipulation of the word of God or by reciting verses of the Bible like robots. God honors the fruit of the labor of His children, which is your tithe and offerings. When you give money to His work, He'll recompense you in many ways. I am hoping you can now see that the prosperity message you are sowing seeds into will never bring a harvest.

Prosperity was restored to us free of charge, two thousand years ago at the cross. All you have to do is to believe God, with a childlike faith, for the things you desire from Him, knowing that it is already done in Jesus name. The Father will grant you your request to glorify His Son.

Though prosperity is not limited to money, alone, more than ever, when the Church speaks about prosperity, the emphasis is always on money and material goods. After many years of receiving the *prosperity teachings,* which were mainly geared towards wealth and material goods, some people may have finally realized that it doesn't work. They have now turn to the cross to get the wealth and riches that they've been waiting on for years because they have learned that we obtain God's blessings only through the finish work of Jesus on the cross. If you are among them, you're going to have to strip the false prosperity teachings out of your mind. Revelation 2:23 says God "searches the heart and tests the mind" God knows the motives with which we give. Your approach to the cross, first and foremost, should be to have a closer relationship with Jesus Christ, to live for Him daily and to maintain a meaningful prayer life before the Lord. You have believed this man- fabricated prosperity gospel, influenced by Satan to steal your money, for years. Now, why don't you turn to the simple truth of the words of Jesus Christ? *"But seek you first the kingdom of God and His righteousness; and all these things shall be added unto you." (Matthew 6:33)* If you are resolute in your heart to do that, then you don't ever have to worry about material goods. You don't have to sow seeds in order to get material things. These things shall be added unto you, (given to you) for sure.

God put you in a material world. He knows you have material needs, such as, money, a house, a car, clothing, etc., and when God gives, He gives the best. He blesses His children every day with material goods. Can you testify that this statement is a reality in your life? The house, the furniture, the car and other things you wanted that you bought were purchased with the money you obtained from the Job He gave you. He protects you every day on your way to work and gives you the strength to perform your duties at work so that He can bless you with the desires of your heart. Think about that! There is no limit to what God can do for His children because of the shed blood of His Son, Jesus, on Calvary's cross.

In retrospect, I now fully understand why the Lord showed me twice in Scriptures that the finished work of Jesus on the cross, where He shed his blood, will deliver me. The formula I was taught all these years, is not what would deliver me but Jesus' sacrifice on the cross alone, with nothing added to it, with no gimmicks attached to it. The added formula was my seed, and my confession of the word.

As I have stated before, there is absolutely nothing wrong with confessing the word of God, and sowing financial seeds to the work of the Lord, but they have their place. They should not be done to show God our faith, nor to move His hand. Everything is done in order in the kingdom of God. Moreover, the pastor of the ministry I was sending my seed said that his ministry was "fertile soil," and since my seed was planted in that fertile soil, my harvest was guaranteed. Looking back, he was saying, his "fertile soil," or his ministry, would bring me the harvest. That statement omits Jesus as the source of the harvest. The words of these pastors are spoken with such craftiness that it is extremely difficult to discern them, when you sit under their ministry. I did what I was taught, and it didn't work. The Lord opened my eyes to see, and to understand, that it is not Jesus and a combination of other things that bring a harvest.

⋏　⋏　⋏

The prosperity preachers do not preach prosperity without showing evidence. They are rich, — extremely rich—and you would think, right away, that they have indeed found the way to the golden pot of heaven, and that if you adhere to their teachings for obtaining wealth, one day the lot would fall in your favor as well.

The prosperity gospel has impoverished some people in the church. They have given the money originally allocated for their mortgage, or car note, to their pastor after hearing him preach a sermon on prosperity, taken out of the Bible that he distorted, and promised them a harvest in days. Often times, the money is collected after a sermon on prosperity is preached, to make sure that a lot of money is given. These kinds of sermons are sweet to the ear, and they are delightful to the heart, but they are just sweet empty words. Although taken from the word of God, they've been manipulated by the kingdom of darkness, to benefit and to maintain the excessively luxurious lifestyle of the men and women who preach them.

The people gave their money because they really believed that their pastor heard the voice of God. There is always a seductive demonic spirit behind these sermons. That's why the people cannot control themselves, and they believe the lie. Then, they find themselves two to three months behind on their mortgage payment, their car note payment, and their utility bills. Next, their car is repossessed, or their house foreclosed. Their pastor's sermon was so convincing that they gave him the money that was going to keep a roof over their head. The harvest never came because it was a lie. God had nothing to do with that lie. He is not going to finance the lies of Satan, using those men and women who have long forgotten the meaning of integrity and honesty.

Furthermore, their pastor tells them, "If the devil has stolen your car or your house, God will give you a better and bigger one." They still believe, and they still continue to sow financial seeds after this big harvest that they're waiting for, but that never comes. They are so addicted to these kinds of teachings that it becomes like gambling. One of Satan's financial bondages in the world to impoverish the addicted person. To recuperate the money, they lost, they have to keep on gambling. As ridiculous as these stories may sound, that is what's going on in many churches, and it does go to that extent. The people are bewitched. Even after such great financial hardships, they can't break loose from those pastors. The prosperity gospel is not helping the believers, but rather keeps them miserable because it keeps them focused so much on material things that they are continuously sowing seeds (money), claiming and naming things, laboring after material goods, and end up not having time to enjoy fellowshipping with Jesus. It takes the joy out of the relationship. They are not resting in Jesus. Just when they thought it was harvest time that they were going to get a breakthrough, they didn't get anything. All they were left with is a broken heart. *"A merry heart does good like a medicine: but a broken spirit dries the bones."* *(Proverbs 17: 22)*

The danger with dry bones in the human body is that they break. This creates a lot of problems. A broken bone can seriously impair one's mobility. It's the same spiritually, it will affect your spiritual walk and can impair it greatly, to the point where you walk away from God.

Does this mean we should not ask God for things that we want? I am not saying that at all. We should ask God for the things that we desire. He is your Father! The difference between putting your faith in Jesus, and His sacrifice on the cross, to receive from God and the teachings of the proponents of the prosperity gospel is that God will always answer you when your faith is exclusively in the shed blood of Jesus Christ on the cross. You sure will get what you ask the Lord for.

You must learn to be satisfied in Jesus Christ, otherwise, you will always feel like you lack something in your life. When you compare what you call lack in your life to the standard of living of a great majority of people around the world, you are a wealthy person. You can work hard to buy all the things you desire (without God's help), like many have done, only to discover the emptiness is still within you. Things from the material world cannot fill the heart. On the other hand, the fulfilled promises of God, and His blessings, provide a merry heart, joy unspeakable and peace.

A A A

The spirit that introduced the teaching of "sowing a seed for a need" in the church is extremely shrewd. Everything is seemingly done in the name of Jesus, but, in reality, that teaching excludes Jesus Christ. The subtle emphasis is always on the amount of seeds (money) you sow, and that's twisting the Scriptures. If you can understand what I just said here, Satan will not take another penny from you because you will stop giving your money to the followers of Jezebel. She pays these ministers well for taking your faith away from Jesus and putting it in your seeds and your confession. Then they blindfold your eyes when they add "In the name of Jesus" to their prayers. You can't use a man-made method, inspired by Satan, add "in the name of Jesus" to it and expect to get good results. That's precisely what's happening in your life. That's why you don't see any good results. Ask the Lord to open your eyes to what I've just said here. That's what will make a big difference for you to be truly blessed by the Lord. Or, you can stay in that vicious cycle, of "Sowing a seed for your need," and obtain nothing.

I believed in what these pastors were teaching because I saw the evidence in their lives. I still had some reserve though, about their method of constantly asking the believers to "sow seeds for their needs." It didn't feel right. This caused me to refrain from applying their method in my own ministry. I was young in the ministry. They were my model; they were my teachers. I bought their tapes and their books to study, and I believed in their interpretation of the Bible. Until, the Lord opened my eyes to see and understand that their prosperity gospel, their "seed for a need" teaching, "confession brings possessions" and many other gimmicks were not of the Holy Spirit.

There are people in the church that are constantly asking God for money in their prayers to give to these prophets and prophetesses of Jezebel, since they have to sow more seeds money in their ministry and churches to get a huge harvest to recuperate what their pastor told them that Satan has stolen. Yes, Satan has stolen your money to give it to your pastor. So that when you lose your house, your car and are in great financial distress, and God does not come to Bail you out you can forget His name. Some believers have resorted to using their credit cards to help them with their financial struggle. With more debt incurred, their financial situation worsens.

This financial crisis creates a perfect atmosphere for Satan to enter the homes and wreak havoc. Situations that have in many cases resulted in divorce, which leads to the destruction of families. Many believers have testified of the financial abuses going on in their church and many more will attest that this is also their story. There are others who have used their credit cards to make purchases beyond their means, in order to live the life of luxury, because they knew that in only a matter of time, God would send them a huge financial harvest. Years have passed by and they have received nothing but some are still believing the lies up until this present hour. They are continuously told that they have to keep sowing seeds (money) regardless if they didn't see the harvest yet, and are in debt. Because it's the seeds they are sowing that will bring them a huge harvest to make them debt free.

The people of God are taught, by these prosperity preachers that to receive something from Him, they have to sow a seed. In other words, they have to give Him money first. In their prosperity verbiage, they call their ministry, or church, the "good soil" in which the people must sow their seed, in order to receive a bountiful harvest. If you gave them your money, and you never received the harvest, it's because you were not sowing into a "good soil," but into a lie. What father would take pleasure in seeing his child bring him an envelope with money each time she needed something, because the child believed that it was the only way she could get his attention or obtain the favor she was requesting from him. And what father would find pleasure in seeing his child sad because she didn't have any money to put into an envelope to bring to him, and she knew that without the money, she stood no chance of getting anything from him.

Is this a healthy relationship between a father and his child? Pastor, is this the kind of relationship you have with your own children? You, as a parent, appreciate it when your child gives you a gift for your birthday, or the Christmas holidays or Father's Day, or Mother's Day. It is a mark of affection and honor. And if you knew that your child didn't have money to offer you a gift, your love for your child would not diminish. The fact that you didn't get a gift or money from her would not prevent you from giving her, your best. Everything that your child needed you would still give it to her.

Jesus made these statements, recorded in the book of Matthew. "Or what man is there of you, whom if his son ask bread, will he give him a stone? *Or if he asks a fish, will he give him a serpent?* **If you then, being evil, know how to give good gifts unto your children, how much more shall your Father which is in heaven give good things to them that ask him?"** (*Matthew 7:9-11*)

Our heavenly Father gives to His children unconditionally! We can obtain what we need from Him in the name of Jesus freely. It is written: *He who spared not His own Son, but delivered Him up for us all,* **how shall He not with Him also freely give us all things?** (Romans 8:32) He did not ask for a financial seed. He gives all things freely. God will never be manipulated by the teachings inspired by the Jezebel spirit. I hope you have already seen how some men and women take the promises of God from the Bible, which are true and misinterpret them for their own personal gain.

According to the word of God, our need is taken care of daily by our heavenly Father. Jesus said, *"(For after all these things do the Gentiles seek :)* **for your heavenly Father knows that you have need of all these things."** (*Matthew 6:32*) Brothers and sisters, these words that came out of the mouth of Jesus were not limited only to the basic necessities of life. They addressed every need of man.

▲　▲　▲

Jesus also told the people how to get their need met. *"He said, but seek you first the kingdom of God, and his righteousness; and all these things shall be added unto you. Take therefore no thought for the morrow: for the morrow shall take thought for the things of itself. Sufficient unto the day is the evil thereof."* (*Matthew 6:33-34)* Jesus is telling us not to worry about tomorrow. Instead of worrying about your needs, and planting seeds to change your circumstances (which will never happen). You should do exactly as Jesus said: Leave your needs in the hands of your Heavenly Father; and trust Him to take care of them. Our heavenly Father knows that we need all these things, because He is omniscient.

All some believers know about Jesus that resonates with them, is that they can get material goods in His name. We just read that Jesus told the people that their heavenly Father was aware of their needs. Then, is it necessary to constantly bombarding them with these "seeds for need" messages like you've been doing for years? Instead, you should be looking after the well-being of their soul, which only a close relationship with Jesus Christ through the cross can produce. Have you become the tares that Jesus doesn't want to uproot now, so that He doesn't harm the wheat and is awaiting harvest time to separate the two?

Let me reiterate: There is absolutely nothing wrong as children of God, to ask Him the material things that we desire. We live in a material world. We need material goods so, we need money to acquire them. We are children of the Most-High God and we do not have anybody else to ask, but Him. What's being addressed in this book is the manipulation of Scriptures, the greed, the lies, the false doctrines, the deception, the constant preaching on materialism, the flesh- inspired methods taught to the children of God to climb the ladder of success, the false promises, the rejection of the preaching of the cross, and the expulsion of the name of Jesus from His church. There are too many issues to mention, I have only mentioned a few.

The children of God need to know that as long as they want to adhere to these teachings, God cannot bless them. You can ask your heavenly Father for whatever you want with a childlike faith in Jesus Christ, and Him alone. Don't bring an envelope with money before God with your request. Instead go under the shed blood of His Son, Jesus that's what will move heaven and earth on your behalf. Stop approaching God with "the seed for need" mentality. It's not working, and will never work since it's a lie. Approach Him by the way of the shed blood of His Son Jesus on Calvary's cross; it will never fail. Amen!

When we have a request before the Lord, and He is working behind the scene to make it come pass, He will put faith in our hearts to continue believing Him for it. He'll give us peace of mind until He grants us that request. The people of God are constantly worrying about tomorrow because faith cannot come from something a lying spirit has concocted. In fact, it will produce worry. If you have given a large sum of money as a seed, you have planted it for something that is of concern to you. When you see that this concern still remains, and the harvest has not come to take care of it, it produces worry.

The only thing you probably have not been asked to plant a seed (money) for is your salvation. They will tell you that it is free. You obtain your salvation at the cross, in the name of Jesus, and it's free. It is also the way you are going to obtain everything else you need from God, at the cross, in the name of Jesus, and it's also free. Even though salvation is a gift from God, there are some pastors that would still ask the people to sow a seed for the salvation of their loved ones. Who wouldn't want their loved ones to be saved from the horror of hell? If the loved one you sowed seeds for to be born again is indeed saved, it wasn't because of the money you gave, but rather because of the grace of God who answered your faithful prayers. Salvation is free! No seed money is needed for God to answer that prayer. It is His gift to all men, women and children of all ages, but only those who have accepted it will receive it.

It is a serious sin in the eyes of God to continue giving your money to the churches and ministries whose teachings are greatly influenced by the Jezebel spirit of Thyatira, who is still at work to this day. When you put your money behind these teachings, you are committing spiritual adultery. The Blessings promised in the word of God are for you, but there are few who benefit from them because too many have left the cross, the meeting place of God with man.

You cannot separate Jesus from the cross. Satan is terrified when we mention "Christ crucified." He will do everything he can to prevent Christians from mentioning the cross. Therefore, if somebody says to you: "we preach Jesus" and they don't mention His sacrifice on the cross as the source of all blessings but rather seed money, and confession of the word. "It is another Jesus, a different Gospel, another spirit." 2 Corinthians 11:4.

In in second epistle to the Corinthians Paul wrote: *"But I fear, lest by any means, as the serpent beguiled Eve through his subtlety, so your minds should be corrupted from the simplicity that is in Christ." (2 Corinthians 11:3)* That's right, the serpent has seduced and corrupted the hearts of many from the simplicity that is in Christ. The simplicity of Christ is His death on the cross to save people from every nation, all races and all languages through the acts of believing in Him, and asking the Father to forgive their sins in His name. The corruption sets in the heart when whoever is preaching the word, start to focus more on materialism than the cross of Christ. When the means to get "your stuff" is by sowing more seeds (money) instead of looking to Jesus, who paid a great price on the cross, to provide us whatever we need from the wells of salvation. The serpent has nothing to do with "Christ crucified," he fights the preaching of the cross in the churches around the world because he knows that he is in danger of losing anyone who invokes the name of Christ crucified and resurrected from the dead in faith.

▲   ▲   ▲

Paul also warned the believers about these deceitful workers. *"For such are false apostles, deceitful workers, transforming themselves into the apostles of Christ. And no marvel; for Satan himself is transformed into an angel of light. Therefore, it is no great thing if his ministers also be transformed as the ministers of righteousness; whose end shall be according to their works." (2 Corinthians 11:13-15)*

How can one reject the teachings of Christ and embrace those of the enemy and think that everything is going to work wonderfully for them? That's what the enemy has been doing since the Garden of Eden. He promises happiness to man, and the opportunity to pass to another dimension in his life, with his own knowledge, and his own method of fixing things, but excluding Jesus Christ the giver of life. Instead he plunges him into a deep black hole of endless despair.

As a matter of fact, those who preach the prosperity gospel, are to a great extent, those who live the luxury lifestyle. With so much money taken every week from the believers, they can increase their salary as they please. Their wealth increases and everything goes well for them. Some have said, they do not take a salary from their church. Why should they? It is because of years of amassing their fortune from their church that they have more money in their bank account than their church has in its bank account.

Many are no longer walking with Jesus, but with their pastor, their confessions and their seeds. Adding "in the name of Jesus" after a prayer does not mean that you have a relationship with him. It's up to you to decide! Are you going to continue to walk with these men and women in their erroneous teachings, and never see the goodness of the Lord in the land of the living? Or are you are going to come out from among them, and go back to the cross to walk with your Redeemer, and experience His love and His blessings of every kind?

The soul of man will never be satisfied, until it is reconciled with Jehovah God his Creator. The disciples of Jesus understood that and their ministry was focused on the Lord. They showed the way that leads towards the heavenly Father, by the way of "Jesus Christ." The enormous price that Jesus paid for the redemption of souls made them conscious of their mission. The disciples' responsibility was to proclaim this truth to people everywhere they went. They never forgot Jesus in their preaching and teaching. Everything they said and did was always about Jesus. They were conscious of the great responsibility that the Holy Spirit had entrusted to them concerning the eternal destiny of man.

Many people that follow these ministries, and attend the churches that are teaching erroneous doctrines, have a void that is never filled up. Therefore, those people go from one religion to another, and from one church to another. They are always in search of the new preacher everybody is talking about, hoping that he or she will bring them relief. Certain pastors avoid the preaching of the cross in order not to offend the congregation, and to maintain a vast crowd. There are also some people who attend these churches that have no intention of becoming attached to Christ and His teachings. They only want to feel good when they come to spend time in church. They always want to hear "God loves you," that "He is going to open the windows of heaven to pour out a blessing for you," and that "you are next in line to receive a big promotion."

All of that can be true for a child of God. It is God's nature to bless His children, however, the majority of times these words are spoken to manipulate the people. They bring a brief sensation of well-being to the soul and they are very pleasing to the ear. When the people hear these words, their emotions are worked up to a point where they can't control themselves anymore. They feel like they are in heaven and, being in such a state of mind, they cannot restrain themselves from opening their wallets and pouring out money they cannot even afford. They don't realize that they are in a hellish environment, where a so-called minister of the gospel is distorting the word of God to do the work of Satan.

▲   ▲   ▲

The saddest part is when you meet these precious souls after the service, and they are on such an emotional high, that they will quickly tell you, "Church was good today." But, if you come back to them a year later, and ask them if any of these promises came to pass in their lives they'll tell you "No." There are some who do not want to hear messages about the cross—the place where the passions of the flesh are mortified. In some churches if the pastor began preaching "Christ crucified." They would take off like a flash of lightning. The cross exposes sin in the life of the believer or non-believer. It is a reminder to every believer of the price Jesus paid to set them free from their habitual life of sin. The cross brings conviction to the heart of man. Instead of running far from it, they should run towards it. It's a place of great triumph. Therefore, the Pastors who are like psychologists and the motivational speakers prefer not to preach the cross, and not to address the issue of sin, for fear of diminishing the number of attendees in their church.

In addition, some attendees do not come to hear the true gospel of Jesus Christ, which has the power to transform them. They come for a psychology session, which briefly mentions the name of Jesus, if at all. However, it would be better for a pastor to go back to "the preaching of the cross," which would produce healthy sheep for the Lord Jesus, rather than to conform to the desire of the people, to preach and to teach what they want to hear. At the end, the pastor will appear alone before Jesus Christ, to give an account to Him, of the ministry that He had entrusted to him.

Many ministers of the gospel proclaim: "We preach the Gospel without compromise." Yet the name of Jesus is hardly mentioned in their messages. When His name is mentioned, it is associated with money. Some Sundays the name of Jesus is not even mentioned once in the sermon, if you think that you are preaching a Gospel without compromise, you are seduced by the Jezebel spirit. She wants nothing to do with Jesus Christ and the cross. She has coerced you into excluding Jesus from His church, in order to give place to the preaching of materialism, you are among those who call Jesus, "Lord, Lord" but you have no relationship with Him.

It's been such a long time that you have been compromising with the Jezebel spirit that your condition has become your very nature. Your conscience is seared. Nothing that you do troubles your mind. You have become like a wild horse, without restraint, in your erroneous preaching and teaching that have gone way beyond the teaching of Jesus Christ. The disciples of Jesus understood that the rich men, as well as the poor ones, must be taught that the answer to their problems is Jesus Christ. Whatever the nature of the problem is. He is the only one who could help the poor people overcome the financial difficulties, they were faced with. They never told to anyone: "If you want to go out of this life of poverty, to have a better life, you must sow seeds or give money to God in our ministry, that's your way out of lack."

▲ ▲ ▲

The Holy Spirit is raising up men and women from the "back side of the desert," from foreign lands, from all over the world, who will once again preach the sound doctrine of "Christ crucified." When a pastor is continuously preaching materialism, psychology, and everything in between that has nothing to do with Jesus Christ, he is not feeding the sheep of Jesus Christ. They are going to be spiritually emaciated. Pastor, you need to go back and listen to your sermons again, you will then see you how far you have drifted from Jesus Christ, and far from what the Lord called you to do in the ministry, that is, to preach the gospel of "Christ crucified" so souls can be saved and the saved ones can have a victorious life in Christ

The hour has come for the church to look up, not look down. When a preacher is continually preaching materialism, you are looking down and when you are constantly looking down, you become empty. That's why, Preacher, when the next guy comes with a new revelation from the pit of hell, it is like fresh manna to you because of your spiritual drought. You embrace the new revelation, run with it, feeding the people of God this toxic revelation from hell, and mixing it with the word of God. The people then take this lethal dose of your teaching, which is keeping them in sin, oppression, and in the bondages of Satan. These types of messages do not glorify God, they do not honor Jesus, and they grieve the Holy Spirit. Go back to "the preaching of the cross!" That's what is going to prepare the church for the return of Jesus Christ.

> *"No man can serve two masters: for either he will hate the one, and love the other; or else he will hold to the one, and despise the other. You cannot serve God and mammon." (Matthew 6: 24)*

It is obvious that those men and women, who are continuously asking for money out of greed, love Mammon more than they love Jesus Christ. They preach about money continuously, but rarely if at all about Jesus' sacrifice on the cross. When Jesus' name is mentioned, often times it's to associate Him with money. Their love is for Mammon. If Jesus had not been to the cross for these proponents of the "prosperity gospel"—to save their souls —they would be lost forever, destined to hell's fire. If Jesus Christ had not made Psalm 113:7 true in their lives, their names would not be famous worldwide. *"He raises up the poor out of the dust, and lifts the needy out of the dunghill." (Psalm 113:7)*

It is because of Jesus death on the cross that they have become who they are. The respect and admiration that these men and women receive from others are because of Jesus Christ. If some of them are still alive, it is because of the stripes Jesus received at the hands of sinners, shedding His blood on the cross to provide their healing, but they have completely forgotten Him. It is reflected in their sermons. The preaching of the cross is foreign to them.

They are doing their own work to accumulate personal wealth and they are no longer doing the Lord's work. Some of them have gone as far as removing His name from their church replacing it with a more modern name. Some pastors teach others that their success depends on their own efforts, and they organize seminars to teach others how to find the way to success without Jesus. They climbed up the social ladder and arrived at a level that has caused them to become egotistical. They'll use anyone, and anything, to get to where they want to arrive, even the enemies of Jesus Christ, who have publicly proclaimed that He is not the only way to God. They have left Jesus, their first love, and have not even realized it. They have been blinded by the mighty dollar. Their platform is so elevated that Jesus has diminished, and they have increased, contrary to what John the Baptist said about Jesus, *"He must increase, but I must decrease." (John 3:30)* To many church attendees, Jesus has become a bleak personality in the background. Their pastors have become the bright shiny superstars of Christianity. They have become the god of their church.

▲　▲　▲

In the midst of all these prosperity messages, and the opulent lifestyle of their pastors, some of the believers who attend their churches are oppressed. They are living a life opposite to that which was promised to them by their pastors. They are in serious debt. They are not living the victorious life Christ died to give to them. They are doing all they can, they are applying their pastor's teachings to their lives and it doesn't work. It's the same deceit week after week, month after month and year after year. These assemblies are exactly where the Jezebel spirit is reigning, when Jesus is excluded from the church, when the preaching of the cross is omitted the only things that are left are Satan, the flesh with its passions, foolishness and insanity.

Peter, inspired by the Holy Spirit, wrote the following about false prophets and false teachers, who will **secretly** bring in damnable heresies into the church. They will use deceptive words to entice you. *"But there were false prophets also among the people, even as there shall be false teachers among you, who* **privily** *shall bring in damnable heresies,* **even denying the LORD who bought them,** *and bring upon themselves swift destruction.* **And many shall follow their pernicious ways;** *by reason of whom the way of truth shall be evil spoken of. And through covetousness shall they with feigned words make merchandise of you: whose judgment now of a long time lingers not, and their damnation slumbers not." (2 Peter 2:1-3)*

These verses of scripture are not referring to some unknown men and women from the extremity of the world. They are referring to those who stand before you, week, after week, on the church pulpit bringing you seductive heresies. Yes, they do deny the Lord, that's why you don't hear any sermons about Jesus, no messages about the cross of Christ. If you are living in this world, you know the way of truth is blasphemed because of their false doctrines, greed and folly. Now after the Holy Spirit has revealed this truth to you, do you think, He is going to finance this exploitation and deception by giving you wealth and riches to continue giving money to these false prophets and false teachers?

It is with sadness that I watched how these preachers went after money on some Christian television stations. During one telethon, I heard a pastor say that God told him that there was a businessman watching and that if he gave one million dollars, he was going to get a multi-million-dollar contract in just days. In order for him to make his pitch for funds in the time slot allotted to him during the telethon, I remember the pastor saying that the business man he was supposedly talking about should call. I believed it back then. He wanted that businessman to call on his clock as proof that he had heard from God. But he didn't call at that time, because it was not true.

If God had truly spoken to him, the businessman would have called to confirm the word of God. They needed the money and they were not going to stop at anything to push this person to give that amount of money. In my opinion, they go to such lengths to raise money for that television station in order to maintain their name on the short list of good fundraisers. That way, they get called back for every telethon, and they maintain their notoriety on that television station.

⋏　⋏　⋏

WEALTH TRANSFER!

There are a couple of pastors in the field whose core message is: "There's a transfer of wealth, which is going to take place, where God is going to take the wealth of the wicked and transfer it to His children." They tell the believers, with certainty, that they would receive this money. To receive their portion of this transfer of wealth, all they would have to do is to sow seeds (money) into their ministry towards this great harvest. Many Christians are waiting for this transfer of wealth to take place. For those who do not follow these men and women's ministries, who are not members of their churches, it is easy to see that this is silly, or to spot the lie right away. However, the followers of these ministries, believe the false teaching so much that they'll stake their lives on the lie, since they believe it to be so true.

One of the verses that they often used to persuade the believers of this fact is: *"A good man leaves an inheritance to his children's children: and the wealth of the sinner is laid up for the just." (Proverbs 13:22)* They would also refer to the Egyptians who gave Israel the wealth of Egypt, when they were leaving Egypt, on their way to the promise land. *"And the children of Israel did according to the word of Moses; and they borrowed of the Egyptians jewels of silver, and jewels of gold, and raiment: And the LORD gave the people favor in the sight of the Egyptians, so that they lent unto them such things as they required. And they spoiled the Egyptians. Now the sojourning of the children of Israel, who dwelt in Egypt, was four hundred and thirty years." (Exodus 12:35-36, 40)*

Friends listen! The children of Israel worked as slaves in Egypt. They were there for four hundred and thirty years. Pharaoh subjected them to hard labor with inhumane conditions and they were hard workers who were not paid any wages. They cried out to God, and He heard them. He sent Moses to deliver them. When the children of Israel had to leave Egypt, the Lord, who is righteous, transferred the wealth of Egypt to them. He had given to them what they were owed. They were not lazy people who confessed the word of God, night and day, dropping a couple of dollars in an offering basket and awaiting the wealth of the wicked. They were not greedy or covetous people who were never satisfied with what they had while they were in Egypt. If this were in the present time, they would not come in agreement with any lying preacher, who came along promising them the wealth of the wicked if they sowed money into his ministry.

It was God's idea that the wealth of Egypt would be transferred into their hands. They had nothing to do themselves to receive it. They didn't know how they were going to get it. They had to continue to work and believe God for their deliverance. When the time had come for God to deliver them, He moved on the Egyptians' hearts, and gave His people favor in their sight. Then, God told Moses what to tell the people to do get the goods.

In this day and age, it is the preachers who are preaching this lie, who are telling the people what to do to get the wealth of the wicked that's coming to them, but they don't even know when that wealth transfer is going to take place. However, they constantly ask the people to sow seeds into their ministry to receive their share. And they don't even care if the people give their entire life savings, and end up with no money to take care of their own needs. As long as they get their money to satisfy the greed of their flesh, they're set. People of God, listen! If a preacher tells you: "God said you have to sow such and such amount of money to get the blessing of the wealth transfer of the wicked." Or, he is personally telling you himself that you have to "sow money to partake of that wealth transfer" he is lying.

If there was going to be a wealth transfer, it would happen in God's timing, and in His way. Then, He would move on the heart of the ones who have the wealth, and He would give His children favor in their sight to obtain whatever He wanted them to have. That's the example set before us in His word. And God doesn't need help from any avaricious, corrupt man, or woman, to make it happen. He wouldn't need us to give money to any ministry or any church in advance in order to receive the "wealth transfer." In other words, He would not need our help. He is God. Whatever He does, He wants the glory for Himself. The children of Israel couldn't come back and say if they had not done this, that or the other, they wouldn't have gotten their share of the wealth transfer of Egypt. No one can get credit for what happened that day, except for God. If there was going to be a "wealth transfer of the wicked" to the children of God, in our times, it would not be any different.

In the New Covenant, everything we receive from God, is given to us because of Jesus Christ' sacrifice on Calvary's cross. He died, not only to save us from our sins, but also to restore everything stolen from us by Satan. So, under the new covenant, which is sealed by the blood of Christ, it's not a question of sowing seed continuously to await the "wealth transfer of the wicked," but rather a matter of returning to the cross. That's where every need in man's life is met.

⅄ ⅄ ⅄

The wealth transfer some pastors have been preaching about, actually happened two thousand years ago at Calvary. Remember what Jesus told His disciples after His resurrection, before He ascended to heaven, "And Jesus came and spoke unto them saying, *"All power is given unto me to Me in Heaven and in earth." (Matthew 28:18)* Everything that we need is under Jesus's power. Satan who is the chief of the wicked was bankrupt after the death of Jesus on the cross, and His resurrection. The children of God are not getting the full benefits of the sacrifice of Jesus on the cross because their pastors have rejected "the preaching of the cross," the place from where all blessings flow, to preach false doctrines inspired by Satan.

Those pastors are promising the children of God a wealth that is no longer in Satan's hand, but under the power of Jesus Christ. Take your eyes away from the wealth of the wicked, put them on the wealth of Jesus. The wealth of the wicked can't come close to what Jesus possesses. He is our Lord and Savior, let us keep our eyes on Him in these perilous times. That's what every child of God ought to do. That's what every conscientious pastor ought to preach.

If the people went back and studied every Scripture that the preachers have quoted to make them give money, they would see, in some cases, the people, or the person, who received the "wealth transfer," did not get a fair share for their hard labor. God gave it back to them by taking it from the hands of those who abused them. He still does this in many ways unknown to man. God does not reward laziness.

Jesus said in *Luke 10:7, "the laborer is worthy of his hire"* meaning that he should get paid fairly for his labor. God is on the side of the worker. If he doesn't get his wages, God will find a way to get it to him. If the people of God would take their time to read the Bible, the Holy Spirit would reveal the truth of His word to them, and they would stop believing the lies and manipulation of these corrupt men and women.

Furthermore, the Bible teaches *"And whatsoever we ask, we receive of Him, because we keep His commandments, and do those things that are pleasing in His sight. And this is His commandment that we should believe on the name of His Son Jesus Christ, and love one another, as He gave us commandment." (1 John 3:22-23)*

The commandment God has given us to receive whatever we asked Him is "Believe on the name of His son Jesus Christ and love one another." If you do not obey this commandment, you will not receive anything from God. Whatever else you do to obtain the favor of God is disobedience to His commandment. When you need anything from God, and you stand in the name of Jesus because of His sacrifice on the cross, God will hear you. John never mentioned money, nor "a seed for a need." Wake up, people of God! You've been robbed by Satan for too long. Believing in Jesus goes hand in hand with loving one another. The love that you have for your brothers and sisters in Christ will prevent you from exploiting them.

You cannot violate the commandment of God by following preachers who have twisted the word of God, feeding you their own formula to receive the blessings of God, and expect to receive God's blessings. I wish from the bottom of my heart that you would see, from the aforementioned verses that it is imperative that you put your faith only in Jesus Christ, the Son of God, with no gimmicks attached. This way you will be able to receive from God and to love one another, because God is love. How could you help your brother, who is in need, if you do not love him? Unfortunately, there cannot be love in an assembly where the Jezebel spirit is reigning. It is confusion, materialism, hypocrisy, and all kinds of turmoil that reign in these assemblies

▲   ▲   ▲

The people are bound. There are evil forces behind these teachings. They are lies from the pit of hell. Their pastor used the word of God to perpetrate these lies. Such pastors are not thinking about the people of God, they are thinking about themselves, their ministries and their families. These men and women need large sums of money to support their luxurious lifestyle and their ministries, for their own glory. Therefore, they are going to get this money any way they can. It is a sad situation, but it is a reality.

Dear child of God, God wants to bless you. He said in His word, *"Who has prevented me that I should repay him? Whatsoever is under the whole heaven is Mine." (Job 41:11)* The precious things He has under heaven are not for the angels; they do not need it, and they are not for the devil either. They are for His children. Brothers and sisters in Christ, you are responsible to stop funding Satan's agenda. Return to the truth, return to the simplicity of the gospel of "Christ crucified."

Satan told Jesus that he would give Him the glory of this world if Jesus would agree to bow and worship him. That's what it would take for Jesus avoid death on the cross. But, He chose to pay the ultimate price for us, so we can be saved, and so that we can obtain what we ask our heavenly Father for in His name. If you take your eyes off the sacrifice of Jesus on the cross, and go before God with the lies you've been taught, your prayers will not be answered. It's up to you to put an end to these abuses.

Brothers and sisters in Christ, The things you want God to do for you that He alone can perform, such as: the salvation of loved ones, victory over hellish situations, a breakthrough in your financial crisis, a reversal of that death sentence from an illness, your healing, deliverance from spiritual drought — everything that you desire— whether it be a husband or a wife, resolution of marital problems, and anything else that affects your pilgrimage on this Earth, the answer is in one person, Jesus Christ!

You must also understand that even though your faith is in Jesus and the cross, it will neither pressure God to answer your prayers overnight, nor will it pressure Him to answer contrary to His will. What interests God the most is your spiritual walk. His priority is that you are transformed into the image of His Son, Jesus. His desire is that you seek first the kingdom of God and its righteousness. In the process of doing so, some of the things that you thought were necessary for your survival, will not interest you anymore. Even if the answer to your prayers takes a little time, if your faith remains anchored in Jesus Christ and His sacrificial death on the cross you will see the promises of God being fulfilled in your life. Your prayers will be answered. That is what glorifies God.

THE MANTLE OF ELIJAH

ELISHA WAS CHOSEN by God to replace Elijah, and it was God who told Elijah to anoint Elisha, along with Jehu and Hazael. The anointing belongs to God. He is the one who chooses whom He wants to anoint for His service. The story of the prophet Elijah, who was taken up in chariots of fire to heaven and passing his mantle to his servant Elisha on his way up is another passage of Scripture that is distorted by some pastors to corroborate their claim that the anointing that is on them can be transferred to their partners in the ministry. God had ordained Elijah to anoint Elisha as prophet, Hazael as king, and Jehu as king before the translation of Elijah took place. Let's read that passage together. *"And the LORD said unto him, Go, return on your way to the wilderness of Damascus: and when you come, anoint Hazael to be king over Syria: And Jehu the son of Nimshi shall you anoint to be king over Israel: and Elisha the son of Shaphat of Abel Meholah shall you anoint to be prophet in thy room." (1 Kings 19:15-16)*

The day Elijah was to be taken up to heaven, he had to cross the Jordan River, and he was with his servant Elisha who did not want to be separated from him. This event is recorded in the Bible as follows: *"And Elijah took his mantle, and wrapped it together, and smote the waters, and they were divided hither and thither, so that they two went over on dry ground. And it came to pass, when they were gone over, that Elijah said unto Elisha, ask what I shall do for you, before I be taken away from you. And Elisha said, I pray you, let a double portion of your spirit be upon me. And he said, you have asked a hard thing: nevertheless, if you see me when I am taken from you, it shall be so unto you; but if not, it shall not be so. And it came to pass, as they still went on, and talked, that, behold, there appeared a chariot of fire, and horses of fire, and parted them both asunder; and Elijah went up by a whirlwind into heaven. And Elisha saw it, and he cried, my father, my father, the chariot of Israel, and the horsemen thereof. And he saw him no more: and he took hold of his own clothes, and rent them in two pieces. He took up also the mantle of Elijah that fell from him, and went back, and stood by the bank of Jordan; and he took the mantle of Elijah that fell from him, and smote the waters, and said, where is the LORD God of Elijah? And when he also had smitten the waters, they parted hither and thither: and Elisha went over." (2 Kings 2:8-14)*

It's a beautiful story of God's power. Elisha asked Elijah for a double portion of his spirit. He, very likely, was asking Elijah for what he had already received from God, when God asked Elijah to anoint him. It probably was not the time yet, for it to be manifested in his life. The answer of Elijah to his request was, "you have asked for a hard thing," because as a man of God, Elijah knew as great as his request was, Elisha was asking him for something that is in the realm of impossibility. When it comes to a man transferring his spirit, or the anointing of God that is upon him, to another man. Elijah never took that initiative in his ministry. It was God who always told him whom to anoint.

As Elijah was taken up to heaven, Elisha tore his own clothes in two pieces. As to demonstrate that he didn't want anything associated with the flesh to hinder this great mantle he was about to receive. He had to make a choice, at that moment, between what made his flesh feel good, protected, and secure, and the anointing of God. The spiritual choice was more precious to him than what made his flesh feel comfortable. At the very moment he did that, it was the greatest sacrifice he could have made, thus showing God that he understood what the anointing was about— that it is holy; it is precious; and it is the power of God in human hands to accomplish great things for Him. Then, Elisha took the mantle (which is symbolic of the anointing) of Elijah that had fallen from him. The mantle fell by itself, and all he had to do was reach out and take it. The mantle was passed onto him effortlessly, by God.

In the Old Testament, Elisha asked Elijah, his master, a man, for a double portion of his spirit. At that time, the Holy Spirit didn't dwell in man. When a man had a special assignment to fulfill for God, the Holy Spirit would come upon him, and anoint him. Once that task was accomplished, He would leave. Elisha, in all probability, didn't understand why it was this way at that time. Although the number of miracles he performed during his lifetime were twice as many as Elijah performed. But what didn't change is that the Holy Spirit could not dwell in him. He came upon him to perform the miracles assigned to him by God, and when he was done, the Holy Spirit left. Just like it was for Elijah, his master. But now, because of Jesus's death on the cross, and His resurrection, those who believe in Him have the privilege of having the Holy Spirit, take up residence in their heart.

The cross, afforded us His righteousness to receive the Holy Spirit's Mighty power. John said Jesus had the Spirit without measure, meaning that there was a continuous flow of the Spirit coming from Him. He sent the Holy Spirit to us, so we can continue to be immersed in that flow. John said Jesus is the baptizer with the Holy Spirit. We receive the baptism with the Holy Spirit with the evidence of speaking in other tongues as the Spirit gives the utterance from Jesus. When Jesus baptizes a believer with the Holy Spirit with the evidence of speaking with other tongues, He doesn't give him a little sprinkle of the Spirit. He receives far greater than what Elisha asked Elijah. He has received God, the Holy Spirit. The giver of the anointing.

Another example we have in regard to God transferring one man's spirit to another is in the book of Numbers. When Moses felt heavy laden with the children of Israel, he cried to God to tell Him the burden was too heavy for him. *"And the LORD said unto Moses, gather unto me seventy men of the elders of Israel, whom you know to be the elders of the people, and officers over them; and bring them unto the tabernacle of the congregation, that they may stand there with you. And I will come down and talk with you there: and I will take of the Spirit which is upon you, and will put it upon them; and they shall bear the burden of the people with you, that you bear it not yourself alone."* (Numbers 11:16-17)

Moses was chosen by God from birth and prepared by God for forty years to deliver the children of Israel from the bondages of Egypt. He was a friend of God, this is the only man of whom God said, "Hear *now My words: If there be a prophet among you, I the LORD will make Myself known unto him in a vision, and will speak unto him in a dream. My servant Moses is not so, who is faithful in all My house. With him will I speak mouth to mouth, even apparently, and not in dark speeches; and the similitude of the LORD shall he behold: wherefore then were you not afraid to speak against My servant Moses?"* (Numbers 12: 6-8)

Of all the prophets, he was the only one the Lord spoke with face to face. Yet, when the burden of the children of Israel was too heavy for him, he cried out to the Lord. He didn't take it upon himself to look for some men in the camp to ask them if they wanted his anointing, and to start laying hands on them to do the work of the Lord. Moses knew the Spirit of the Lord that was upon him to do God's work didn't belong to him. He respected, and honored, the Spirit of the Lord who was upon Him. The Lord told Moses in *Numbers 11:17 "I will take of the Spirit that is upon you and will put the same upon them; and they shall bear the burden of the people with you, that you may not bear it yourself alone."* The same Spirit that was upon Moses was put upon the seventy elders by God Himself. It was not a different Spirit; it was not a different anointing. These men were not prepared as Moses was; Moses's task was unique, he walked in a greater anointing. God took what was upon Moses and put it upon them to enable them to do His work.

The same as the Lord took of His Spirit that was upon Moses and put it on the seventy men to do His work, He imparts the anointing that was upon Jesus to those He has called to do His work. The anointing is given by the Holy Spirit alone, because it belongs to Him. We are anointed through Jesus Christ. The word "anointing" by itself cannot heal cancer, or any other diseases but Jesus, the anointed one can. We are healed by the stripes of the anointed one. The word "anointing" by itself cannot deliver anyone from the bondages of sin, but Jesus the anointed one can.

A lot of people are running after "the anointing." They seek the anointing, the power of God more than they seek having a closer relationship with Jesus, but that's not going to happen. I am talking about Christians and even some ministers of the gospel who have no reverence for Him, and are not living for Jesus, through whom we are anointed. The Holy Spirit anointed Jesus and will continue to anoint the body of Christ through Him. You cannot pursue a greater anointing. It's up to God to anoint you, to equip you, for what He has called you to do. You must pursue a closer relationship with Jesus

Christ through the cross. The Bible does not teach for the believer to tap into the Holy Spirit's power daily, but rather for the believer to take up his cross daily and follow Jesus. (Luke 9:23) Then, the power of the Holy Spirit will be available to the believer daily through the cross.

▲ ▲ ▲

In the Old Testament, there were three kinds of people who were anointed. They were: the prophet, the king, and the priest. All three were anointed with oil by a person designated by God. But, it was different with Jesus. No human hands had anointed Him with oil, and he held all three offices, King, Prophet and He is our High Priest. In Luke 4:18, we read how He stood up on a Sabbath day in the temple. He read from the book of the prophet Isaiah, and said: "The Spirit of the LORD is upon Me, because He has anointed Me…" no one before Him was anointed as He was. No man can fully comprehend the anointing of the Holy Spirit in depth. We're talking about the power of the almighty God. Nonetheless, God simplified it for the human mind to comprehend it through Jesus. All you need to know is that Jesus is the anointed one and that you are anointed through Him. I have heard preachers say things about the anointing that confuse people more than clarifying what it is. The anointing that was upon Jesus is the power of God that the Holy Spirit imparts to a chosen vessel enabling him to accomplish great things for Him.

A preacher is doing a disservice to the body of Christ when he speaks about the anointing as if it were something one can get based on his relationship with the Holy Spirit. If a minister of the gospel rejects the cross of Christ and is seeking a greater anointing, it will not happen. There is no anointing apart from the cross. The Holy Spirit imparts Jesus's anointing to us because of His death on the cross. The anointing is holy. Jesus gives us His righteousness, thus enabling us to receive the anointing of God. The anointing must be maintained at the cross.

▲ ▲ ▲

Many have said that God called them into the healing ministry, yet they are dishonest, and are liars. The truth is, they know about Jesus but, they've never been with Him, the one who could really transform them. "Jesus never calls anyone into the healing ministry, or any particular ministry, but rather to Himself."

Young man, young lady, let me repeat this to you: The call of God you feel on your life is to Himself. Make it your preoccupation, to take up your cross daily and follow Him. Submit your will to Him every day. Live for Him. Seek a closer relationship with Him through prayer and the reading of the word. He, then will direct you to the ministry in which He wants to use you.

The Bible says, *"And He (Jesus) goes up into a mountain, and **called unto Him** whom He would: and **they came unto Him**. And **He ordained twelve**, that they **should be with Him**, and that He might send them forth to preach, And to have power to heal sicknesses, and to cast out devils." (Mark 3:13-15)*

He went up the mountain top and called whom He wanted. (Every true servant of the Lord has heard that call.) They had to climb the mountain one by one to meet the Lord. It was not easy for them to climb that mountain. They probably encountered some obstacles on their way to Jesus, but they kept on climbing because He was calling them. Some probably slid back when they almost reach the top of the mountain where He was and had to begin climbing again. They were not looking at who had arrived but were concentrating on the One, who was calling them. Jesus called some of the disciples by the beautiful, peaceful seashore but they all had to climb the mountain *to be with Him* and *to be ordained by Him.*

Afterwards, He ordained twelve so that they should be with Him. Then, Jesus sent them to do the work of the ministry, which was to "preach, and to have power to heal sicknesses, and to cast out devils." Anyone can leave their net by the beautiful seashore and follow Jesus. Anyone can give up their career and follow Jesus when they're looking at the fame and huge amounts of money involve that the con artists in the ministry are portraying. But, the true disciples of Jesus Christ are those who have been climbing the mountain, even when their lives, at times, seemed without purpose because there was nothing in sight that showed a better future, yet they kept on believing. Their faith was anchored in Him and His sacrifice on the cross. These are the disciples whom the Holy Spirit is going to impart a greater anointing to, in these last days, to usher in a multitude of souls into the kingdom of God with power to heal the sick, to preach and to cast out devils.

The Holy Spirit imparts His gifts, including the gift of healing, only to those who have been with Jesus. Some people claim to know Jesus because they can quote a few verses of the Bible. If they really knew Jesus, they would seek Him to help them deal with issues in their character that are not pleasing to the Lord. They would also know that Jesus is not going to send any first-class liar, or con artist, to "preach, and to have power to heal sicknesses, and to cast out devils." Jesus never sends sons of Sceva into the ministry. It is recorded in the book of Acts, *"Then certain of the vagabond Jews, exorcists, took upon them to call over them which had evil spirits the name of the Lord Jesus, saying, we adjure you by Jesus whom Paul preaches. And there were seven sons of one Sceva, a Jew, and chief of the priests, which did so. And the evil spirit answered and said, Jesus I know, and Paul I know; but who are you? And the man in whom the evil spirit was leaped on them, and overcame them, and prevailed against them, so that they fled out of that house naked and wounded." (Acts 19:13-16)* Know that He didn't call you into the healing ministry, or any specific ministry, but rather He calls people to Himself to be with Him and afterwards gives them assignments. A lot of people want to give themselves assignments that Jesus never gave them. They rather imitate what someone who has been with Jesus, is doing but they don't want to climb the lonely mountain to get their assignment from Him. Since they are fake, Satan gets into whatever they assigned themselves and creates all kinds of problems for them and for the body of Christ.

If you reject the cross of Christ, the daily meeting place and are chasing after the anointing of God, Satan will offer you a counterfeit anointing. He will infiltrate your ministry with fake healing, and demonic signs and wonders. When the people who stood before you, and tell you that they were healed, only to find out afterwards that they were not, or their situation has not changed as you have prophesied, they will tell others you're a false prophet, including the media. The body of Christ is anointed through Jesus. The Holy Spirit doesn't have a separate anointing to impart to anyone.

▲   ▲   ▲

Jesus had the Spirit without measure like none before Him. John said of Jesus, *"For He whom God has sent speaks the words of God: for God gives not the Spirit by measure unto Him." (John 3:34)* Even though He had the Spirit without limitation, He never did anything without the approval of His Father. Listen to what Jesus said: *"Then answered Jesus and said unto them, Verily, verily, I say unto you,* **The Son can do nothing of Himself, but what He sees the Father do***: for what things so ever He does, these also do the Son likewise. For the Father loves the Son, and shows Him all things that Himself does: and He will show Him greater works than these, that you may marvel. For as the Father raises up the dead, and quickens them; even so the Son quickens whom He will." (John 5:19-21)*

He never took it upon Himself to do anything without first consulting with His Father. Jesus was a man of prayer. He was constantly communicating with His Father. Everything He did, and accomplished in His earthly ministry, was approved by His Father. This is Humility, and no one demonstrated it better than Jesus.

After His resurrection from the dead, He gave a great commission to His disciples, who have climbed the mountain and have been with Him and He knew they needed the power of the Spirit to fulfill it. He didn't take it upon Himself to baptize them with the Holy Spirit at that moment. He told them to wait for the Holy Spirit. The gospel of Luke records the words of Jesus: *"And, behold, I send the promise of My Father upon you: but tarry you in the city of Jerusalem, until you be endued with power from on high." (Luke 24:49)*

I hope, by now you have seen that when you hear preachers selling the anointing they say is upon them and their ministry for a seed (money) yes, that's what they say— you can partake in their anointing, when you plant your seed in their ministry. It is a lie. Jesus, the Son of God, who John said baptizes with the Holy Spirit, was fulfilling His mission on earth as a man. But you can see how cautious, He was with The Spirit of the Lord and the anointing that was upon Him. He walked with twelve men for three and a half years. He offered none of them neither the baptism of the Holy Spirit nor His anointing.

They were not yet prepared for it; they couldn't receive it. He told His disciples to wait until He entered His glory, and was in accord with His Father, to send the power from on high to the church. Jesus did not handle the anointing that was upon Him frivolously, as most preachers are doing today. The Holy Spirit is greater than the anointing. He anoints for service. The anointing comes from Him. Some worship the anointing more than God. No one can do the work of God without the anointing of the Holy Spirit. Jesus is God, and as God, He didn't need the anointing. However, to accomplish His mission on earth as a Man, He needed it. It was such an important aspect of His earthly ministry that the Holy Spirit inspired the prophet Isaiah to prophesy about Him being anointed in Isaiah 61:1-2. When that prophecy was to be fulfilled, Jesus went to the temple on a Sabbath day, it is recorded in Luke 4: 18-21. They handed Him the book of the prophet Isaiah, He read from the passage that prophesied about Him. Then, He told the congregation, "Today this Scripture is fulfilled."

On that day, Jesus confirmed He was the One whom the prophet Isaiah prophesied about when he wrote that passage of Scripture. In order for Jesus to preach, to heal the sick, to give sight to the blind spiritual sight and natural sight, to set the captives free, to deliver the oppressed and to perform all the miracles in His earthly ministry, He needed the anointing of the Holy Spirit. Jesus, knowing that it would be impossible for His disciples to do the work of the Lord without the anointing of the Holy Spirit, commanded them not to depart from Jerusalem, but to wait for the Promise of the Father. *"And, being assembled together with them, commanded them that they should not depart from Jerusalem, but wait for the Promise of the Father, which, said He, you have heard of Me. For John truly baptized with water; but you shall be baptized with the Holy Spirit not many days hence. (Acts1:4-5) The* disciples received the power from On High on the day of Pentecost, and they changed the world. And to this day, no one can do an effectual work for the Lord without His anointing.

⚔ ⚔ ⚔

The created angel, named Lucifer, was the highest-ranking angel. He was anointed by God to perform the duties assigned to him. The description given in the book of Ezekiel chapter 28 is none other than Lucifer, whom later became known as Satan. This prophecy was addressed to the king of Tyre. However, in this passage of Scriptures, the king of Tyre is a symbol of Satan. *"You are **the anointed cherub** who covers; and I have set you so: you were upon the holy mountain of God; you have walked up and down in the midst of the stones of fire. You were perfect in your ways from the day that you were created, till iniquity was found in you. By the multitude of your merchandise they have filled the midst of you with violence, and you have sinned: therefore, I will cast you as profane out of the mountain of God: and I will destroy you, O covering cherub, from the midst of the stones of fire." (Ezekiel 28:14-16)* I believe; we can conclude that the anointing is God's stamp of approval for service.

The power from on high that Jesus told His disciples to wait for, which came on the day of Pentecost is available to every believer who yields himself to Him. Moreover, the Holy Spirit still continues to greatly anoint through Jesus men and women that He has chosen, and prepared, for greater responsibilities in His work.

There is no greater work, any man can perform in quality, beyond what Jesus did on earth. Jesus declared: *"Verily, verily, I say unto you, He that believes on me, the works that I do shall he do also; and **greater works than these shall he do**; because I go unto my Father." (John 14:12) When* He baptizes us with the Holy Spirit, He imparts the same Spirit, and anointing that was upon Him, to fulfill the great commission He has given to us. Therefore, we must look to Jesus for the Holy Spirit and His anointing, not to any human being. This is the great commission Jesus assigned to His disciples, which is really to the church. *"And He said unto them, Go ye into all the world, and preach the gospel to every creature. He who believes and is baptized shall be saved; but he who believes not shall be damned. And these signs shall follow them who believe; In my name shall they cast out devils; they shall speak with new tongues; They shall take up serpents; and if they drink any deadly thing, it shall not hurt them; they shall lay hands on the sick, and they shall recover." (Mark 16:15-18)*

In His earthly ministry, Jesus could be at one place at a time, thus limiting the number of people he could reach. He assigned us to do greater work, firstly, because of His death on the cross and His resurrection, the Holy Spirit can dwell in the hearts of the believers thereby allowing His servants to have access to His power at all times. Additionally, the ability for His servants to touch so many lives in His name in a matter of an hour. He knew that knowledge was going to be increased in the last days. He foresaw the technology era. This generation has the capacity to reach billions of people with the gospel in an hour because of television, the Internet, the radio and all the other social media. People can be saved, healed, filled with the Holy Spirit and be set free, wherever they are in the world.

No man can fulfill the great commission Jesus gave to the church without the anointing of the Holy Spirit. No man can receive the anointing of the Holy Spirit if he has never accepted Jesus in his heart as his Lord and Savior. Therefore, forget about having a relationship with the Holy Spirit without Jesus.

If you are not rightly related to Jesus Christ, and you've been to a crusade, where the preacher laid hands on you and told you, you could have his or her anointing and after he has done so, you start seeing some manifestations in a ministry you have yourself begun. These are not the manifestations of the Holy Spirit, but of the flesh or Satan. It is impossible to receive the anointing of The Holy Spirit if you are not rightly related to God through the blood of Jesus. There are some that are in the ministry who pretend to be anointed. The truth is, they have never been born again.

As awesome as the story of Elisha receiving the mantle of Elijah in the midst of the horses and chariots of fire from heaven was, it cannot be compared to what we have received in the New Testament because of the cross of Christ. The Supreme Being who was responsible for all that glorious manifestation, now dwells in the heart of the believer. We have access to Him any hour of the day, or the night. But, when men and women start compromising the gospel and letting the desires of the flesh get in the way, the flow of the Spirit in that life is hindered.

I can never stress this too much: The crisis we are facing in Christianity is, in part, due to pastors that pretend to have a great anointing upon their lives, offering the anointing of the Holy Spirit, to people they don't even know, and who don't have a clue as what the anointing is for, except for people to fall on the ground when they lay hands on them to demonstrate their own power. These pastors tell the people, and some who are probably not even born again if they sow seeds (money) in their ministry, they can partake of their anointing. Remember! The Lord told Moses, "gather to Me seventy men of the elders of Israel, *whom you know* to be the elders of the people and officers over them" Moses didn't choose any one he just met in the camp. The Lord was specific in His choice of men. *Moses had to choose men he knew.* They were already doing the work of the Lord and God Himself promoted them. As I said, the Lord didn't leave up it to Moses, to impart the Spirit of the Lord, who was upon him, to the seventy men. God came down to do it Himself. Wake up, People of God! No man's anointing can come upon you because you are a partner of his ministry, or you sow seeds in his ministry.

There are ministers of the gospel who are not willing to sacrifice anything like Elisha did to walk in a greater anointing. The anointing is freely given to the believers. Jesus paid the debt of sin with His blood for His servants to receive it. However, you can't just live anyway that is gratifying to the flesh, and expect to be greatly anointed. Some preachers who claim to have a great anointing upon their lives use what they call "the anointing" to deceive and manipulate the people of God and if they have to lie to them to get their money, so be it.

These preachers are not willing to walk away from their luxurious lifestyle that they have grown so accustomed to. Men and women who have given priority to material wealth, which they have obtained by using the word of God to play in the people's emotion to rob their money for personal gain, or have compromised the gospel and used it as a ladder to arrive at the top of a corrupt world in order to be in the company of the rich and famous, cannot be greatly anointed. Men and women who are in competition with each other for the biggest house, the most expensive jet, the latest models of luxurious cars, and the priciest diamond jewelry cannot be greatly anointed. Beware, people of God! You may be sitting under a counterfeit anointing.

The body of Christ is not experiencing the true glorious anointing of God. However, that's about to change. God is rising up an army of men and women, from all over the world, who will preach Jesus Christ, and the cross and seek a closer relationship with Him through prayer. And humbly ask Him, to visit us once again with a mighty move of the Holy Spirit. Men and women who will be willing to part ways with the world, with what makes the flesh feel good in order not to disgrace the anointing of the Holy Spirit that is upon them. In doing so, they'll show the world, once again, what the anointing was like in the time of Elijah, Elisha, and in the book of Acts.

Since Elijah was taken to heaven, Elisha had to continue the work of the Lord. The mantle is a symbol of the anointing. The mantle was imparted to him by God who had previously prepared him by asking Elijah to anoint him. Now when Elisha had to go back to Jericho, he stood by the bank of the Jordan, he used the mantle, like Elijah did, and I like what he said, "where is the LORD God of Elijah?" Even though God can use a man or a woman to accomplish great things for Him with His anointing, we must never take our eyes off of Him, to whom the anointing belongs. Elisha recognized the power was not in the mantle, but in the LORD God of Elijah. Elijah trained him well. He had seen Elijah perform unprecedented miracles, but Elijah had never become a superstar in his eyes. Elijah probably did let him know that the power, by which he was operating these miracles, belongs to God.

⋏　⋏　⋏

Now that Elijah was gone, Elisha was putting what he learned from his master into practice. He witnessed an event that no other human being had ever seen before. He saw chariots of fire and horses coming down from heaven to pick up a man, and watched him translate in a whirlwind right before his eyes. If he had not received the proper teaching from Elijah, he would have put his faith in him, seeing him as a great man, full of power. After Elijah was taken away, Elisha would have probably called on the name of Elijah to cross the Jordan River. And I am almost certain that if he had done that, he would have been stuck by the bank of the river. Even though he struck the water with the mantle and the water parted for him to cross on dry ground, the mantle itself could not part the river. It was the hand of God that parted the Jordan River.

What happened that day was not between two men deciding about the transference of his anointing, from one to the other. There was the unseen hand of God behind what was taking place. Dear brothers and sisters, a pastor cannot transfer his anointing to you by laying his or her hands on you. When the Bible speaks of laying hands to receive from another person, it's in reference to the stirring of the gift that the Holy Spirit has already deposited in that person. Paul said to Timothy, *"Therefore, I remind you to stir up the gift of God, which is in you through the laying on of my hands." (2 Timothy 1:6)*

When a pastor, or bishop or whatever title he may hold, is laying hands on you he is not transferring any gift to you. The gift is already in you, placed there by God Himself. I warn you not to let any corrupt minister lay hands on you. The Holy Spirit will not use a corrupt vessel to stir any gift in an obedient servant he has prepared for ministry. A pastor can't give you his anointing by blowing on you, or taking off his jacket and hitting you with it, or wrapping a mantle around you or by calling fire to come down from I do not know where. In the new covenant, the anointing is obtained by faith in Jesus Christ and His sacrifice on the cross and must be maintained at the cross.

THE PERPETUAL SACRIFICE

AFTER ADAM AND Eve's fall, God instituted the sacrificial system. Animals had to be offered up as sacrifices, and the blood of these animals provided a temporary forgiveness for sins, but it could not take away sin. God ordered Moses to offer two lambs on the altar daily in the morning and in the evening, and it was to be a perpetual sacrifice. It is written in the book of Exodus: *"Now this is that which you shall offer upon the altar; two lambs of the first year day by day continually. The one lamb you shall offer in the morning; and the other lamb you shall offer at even. This shall be a continual burnt offering throughout your generations at the door of the tabernacle of the congregation before the LORD: where I will meet you, to speak there unto you. And there I will meet with the children of Israel, and the tabernacle shall be sanctified by My glory." (Exodus 29: 38- 39, 42-43)*

The times at which the lambs were sacrificed portrayed a perfect picture of Jesus Christ the Lamb of God who would give His life as a sin offering on the cross. Matthew Henry wrote in his commentary on the Bible about, "The Crucifixion; The Death of Christ." 'Between the third and the sixth hour, that is, between nine and twelve o'clock, as we reckon, he was nailed to the cross, and soon after the ninth hour, that is, between three and four o'clock in the afternoon, he died. That was the time of the offering of the evening sacrifice, and the time when the paschal lamb was killed; and Christ our Passover was sacrificed for us and offered himself in the evening of the world a sacrifice to God of a sweet-smelling savor. It was at that time of the day, that the angel Gabriel delivered to Daniel that glorious prediction of the Messiah, Dan. 9:21, 24, etc. And some think that from that very time when the angel spoke it, to this time when Christ died, was just seventy weeks, that is, four hundred and ninety years to a day, to an hour; as the departure of Israel out of Egypt was at the end of the four hundred and thirty years, even the self-same day, Ex. 12:41." (Matthew Henry's Commentary on the Whole Bible (1721) (Matthew 27:50)

Jesus was nailed to the cross around 9AM. The hour the lamb for the morning sacrifice was placed on the altar. And He died at 3 PM. The hour the lamb for the evening sacrifice was placed on the altar. I have been blessed reading Matthew Henry's commentary on this passage of Scripture and see how those events in the Old Testament were pointing to Jesus, and how He fulfilled the Scriptures to the dot.

When God gave instructions to Moses, concerning the sacrifice of the lambs in the morning and the evening, He used the word continually, meaning in perpetuity. However, when Jesus said on the cross, "It is finished." It was the end of these sacrifices. Because the brazen altar upon which the lambs were sacrificed, typified the cross upon which Jesus, the Lamb of God was sacrificed.

"The brazen altar or bronze altar, was located in the courtyard of the tabernacle. The tabernacle was the place where God told Moses He would speak to him, and meet with His people. The altar was raised higher than all the other vessels of the tabernacle and it rested on heaps of earth. The heaps of earth symbolized fragmented humanity. Adam, the first man was formed with the dust of the earth. The altar that is resting on the heaps of earth represents the cross resting upon humanity. It is through the cross the human race is made whole again. It is also the bridge that connects man with his Creator.

The cross was lifted up from the earth at Calvary. Just as the brazen altar, which typified the cross was lifted higher than the other vessels of the tabernacle. The cross of Christ must be lifted up in order for Jesus to attract all men unto Himself. (John 12:32) Unfortunately, the cross is rejected in most churches.

Jesus was the last Lamb who was sacrificed on the altar— the cross —to redeem mankind. Never again would anyone need to bring an animal to a priest as a sacrifice for the forgiveness of their sins.

Jesus is the only one who didn't inherit the sin nature. Therefore, He was the only one qualified to take away the sin of the world. It is recorded in the book of John: "The next day John sees Jesus coming unto him, and said, Behold the Lamb of God, who takes away the sin of the world." (John1:29) John was talking about the sin nature. The sins that man commits are the symptoms of the disease called "the sin nature". Jesus came to take away the sin nature, which means to eradicate it from the human race.

In the New Testament, the meeting place is at the cross. It is at the cross that God will meet with those whom He has chosen to lead His people. It is where He will speak with them, and it is where He will meet with His people, at the cross in perpetuity.

Jesus asks us to take our cross daily and to follow Him. We have daily needs that can only be met at the cross. In the Old Covenant the lambs were put on the brazen altar daily. God wants to have a daily relationship with His children, not once in a while when they need something from Him. That doesn't mean for you to go buy a cross and bow before it to speak with God. However, you must perpetually keep your faith anchored in Jesus Christ and His sacrifice on the cross. You must approach the throne of grace with humility, knowing it is the sacrifice of Jesus on the cross, that gives you access to Him. Don't quote Scriptures to God boasting arrogantly, acting like God owes you the world because you know the right Scriptures, or you want to impress Him with your knowledge of Scriptures.

Preacher, it's not going to work! People of God, it's not going to work! *The cross is the meeting place, where God speaks. He does the speaking, and the spiritual leader humbly listens to what He is saying.*

That's where He gives the leader direction to lead His people. Remember, what He told Moses, about the tabernacle of meeting where the brazen altar which typified the cross was located. *"I will meet you to speak with you. And there I will meet with the children of Israel."* That location has been replaced by the cross. And at the cross, the children of God must also listen with a humble heart to what God is saying to them.

When the cross is rejected, the preacher can't hear the word God is revealing to him to lead the people. He must rely on his own ingenuity, or other people's revelation that sounds like it came from heaven to lead and feed the people spiritually. Most of the time that results in the preacher teaching erroneous doctrine.

The cross must be your daily connection to Jesus Christ. It is by the sacrifice of Jesus on the cross that mankind, in all generations must be born again. Therefore, man will always need the cross. The glory of God has never departed from the cross. That is why, after two thousand years, it still attracts man. The cross of Calvary, upon which the blood of Jesus ran, gives man access to God and God access to man, eternally. Do you now understand why Satan does his best to divert the pastors, and the people of God, from the cross? God has not appointed another place or methods for His servants or His people to meet with Him but at the cross daily and perpetually.

When a servant of God stops preaching Jesus Christ and His sacrifice on the cross, there are hardly any conversions to the Lord. Healing stops, deliverance stops, the spiritual growth, the well- being of the Christian and his walk with the Lord are all affected. When the cross is despised, nothing works, to keep some ministers of the gospel hostage in their deception, the enemy will suggest they put another title before their name. Believing this lie, they think it's a promotion that will change things. They give themselves titles, and they appoint themselves to the five-fold ministry, (Ephesians 4:11) *It* is solely God's responsibility to put a man or woman in the office which He Himself has chosen for them. When God places a person in an office, He anoints him, blesses him, and gives him grace to overcome the difficulties that he will encounter by exercising his ministry. These days, we find a lot of ministers of the gospel who take the responsibility of choosing an office upon themselves. They put themselves in the office that they want to occupy. Those who were evangelists make themselves pastors, those who were pastors make themselves bishops, and apostles, etc. They promote themselves to a new office, but their ministry remains the same.

Dear servants of God, you do not need another title, which is of no use, since the promotion did not come from God, but from the flesh. What you need is the power of the Holy Spirit to cast out demons, to heal the sick, to resurrect the dead, and for lost souls be born again. When you despise the cross, you are without direction, you embrace other methods, which are not in the word of God, to supposedly work miracles. You attract demon spirits into your ministry and the consequences for you can be devastating. Servants of God, the solution is simple: Go back to the cross! To make exploits with God.

▲　▲　▲

Still others will pretend to preach the cross and even write books on this subject, but the people will recognize they are counterfeit when they continue asking you to plant seeds to be able to benefit from the cross. They will find a way to introduce this doctrine of endlessly planting seeds (money) in order to receive from God.

I remember vividly a preacher who wrote a book about the cross. I thought he had a revelation from the Holy Spirit and was convicted that he should return to the cross. One day, I received a letter from him in the mail, soliciting money with a piece of white cloth as a point of contact to pray for me. I was instructed to send that piece of cloth back to him, with my seed (money), and after he prayed over it, he would send it back to me to keep. My miracle was supposedly in that piece of cloth. Before I understood the benefits of the cross of Calvary, I would have sent it back to him with my seed. Very few adults who are living on this planet probably feel that they do not need a miracle from the Lord. We always have issues before us that require divine intervention. That's why these gimmicks are a great source of income for these pastors.

The sacrifice of Jesus on the cross does not need to be accompanied with any piece of cloth, holy water, with absolutely nothing. It is sufficient by itself to address every need of man. Things like that are scams, they are deceitful, and it's all done for money. It will never, never, accomplish what was promised because God has nothing to do with these lies. He deplores them. The cross is sufficient, as Jesus said, "IT IS FINISHED!"

THE BLESSINGS OF SOLOMON

AMONG THE SONS of David, Solomon was the one who was chosen by the Lord to build Him a temple. Let us read the statements of David concerning God's choice: *"And of all my sons, (for the Lord hath given me many sons,) He has chosen Solomon my son to sit upon the throne of the kingdom of the LORD over Israel. And He said unto me, Solomon thy son, he shall build My house and My courts: for I have chosen him to be My son, and I will be his Father. (1Chronicles 28:5-6)"*

Solomon succeeded his father David and became king of Israel. He had set in his heart to seek the LORD. He gathered all the people of Israel to go with him to Gibeon where the tabernacle Moses made was located. He knew God had told Moses it was to be a meeting place with him and with the people. It was there that Solomon offered a thousand burnt offerings on the brazen altar which pleased God. "In that night did God appear unto Solomon, and said unto him, ask what I shall give you." (2 Chronicles 1:7)

And Solomon said to God: *"Give me now wisdom and knowledge that I may go out and come in before this people: for who can judge this Your people that is so great?" (2 Chronicles 1:10)*

Then God said to Salomon: *"And God said to Solomon, Because this was in your heart, and you have not asked riches, wealth, or honour, nor the life of your enemies, neither yet have asked long life; but have asked wisdom and knowledge for yourself, that you may judge My people, over whom I have made you king: Wisdom and knowledge is granted unto you; and I will give you riches, and wealth, and honour, such as none of the kings have had who have been before you, neither shall there any after you have the like." (2 Chronicles 1:11-12)*

Solomon was very generous in his offering to God because we serve a Mighty God. He deserves our absolute best. We can never give Him more than He can give back to us. Solomon learned from his father, David, that when it comes to giving to God, he should give is best offerings. He always wanted to give to his God his absolute best, offerings worthy of a Mighty God.

The word of the Lord came to David, via Gad, to build an altar to the Lord on the threshing floor of Araunah. This would stop the plague that had hit the nation of Israel when he numbered the people against the command of God. When he went to Araunah, he (Araunah) wanted to give him the threshing floor, the animals, and the wood required for the burned offering for the sacrifice. David refused. *"And the king said unto Araunah, Nay; but I will surely buy it of you at a price: neither will I offer burnt offerings unto the LORD my God of that which does cost me nothing. So David bought the threshing floor and the oxen for fifty shekels of silver." (2 Samuel 24:24)*

Although Solomon had honored the Lord with this great offering, it was not the reason why God appeared to him. The Lord appeared to Solomon because, first of all, Solomon and the people were seeking Him. God said in His word: *"And you shall seek Me, and find Me, when you shall search for Me with all your heart. (Jeremiah 29:13) The* Lord is never moved by what the hands give. If one's motives are not pure, and if the heart is not right before Him, He is not going to let anyone manipulate Him with large, medium, or small offerings. God would not have appeared to Solomon if he had not offered these burnt offerings on the brazen altar, at the tabernacle, ***to make peace with God***. He had to have a personal relationship with the Lord. He had to seek God himself. The offerings of his father David were not going to give him a free ride to God. He had to access God himself, and it was going to be done how the Lord intended it—through the blood. It was not because of the number of animals Solomon sacrificed that the Lord appeared to him, as the proponents of the prosperity gospel explain, but rather what they represented.

▲ ▲ ▲

These "burnt offerings" were not seeds given to the Lord to reap riches, wealth and honor. Solomon knew that the tabernacle was God's meeting place with the people and their leader. Although the Ark of the Covenant at that time was in Jerusalem, God is omnipresent, He was where Solomon and the people were on that day, because Salomon and the people were in one accord, searching God with all their heart. Solomon was a young man with a huge responsibility to reign over the multitude. He needed to hear the voice of God. He had to be sure that God was with him. It's a great thing when God exalts a servant as His ambassador. But, when one hears His voice and feels His presence, it's an indescribable experience which cannot be put into words.

The words that came from Solomon's mouth revealed what was in his heart. *"For out of the abundance of the heart, the mouth speaks." (Matthew 12:34)* Matthew Henry said, "Men's characters appear in their choices and desires." Solomon asked God for wisdom and knowledge to lead the people. This request pleased the Lord very much, because Solomon had neither desired material goods, nor did he hold a grudge in his heart for his enemies. Instead he sought after the spiritual things. *"For the Lord, gives wisdom; from His mouth come knowledge and understanding." (Proverbs 2:6)* Solomon had asked for nothing for himself as his request was directed towards the welfare of the people of God. His motives were pure. He did not even consider becoming rich by exploiting the people due to his position. This unparalleled earthly glory, which God had bestowed upon him, was pointing to the eternal glory of Jesus. But, Solomon's glory was pale in comparison to Jesus' glory.

After Salomon had finished building the temple of the Lord, on the day of the dedication, the Bible states, *"Also king Solomon, and all the congregation of Israel who were assembled unto him before the ark, **sacrificed sheep and oxen, which could not be told nor numbered for multitude."** (2 Chronicles 5: 6) **All**that took place on that day was a perfect picture of Jesus Christ the Lamb of God, and His death on the cross, where the souls of man (an amount impossible to count, or number), were saved because of His shed blood. We read many generations later, in the book of Revelation, *"After this I beheld, and, lo, a great multitude, which no man could number, of all nations, and kindreds, and people, and tongues, stood before the throne, and before the Lamb, clothed* *with white robes, and palms in their hands; And one of the elders answered, saying unto me, what are these which are arrayed in white robes? And whence came they? And I said unto him, Sir, you know. And he said to me, these are they which came out of great tribulation,* **and have washed their robes, and made them white in the blood of the Lamb.** *(Revelation 7: 9, 13-14) Not only have those who came from the great tribulation washed their robes* in *the blood of The Lamb, but every believer has obtained the righteousness of Christ through His blood.*

▲   ▲   ▲

This great multitude who are before the throne of God and before the Lamb whitened their robes in the blood of the Lamb—a single Lamb, the divine Lamb of God who is Jesus Christ. What the blood of thousands upon thousands of animals could not do, the blood of Jesus did. He took away the sin of the world!

"Now when Solomon had made an end of praying, the fire came down from heaven, and consumed the burnt offering and the sacrifices; and the glory of the LORD filled the house. And the priests could not enter into the house of the LORD, because the glory of the LORD had filled the LORD's house. And when all the children of Israel saw how the fire came down, and the glory of the LORD upon the house, they bowed themselves with their faces to the ground upon the pavement, and worshipped, and praised the LORD, saying, For He is good; for His mercy endures forever." (2 Chronicles 7:1-3)

The fire came down from heaven and consumed the sacrifices. God made peace with man through these sacrifices. He answered the prayers of Solomon, His glory had manifested and it filled the temple. The glory had manifested in such an intensity that even the priests could not behold it. The only High Priest who can stand in the fullness of God's glory is Jesus. The only way any man can behold the glory of God is through the blood of Jesus.

This Holy manifestation could not take place if the blood of these animals had not been shed on the altar. The blood of these animals allowed the people to stand in the presence of God, permitting them to see the fire, and the glory of God, coming down on the temple—not to consume them in judgment, but as a sign of His approval and to accept them into His fellowship. The sacrifices, the burnt offerings upon the brazen altar, pointed to the cross, where Jesus, the perfect and last sacrificed Lamb, would die and give those who have put their faith in Him access to the throne of God.

The proponents of the prosperity gospel have amassed, and are still amassing, multiplied millions of dollars with this passage of the Bible by showing the people of God that He gave riches, wealth, and honor to Solomon because of the multitude of animals Solomon sacrificed to God. They teach that God would give His children wealth and riches as well if they planted a large amount of seed, i.e. if they give a (significant amount of money), What took place was a foreshadowing of things that were to come, and have come. After the dedication of the temple, God appeared to Solomon a second time to tell him that his request had been granted. The Lord God is omniscient. He knew the tendencies of Solomon's heart. This second appearance was to warn him, to give him instructions and to tell him what would happen to him and the majestic temple if in his heart he should turn away from the Lord.

THE QUEEN OF SHEBA AND THE KING

THE QUEEN OF Sheba heard of Solomon's greatness, and decided to visit him. She took a huge entourage, including camels loaded with gifts of spices, gold in great quantities and precious stones with her. Solomon made a big impression on the queen of Sheba during their encounter. She revealed all that she had in her heart, and Solomon answered all her questions. She saw the house that he had built, the kind of food that was on his table, the well-tailored uniforms of his servants and cup bearers, the animal sacrifices, which he gave to the house of the Lord, and his great wisdom. It was an amazing sight that overwhelmed her. The book of 1 Kings Records:

> *"And she said to the king, It was a true report that I heard in my own land of your acts and of your wisdom. Howbeit I believed not the words, until I came, and my eyes had seen it: and, behold, the half was not told me: your wisdom and prosperity exceed the fame which I heard. Happy are your men, happy are these your servants, which stand continually before you, and that hear your wisdom. Blessed be the LORD your God, which delighted in you, to set you on the throne of Israel: because the LORD loved Israel forever, therefore made He you king, to do judgment and justice. And she gave the king a hundred and twenty talents of gold, and of spices very great store, and precious stones: there came no more such abundance of spices as these which the queen of Sheba gave to king Solomon." (1 Kings 10: 6- 10)*

She was "beside herself" when she saw the glory of Solomon. We, too, will be beside ourselves when we see the glory of Jesus. What she saw was nothing compared to what is reserved for those who have accepted Jesus Christ as their Savior and Lord. *"But as it is written, Eye has not seen, nor ear heard, neither have entered into the heart of man, the things which God has prepared for them that love Him." (1 Corinthians 2:9)*

We can begin to have these things here on earth, as a foretaste of what awaits us because of the sacrifice of our Lord. What a glorious privilege it will be to stand continuously before the throne of God, to gaze upon His face and to serve Him.

Despite being a queen with pagan belief, she recognized that God was with Solomon and that he was elevated to the throne by God, to rule with justice and righteousness over His people. The queen of Sheba blessed the LORD God, who placed Solomon on the throne of Israel as king. Every day we should bless God, who made His Son, Jesus, our King. Through her gifts, she revealed her respect and admiration for Solomon. Each gift that she brought him has a meaning. She brought one hundred and twenty talents of gold—precious metal worthy of a king. Just as she offered gold to the king, we should give our life entirely to Jesus, the King of kings. When we do, it is as precious as gold to Him because He loves us. Then, we will remain forever in His sight, *"The precious sons of Zion, comparable to fine gold..." (Lamentations 4:2)*

▲ ▲ ▲

She also brought a ***large quantity of spices***. There were no spices like she gave him. The Bible didn't tell us the amount she gave—spices are symbolic of worship. When you worship the Lord with a sincere heart, it is priceless in His sight, it is unique to Him, it cannot be measured and He will not compare it to anyone else's worship. Hence, our King is unique. He is incomparable to anything, or anyone. We must worship Him, and Him alone.

Lastly, she gave him precious stones to reflect the beauty of the king and his kingdom. The amount she gave was also not revealed. Our Lord is "beautiful beyond description" as the Christian hymn says. His beauty cannot be compared with anyone, nor can the glorious majesty of His kingdom be compared to any earthly kingdom.

Solomon's kingdom was temporal. Our appreciation for Jesus' kingdom should far outweigh the queen of Sheba's appreciation for Solomon's kingdom because Jesus' kingdom is eternal, and nothing can be compared to His Majesty. Her gifts were an impetus of the heart, which meant a lot to Solomon. There was no intention of manipulating the king with her seeds. In response to her gestures, the Bible said, *"And King Solomon gave unto the queen of Sheba all her desire, whatsoever she asked, beside that which Solomon gave her of his royal bounty. So she turned and went to her own country, she and her servants." (1 Kings 10:13)*

One can have wealth to buy all that they need, but there are desires of the heart that money cannot buy, only God can fulfill them. That's the reason why some people who are extremely wealthy are very miserable. Their hearts desire things that their money can't buy. "Solomon gave the queen of Sheba all she desired." She touched the heart of this earthly king. She did not come before him with empty hands, and she did not return to her country with empty hands. This is the beauty of giving to the Lord with a pure heart and with joy. He knows the motives with which we give and, consequently, the recompense is always far greater than that which has been given.

The queen of Sheba praised the Lord for what He had done for King Solomon. She was not looking at his prosperity with covetous eyes. She brought him gifts worthy of a king, to honor him. There was no flattery or manipulation in hope of personal gain. She saw God as the giver of Solomon's wealth, glory, and honor. Solomon was very generous towards her. He gave her gifts that only a king could give. In addition, she received all she asked for, and all she desired. There is no one who approaches Jesus, the King of kings, with pure motives, worshiping and praising Him, who returns with empty hands. Their requests are always granted in His time. Ephesians 3:20 says: "He is able to do exceedingly abundantly above all that we ask or think." The gifts of the queen of Sheba to King Solomon speak of respect, admiration, and reverence.

She is a good example of what it is to give honor and reverence to a king, and it was an earthly king. How much more should we give honor and reverence to Jesus our King? Everyone cannot give gold and spices to our King Jesus, like the queen of Sheba gave to Solomon, or, a large sum of money in present time, but everyone, whether rich or poor, can give Him their heart. The riches of Salomon, and the glory of his kingdom, although temporary belonged to God. They were the shadow of the riches and the glory of Jesus in heaven. Where are they now? They've been long gone. However, the riches, the prosperity, the wealth, the honor, the holiness, the joy, the peace and all the glory of the kingdom of Jesus are eternal.

In the last prayer Jesus prayed, before His trial, which would ultimately lead to the cross, He, more than once, made reference to His glory. Jesus prayed to His Father that all who have accepted Him as their Lord and Savior would come to see His glory. *"Father, I will that they also, whom You have given Me, be with Me where I am; that they may behold My glory, which thou have given me: for You loved Me before the foundation of the world." (John 17:24)*

The prayers He addressed to His Father were always granted. Therefore, we know those who have accepted Him as their Lord and Savior will definitely be with Him to see His glory. We will one day behold the glory of our King and Lord Jesus. What a glorious day it will be!

ᴧ ᴧ ᴧ

THE KING AND HIS WIVES

The first time God appeared to Solomon and told him to ask for what he wanted, Solomon asked Him for wisdom and knowledge to lead the people. But, did he ask the Lord for everything that he needed to fulfill his duty as king over the people, and to remain loyal God? Let's read the advice given to Solomon by his father David in regard to his walk with God: *"And you, Solomon my son, know thou the God of your father, and **serve Him with a perfect heart and with a willing mind:** for the Lord searcheth all hearts, and understand all the imaginations of the thoughts: if you seek Him, He will be found of you; but if you forsake Him, He will cast you off forever." (1 Chronicles 28:9)*

Along with wisdom and knowledge to lead the people, Solomon should have added *"a perfect heart or a loyal heart and a willing mind in his request."* This is the greatest thing a man can ask God for. Wisdom and knowledge are divine gifts of God that are given to the man who is pleasing unto Him. It is written, *"For God gives to a man that is good in His sight wisdom, and knowledge, and joy..." (Ecclesiastes 2:26)* When Solomon asked the Lord for "wisdom and knowledge", he was seeking the Lord. Wisdom and knowledge would have been given to Him without him even asking for it, for the Lord knew he needed it to exercise his duty as a king. He asked the Lord for something that is His will for man to have, so it pleased the Lord to give it to Him.

God will give exceedingly above anything a man or a woman asks. However, when it comes to the heart of man, God will neither force nor influence a man or a woman under any circumstances to have a "loyal heart, and a willing mind" towards Him. He lives it to the person to choose to give Him those aspects of their lives so that they can serve Him faithfully. If you ask God for a "loyal heart and a willing mind" towards Him, He is able to guard your mind and your heart when pressures come from all sides to cause you to be unfaithful to Him. I think if Solomon had asked the Lord for a "loyal heart and a willing mind," like his father advised him, his story would have a better ending.

A selfless leader will always put the interests of his subordinates before his own, and that's an excellent quality. He can be well equipped to lead his people, However, that's not enough to help him personally when pressures and temptations are coming from all sides. It's in moments like this when a "loyal heart and a willing mind" will be of tremendous help to Him. He will be in a better position to resist the temptations of the enemy in every area of life, just like Joseph resisted the temptation of Potiphar's wife who had asked him to sleep with her. His loyal heart towards God made him say "no." His response to her was, *"There is none greater in this house than I; neither has he kept back anything from me but you, because you are his wife: **how then can I do this great wickedness, and sin against God?**" (Genesis 39: 9)*

A loyal heart will put God first, before the desires of the flesh. That is why it is of utmost importance that we keep our faith anchored in Jesus Christ and His sacrifice on the cross daily and to find strength to maintain a "loyal heart and a willing mind" towards God when temptation comes. David, made great exploits with God. From his past experiences with Him, he knew that "a loyal heart and a willing mind" are what would help his son Solomon when temptations come.

The following is what God said to Solomon when He appeared to Him the second time: *"And as for you, if you will walk before Me, as David your father walked, and do according to all that I have commanded you, and shall observe My statutes and My judgments; Then will I establish the throne of your kingdom, according as I have covenanted with David your father, saying, there shall not fail you a man to be ruler in Israel. But if you turn away, and forsake My statutes and My commandments, which I have set before you, and shall go and serve other gods, and worship them; Then will I pluck them up by the roots out of My land which I have given them; and this house, which I have sanctified for My name, will I cast out of My sight, and will make it to be a proverb and a byword among all nations." (2 Chronicles 7:17-20)*

David was not a perfect king, he wrote Psalm 51 in repentance after he sinned with Bathsheba and killed her husband Uriah. He humbly sought the Lord for forgiveness, and he always took full responsibility for his actions instead of pointing fingers at others for his failures. Even though he sinned in the eyes of God, *his heart was loyal to God.* He never served other gods and He was never involved with doctrines of demons. I believe that's why God said the following about David: *"And when He had removed him, He raised up for them David as king, to whom also He gave testimony and said, "…I have found David the son of Jesse, **a man after My own heart** which shall fulfil all my will." (Acts 13:22)* I believe, of all the sins that a man can commit, serving other gods, worshiping them and being involved with doctrines of demons are the most abhorrent to the Lord.

⋏　⋏　⋏

The proponents of the prosperity gospel are constantly pointing to the wealth of Salomon, to motivate the believers to sow financial seeds to the tune of multi-millions of dollars so that they can get wealth similar as his. Have they taken the time to explain to the believers how Solomon's story ended? Let's read what's recorded in the Bible.

*"For it came to pass, **when Solomon was old, that his wives turned away his heart after other gods: and his heart was not perfect with***

*the Lord his God, as was the heart of David his father. For Solomon went after Ashtoreth the goddess of the Zidonians, and after Milcom the abomination of the Ammonites. And Solomon did evil in the sight of the LORD, and went not fully after the LORD, as did David his father. And the LORD was angry with Solomon, because **his heart was turned from the LORD God of Israel, which had appeared unto him twice**, and had commanded him concerning this thing, that he should not go after other gods: **but he kept not that which the LORD commanded.** Wherefore the LORD said unto Solomon, forasmuch as this is done of thee, and you have not kept My covenant and My statutes, which I have commanded you, **I will surely rend the kingdom from you, and will give it to your servant**. Notwithstanding in your days I will not do it for David your father's sake: but I will rend it out of the hand of your son." (1 Kings 11: 4-6, 9-12)*

Solomon received wisdom and riches from the Lord, which exceeded that of any other king before, or after him. Nonetheless, **he turned his heart away from the Lord, who had given him these blessings, to serve other gods.** He became attached to doctrines of demons. His prosperity, his glory and his wisdom didn't cost him anything as they were gifts from God. As a consequence of Solomon's actions, the kingdom was then divided after Solomon's death.

God kept the kingdom until his death because of His loyalty to David. Jeroboam, Solomon's servant, was chosen by God to reign over ten tribes. Solomon tried to kill Jeroboam, and in order to save his life, Jeroboam had to flee to Egypt, where he stayed until the death of Salomon. If God had not been with Jeroboam, Solomon would have had another title added after his name: "murderer" This is the end of Solomon's glory. Although he had repented and had returned to God, it didn't change the sad ending of his glorious kingdom. The Scriptures that speak of Solomon's riches are greatly distorted, they are turned into "money Scriptures" for self-gain. You are wasting your money when a pastor asks you to sow seeds (money) to be as blessed as Solomon was. Children of God, it's far better to have a "loyal heart and a willing mind" towards God then to possess all the wealth of Solomon. That's what every loyal pastor ought to preach.

▲   ▲   ▲

I like these words spoken by Jesus about the queen of the south, who is the queen of Sheba, who went to see Solomon. *"The queen of the south shall rise up in the judgment with this generation, and shall condemn it: for she came from the uttermost parts of the earth to hear the Wisdom of Solomon; and, behold, a greater than Solomon is here." (Matthew 12:42)* Jesus said, "A greater than Solomon is here."

He said this about Himself. We can then conclude that the riches, the wisdom, the honor and the glory of Jesus' kingdom cannot be compared to Salomon's kingdom in beauty, nor in splendor. You must be born again to reign with Jesus in His glorious kingdom. It is so glorious, that the natural sinful flesh would not be able to withstand its glory. It is at the resurrection that those who have accepted Jesus as their Lord and Savior will be given a glorified body, so we can behold the splendor of Jesus' glory. Beloved, everything on this earth is ephemeral; no matter the splendor of the glory, the amount of wealth, and the depth of wisdom, the duration of these things is as a vapor. Jesus' glory is eternal. It is in heaven and out of reach of evil forces. Nothing on earth, or in hell, can tarnish the splendor of His kingdom.

You Have Not Asked In My Name

MANY CHRISTIANS HAVE prayed to God the Father, for many years. For ten to fifteen years, some of you have asked for the same things over, and over again. Then, you always add "in the name of Jesus" at the end of your prayers. However, when you read the following verses of the Bible, you may quickly say, "oh, they don't apply to me." Jesus made this statement, *"And in that day you will ask Me nothing. Most assuredly, I say to you, whatever you ask the Father in My name. He will give you. Until now, you have asked nothing in My name. Ask, and you will receive, that your joy may be full." (John 16: 23-24)*

Because you 've always added, "In Jesus' name" at the end of your prayers to your heavenly Father, you probably thought the answer to your prayers was guaranteed according to how you prayed. If you stand before God, with an envelope that has seeds (money) in your hands, and you start quoting scriptures, in Jesus' name, thinking, that's what's going to make God answer your prayers, however sincere you may be, God is not going to answer these kinds of prayers. The methods you have been taught, and that you have applied, are exactly why your prayers are not being answered. In these kinds of prayers, "in Jesus' name" becomes a cliché instead of a powerful name, at the mention of which demons tremble.

Asking in Jesus' name is when you approach God in faith, believing that, because of the shed blood of Jesus on the cross, God hears you. Since it is Jesus' sacrifice on the cross that gives you access to Him. Your prayer can be a simple childlike prayer, addressed to the Father, with no money attached to it and it would be answered when it is addressed to the Father based on the sacrifice of Jesus on the cross. That's what it means to pray in Jesus' name. He has given you, His righteousness so that you can approach the Father in His name. When you apply a man-invented method that has grossly distorted the word of God to turn it into a money- making machine, you are not asking in Jesus' name. Jesus is directly talking to you when He said: "Until now, you have asked nothing in My name."

If you are praying to God, according to the teachings of man, it produces nothing but frustration and despair. You must get rid of the man -fabricated method of approaching God constantly with an envelope of money as your seed for your prayers to be answered. When you do that, you will see the difference. In the gospel of John, Jesus said, *"And whatever you ask in My name, that I will do, that the Father may be glorified in the Son. If you asked anything in My name, I will do it." (John 14:13-14)* Always remember the word of Jesus, He will keep His promise.

▲   ▲   ▲

I heard a pastor with an earned doctorate on Christian television teaching that when we approach God, we can address Him as "Daddy"— that He is our "heavenly Daddy." It was explained that it was equivalent to when Jesus called His Father, "Abba Father." For a while, I thought that I could call God "Daddy" until the day the Lord allowed me to comprehend, in my frail human mind, the grandiosity of His Majesty.

Easton's Bible dictionary defines the word "Abba" in the following way: "Abba: this Syriac or Chaldee word is found three times in the New Testament (Mark 14: 36, Romans 8:15, Galatians 4:6) and in each case is followed by its Greek equivalent, which is translated "father." It's a term expressing warm affection, and filial confidence. It has no perfect equivalent in our language. (M.G. Easton M.A., D.D. Illustrated Bible Dictionary, Third Edition, published by Thomas Nelson, 1897)

According to this description of the word, "Abba" is a term expressing warm affection and filial confidence. It's an affectionate term, which expresses how we should rest in God in any difficult situation we are facing. It expresses total submission to His will, and our outmost confidence in Him. The words "Abba, Father" were used by Jesus when He was praying to His Father in the garden of Gethsemane to take the cup away from Him. This is the prayer Jesus prayed: *"Then they came to a place which was named Gethsemane; and He said to His disciples, "Sit here while I pray." And He said, "Abba, Father, all things are possible for you. Take this cup away from Me; nevertheless, not what I will, but what you will." (Mark 14: 32, 36)*

Paul reminds us of that term used by Jesus in his epistle to the Galatians. He wrote: *"and because you are sons, God has sent forth the Spirit of His Son into your hearts, crying out, "Abba Father!" Therefore, you are no longer a slave but a son, and if a son, then an heir of God through Christ." (Galatians: 4:6-7)* Paul is telling us that because we are sons by adoption through Christ, we can express the same warm affection towards our Father, knowing that He will work out any difficult situation in our favor.

We cannot address God with a nickname with which we address mortal men. I want to emphasize the following words in the definition of the word "Abba: ***it has no perfect equivalent in our language.*** " Our human mind cannot conceive this expression of love and confidence Jesus expressed towards His Father in that critical hour of His earthly ministry. Therefore, no one should attempt to give it an equivalent in our language. We should leave it as "Abba, Father!" Moreover, once its meaning is understood, there is no need to change it to our limited terminology.

Paul never did that. He explained in Galatians 4:6, he explained this wonderful expression and told us it was ours to use to express the same love and the same confidence in God in our most difficult situations. Therefore, I think it's blasphemy to call our heavenly Father "Daddy." He cannot be compared to any "Daddy" on the Earth. The very best Daddy cannot be compared with God. He cannot be compared with anyone, anything, and anywhere. This is the kind of familiarity that these men seek to have with God, and are teaching to the body of Christ, which produces the irreverence towards Him that we are seeing today. He is the Most-High God, His Majesty is above the heavens! Jesus, in His last prayer before He went to the cross, called Him, "Holy

Father, Righteous Father." He is not our "Daddy." He is our "Holy Father. Our Righteous Father, our Abba Father."

⋏ ⋏ ⋏

The title "Holy Father" should not have been given to any mortal man, to the Pope or anyone else. It is blasphemy to call a mortal man, created by God, "Holy Father." That's not my opinion. It is written in the word of God, *"Do not call anyone on earth your father; for one is your Father, He who is in heaven." (Matthew 23: 9)* God is not telling us not to call our earthly father, "father." That's the name God appointed to call him. What is being said here is, to not bow before any man nor exalt him and call him "Holy Father" with the same reverence as you would call God, your heavenly Father. This title belongs to God and God alone. It's a sin in the eyes of God to call the pope, "Holy Father." Our heavenly Father is awesome! I like the following verses written by the prophet Jeremiah. *"Inasmuch as there is none like You, O LORD (You are great, and Your name is great in might). Who would not fear you, O King of the nations? For this is Your rightful due. For among all the wise men of the nations, and in all their kingdoms, there is none like You." (Jeremiah 10: 6-7)*

These preachers have not realized the damages they have caused to the body of Christ with their false teachings. More than any past generations, their teachings have created a new generation of spiritual beggars, who are constantly asking and believing Him for "Stuff." It's a generation that wants to play the game of "Let's make a deal with God. They'll tell Him, "I'll sow the large quantity of seeds (money) you have asked, but I am sowing for this, and that, and I am expecting you to bring me my harvest." They are not children of faith, who would seek their heavenly Father's face in prayer to know Him, and seek Him to know if He approves of the things they are sowing seeds for. They are not children who would pour their love and admiration on their heavenly Father, thanking Him for the sacrifice of Jesus on the cross, telling Him "Father it works. I've been changed. It's glorious. Thank you! Thank you, Jesus for the cross! Thank you for the Holy Spirit, my counselor, my helper, my comforter."

The church of Jesus Christ does not run on lies and manipulation. In some churches and ministries, it's not about Jesus anymore but rather about self and the pastor's ego. Jesus' name is being used as a shield to operate in darkness, which can never be done. He is the light. That's why these false preachers are being exposed. The Holy Spirit is calling the elect to come out from among them. He is opening their spiritual eyes to see the lies and the deception that has become the norm in their churches and ministries. The reason why they distort the Scriptures is to take your money to maintain their luxurious lifestyle, including traveling around the world in their private jets, to bring the lies, and the false doctrines of the Jezebel spirit, to the people of God all over the world. And you are paying for it with your seed (money).

▲　▲　▲

I have received letters in the mail from people who were soliciting me for money, telling me that I won a big prize, but in order for me to claim it, I had to send money to them so that they could process it on their end. For me, these kinds of letters are classified as junk mail and they went in the garbage every time I received them. If a person, can find my address to write to me and tell me that I won a prize, why couldn't he put that check in the mail for me? Why would I have to send him my money to receive the prize he claimed I won? It has been proven that these letters are scams. Their intent is to steal people's money. I have also received a few notices like this in my e-mail. When I receive these kinds of solicitations, I identify and classify them as "Phishing scam." I am sure some of you know what I am talking about, and have done the same thing. However, some of you have probably been taken by these scammers.

If we can weed these scammers out in the natural, why are we continuing to allow scams by false preachers, who have lost their way and have compromised the gospel of Jesus Christ? "Sow a seed for your need" and "The wealth transfer of the wicked coming to your hands" are just two the many scams they use. It's time for you to start checking "Phishing Scam" when you hear these kinds of appeal for money. Every few years these false teachers come up with another scam.

They used to call their teaching the prosperity gospel and they were not ashamed of it, even displaying their riches before our eyes. Some have said that they were "loaded with money" and so forth. Some have dropped the title "Prosperity Gospel" and have embraced the title "Grace Gospel." They've changed the name, but they still distort the Scriptures. The name has changed, but their mentality has not, and it is still all about money. The devil will inspire them to name the gospel anything, as long as they stay away from the cross. Satan knows that he can't mess around with the cross of Christ because that's where he was defeated. He is terrified of the "preaching of the cross" and so are his ministers.

There is one Gospel, and that is the Gospel of "Christ crucified." Everything we receive from God —from His precious grace, to the least of our needs—could not be given to us if Jesus had not died on the cross. It is written: *"I thank my God always concerning you **for the grace of God which was given to you by Christ Jesus, that you were enriched in everything by Him** in all utterance and all knowledge." (1Corinthians1:4-5)* What the believers need to watch out for is that the prosperity preachers don't take the portion **"that you were enriched in everything by Him"** and turn it into a "sowing seed" (money) verse. Twisting it to say, "By His grace, you'll be rich when you sow seeds (money) in our ministry, or our church." That's their "Modus operandi, their method of operation." They'll take a portion of scripture, turn it into a money verse and rake in millions of dollars. In addition, they'll always find a way to tie money in with the message of grace. They may have various names for their gospel, but they will not preach the cross, they will not preach Jesus Christ. They may include the name of Jesus here and there in sermons as a cover up for these deceptive teachings.

Grace and the cross of Christ are one. The grace of God sent Jesus to the cross to die for us to save us. The grace of God can be given to man only through the cross of Christ. It's extended to all aspects of our lives so that we may be enriched in everything by Jesus. Any preacher who is preaching grace but rejects the cross of Christ or not preaching any sermons about Jesus and

His sacrificial death on the cross as the source of the grace of God is a fraud. Those preachers want the grace (which has been turned into a "license to sin" message) but they don't want the one who gives it, nor the cross that provided for it. Therefore, they are frauds.

▲ ▲ ▲

FORGIVE ME LORD!

Forgive me, Lord! These words are the key that opens the door to the kingdom of heaven to a sinner. When a person humbly utters these words to ask God, the Father, to forgive their sins, and puts their faith in Jesus Christ, they acknowledge that they are sinners. They have done wrong, in the sight of God. They recognized that the One they are asking to forgive their sins is greater than them, and He has the power to forgive and cleanse anyone from all unrighteousness through the shed blood of His Son Jesus. Many will go to hell because of pride. They never want to admit that they have done anything wrong, or they are so self-righteous that they don't see the need to ask God for forgiveness. They have their own rules and ideology that they abide by. So, that makes them perfect in their own eyes and they think they can bring God down to their level of self-righteousness and make Him approve their way of living. The religious ones, who are so into their religion, think that once they perform the duties of their religion they don't need to ask God for forgiveness, because they are faithful to their religion, or their church, and they are therefore justified. Some were taught an erroneous doctrine which omits that the first step toward a relationship with God begins with these words, "Forgive me, Lord" and accepting Jesus as their Lord and Savior.

Moreover, some of the grace gospel preachers have excluded the words "Forgive me, Lord" from their teachings. The people are taught that their sins were forgiven once and for all when they were born again. Therefore, if they sin against God after their salvation, it's not necessary to ask Him for forgiveness. It is true that all of our sins are forgiven once we ask God to forgive us and have accepted Jesus as our Lord and Savior. However, we will get rid of the sin nature when we receive our glorified body. Until that happens, while we are living on earth, all human beings will sin. John wrote: *"If we say that we have no sin, we deceive ourselves and the truth is not in us. **If we confess our sins,** He is faithful and just to forgive us our sins and to cleanse us from all unrighteousness. If we say that we have not sinned, we make Him a liar, and His word is not in us. My little children, these things I write unto you, that you sin not. And if any man sin, we have an Advocate with the Father, Jesus Christ the righteous."* *(1 John 1:8-10, 2:1)* These verses are addressed to born again believers on how to deal with sins when we fail God.

Once we are convicted by the Holy Spirit that we have done something wrong, all we have to do is to confess that sin by saying: "Forgive me Lord." If forgiveness is sought with a repentant heart, He will forgive you. The believer must not continue living a life of sin. The Holy Spirit resides in you and when your faith is anchored in Jesus Christ and His finished work on the cross, the Bible says, "For *sin shall not have dominion over you…*" (Romans 6:14)

The teaching that says that believers no longer have to ask God for forgiveness is another ploy of Satan to mislead the people of God and to harden their hearts. If you practice what these preachers are teaching, you will become a person who has no boundaries. If you keep on sinning and never ask God for forgiveness, you'll get to the point where you won't not know right from wrong. It can be even worse for you, then before you were born again. The Bible says, *"Take heed therefore, that the light which is in you be not darkness." (Luke 11:35) The* light that is in you can become darkness. That can happen to you when you reject the cross of Christ, and when you no longer recognize that you have crossed the line and that you need to go to God in prayer to make things right. These kinds of teachings that tell you that you no longer need to ask God for forgiveness after salvation have a powerful, seductive demonic, arrogant and prideful spirit behind them. It is written: *"For **there are certain men crept in unawares,** who were before of old ordained to this condemnation, ungodly men, **turning the grace of our God into lasciviousness,** and denying the only Lord God, and our Lord Jesus Christ." (Jude 1:4)* These men are among those that call Jesus Lord, but don't really know Him. With subtlety, they crept among the Christians, bombarding them through

Christian television and other forms of media with their hyper grace message that they have turned "into lasciviousness." So, this insanity you are hearing on Christian television is not new. The devil has had men in all generations who were, and still are, willing to compromise the grace of God that Jesus died to extend to all, for fame and money. Don't be astonished when some say that they don't get a salary from their church. The church pays for the television times in the countries they have invaded to spread their deceitful grace message.

They write books and advertise them on their television programs, and with such a huge audience, they sell millions of books that they've written about their erroneous grace doctrine, and many other subjects. They then, keep the money to themselves. After all, it's their books and they are entitled to keep their money. The Jezebel spirit, who is Satan, who inspired them to teach the people of God false doctrines pay them, one way or another, for a job well done.

One hyper grace message preacher said: "Your miracle is in your mouth." That is wrong! Your miracle is in your faith in Jesus Christ and His sacrifice on the cross. Period! This too is worth repeating: God will move heaven and earth to honor Jesus' sacrifice on the cross. Therefore, your miracle is not in what comes out of your mouth but rather in whom you put your faith. Once again, that is Jesus Christ and the cross. If one would take the time to study these false teachers' materials, they would discover that their books and sermons really have nothing to do with neither Jesus Christ nor His finished work on the cross, the source of all blessings for the believers. His name may be mentioned as a deception cover-up, but it's really not about Him.

The ministers of the gospel who are teaching the hyper grace message are deceived. The people who are hearing it and believe it are deceived. If you are sitting under a preacher who teaches this erroneous doctrine, you need to ask the Holy Spirit to open your eyes to the truth before it's too late for you. You cannot love your pastor more than God and more than your soul. You need to ask the Holy Spirit to open your spiritual eyes to the truth and, He will do it.

Recognition that you have sinned brings humility to the heart. Since the Holy Spirit is the one who convicts of sin, when the believer confesses that sin, it means that he is in agreement with the Holy Spirit that he is indeed wrong. Being under the conviction of the Holy Spirit brings repentance to the heart and causes the believer to say, "I am not going to continue down that path but rather the way of the cross." The teaching that you don't need to ask God for forgiveness if you sin can leave you with a prideful and arrogant attitude.

▲   ▲   ▲

The greatest prayer of repentance in the Bible is Psalm 51 written by David. He humbly sought the forgiveness of God after he had sinned with Bathsheba. The believer should ask the Lord in prayer, to search his, or her, heart to bring light to any hidden sin. The following verses in these Psalms were written by David as well. A man about whom God said is a man after His own heart. He understood the importance of having a pure heart before the Lord and he sought God in prayer to help him in that aspect. These verses should be the prayers of every believer, asking the Lord to enlighten any trace of darkness within their hearts. To allow them to see the light through His light and to search their hearts for any wicked way that may be in them, so that the Holy Spirit can lead them in the everlasting way. These were the words of a man who knew God, who walked with God all the days of His life. I would take his words a million times over those of the hyper grace revolution preachers.

> *"For You will light my candle: the LORD my God will enlighten my darkness." (Psalm 18:28) "For with thee is the fountain of life: in thy light shall we see light." (Psalm 36:9)*
> *"Search me, O God, and know my heart: try me, and know my thoughts: And see if there be any wicked way in me, and lead me in the way everlasting." (Psalm 139:23-24)*

The Holy Spirit will remain silent after you have ignored His prompting warning you that you are heading the wrong way. Since He has remained silent, the devil will make you think, it's okay to continue in your sin because you are forgiven. That's why you are at peace. If you don't ask God for forgiveness and access His provision for the forgiveness of sins, it will progress in your life. And that sin can destroy your reputation, your ministry; it can cost you your family, your Job and even your life.

The following is an excerpt taken from my favorite timeless classic devotional, *"My Utmost For His Highest"* by Oswald Chambers. These are the most profound words I have ever read about repentance. "The entrance into the Kingdom is through the panging pains of repentance crashing into a man's respectable goodness; then the Holy Ghost, Who produces these agonies, begins the formation of the Son of God in the life. The new life will manifest itself in conscious repentance and unconscious holiness, never the other way about. The bedrock of Christianity is repentance. Strictly speaking, a man cannot repent when he chooses; repentance is a gift of God. If ever you cease to know the virtue of repentance, you are in darkness. Examine yourself and see if you have forgotten how to be sorry."

When a person has sinned and goes to God and says, "I am sorry. Forgive me Lord, I have done wrong in your sight," like David did in Psalm 51. That places God above that individual because they recognize that they have offended Him and that they need Him to pardon them. There is no greater proof of humility and fear of the Lord than when you can bow before Him and seek His forgiveness. Your sins are certainly under the blood of Jesus. The fact that you recognize you have done wrong is proof that the Holy Spirit is alive and well in your life. It is His job: to bring conviction when we've sinned. Our responsibility is to ask God for forgiveness. The Holy Spirit, then, can begin to work in us to forsake that tendency that brought us to that place. That's the progressive work of sanctification that the Holy Spirit operates in the life of the believer. To ignore that, is spiritual suicide.

Preacher, you can wrap your hyper grace message in any package you want, but the cross of Christ will expose you and in the end, it will swallow every false doctrine inspired by the Jezebel spirit, who has been corrupting the servants of God beginning in the church of Thyatira (Revelation 2:18-29), up until now. The seed (money) you are giving to such men is the riches that the spirit that was behind Bera, the king of Sodom (who is Satan himself), has promised to give to them, in exchange for the "persons" which is really to teach them false doctrines. You are paying these men to mislead you. That's the purpose of all false doctrines. One should seek the Holy Spirit to enlighten him or her concerning the hyper grace teaching that has fallen into the category of insanity. All false doctrines have some truth to them, which is why it's difficult to recognize them. But if you call on the Lord, He'll open your eyes to separate the truth from the lies.

Often times you hear some people say, "You are not giving your money to pastors. You are giving it to God." So, it doesn't matter what they do with it, once you know you've given it to God." However, that is wrong! Yes, it does matter what they do with it because we want our money to be used as God intended. The money we give should be used to take care of the necessities of the church, so that lost souls can come and hear about Jesus Christ and be born again. If nobody is being saved, it's because they have put Jesus out of their church. If that is the case, it's not the work of God. It's the work of man and you should not give your money to the work of man.

⋏ ⋏ ⋏

There is a big difference between a church that is filled with attendees and a church that has saved Christians. A church that has saved Christians is the church where the pastor preaches Jesus, the blood, and the cross. Such a pastor loves Jesus and this love is reflected in his work. He is conscientious about the work God called him to do. It's the only work on planet earth that has an everlasting impact as it entails the eternal destiny of the souls of men, women and children. You will not hear Him constantly bombarding the believers with messages on material wealth and lying to them by promising them wealth for the seed they sow to rob them. Taking everything into account, it does matter what the church does with the money.

God is not a thief. He would never lie to you, or manipulate you, in order to take back the money He gave to you in the first place. Whether you want to admit it, or not, when you are sowing money into a lie, you are giving your money to the pastor because God will not bless a work where a lying spirit reigns. When you are looking at it with natural eyes, it may look like the church is blessed but spiritually speaking, it's a dead church.

No pastor can deliver the souls of the people of God to the Jezebel spirit, nor to the spirit who possessed Bera, the king of Sodom who wants the people in exchange for riches. However, the people are oppressed, discontent, tormented, and worried. These believers will say, "We are blessed," but they are not living a blessed life, which is contentment in Jesus Christ, and leave the increase up to Him, according to His will. These pastors have stolen this privilege from them. Because their heart is always longing after the lifestyle of the rich and famous promised to them, if they give a lot of money in the offering, and that promise is never fulfilled.

BRING THE FISH!

W HEN I WAS a little girl, I remember one Sunday afternoon my mother
sent me for a walk with a maidservant from our home. She took me
to the pier. Where I saw a fisherman who was fishing. He had thrown the
hook into the sea, and he caught a fish, and he then put it in a bucket that
was near him. The fish jumped out of the bucket and was flipping around on
the floor. I was scared so I took a couple of steps back, holding on to that dear
lady. I kept watching attentively as the fisherman remained calm, and kept on
fishing. He let the fish do its gymnastics on the dock, but a couple of minutes
later, it did not jump anymore since it died. He calmly reached out, grabbed
the fish and put it back in his bucket.

Jesus' appearance to His disciples on the sea shore after His resurrection
reminds me of this story of my childhood. *"But when the morning was now
come, Jesus stood on the shore: but the disciples knew not that it was Jesus. Then
Jesus said unto them, Children, have you any meat? They answered him, No. And
He said unto them, Cast the net on the right side of the ship, and you shall find.
They cast therefore, and now they were not able to draw it for the multitude of
fishes. Therefore, that disciple whom Jesus loved saith unto Peter, it is the Lord.
Now when Simon Peter heard that it was the Lord, he girded his fisher's coat unto
him, (for he was naked,) and did cast himself into the sea. And the other disciples
came in a little ship; (for they were not far from land, but as it were two hundred
cubits,) dragging the net with fishes. As soon then as they were come to land, they
saw a fire of coals there, and fish laid thereon, and bread. Jesus saith unto them,
bring of the fish which you have now caught. Simon Peter went up, and drew
the net to land full of great fishes, a **hundred and fifty and three**: and for all*

there were so many, yet was not the net broken. Jesus said unto them, Come and dine. And none of the disciples asked Him, Who are You? Knowing that it was the Lord. Jesus then comes, and takes bread, and gives them, and fish likewise." (John 21: 4-13)

When a fish is caught from the sea, and is brought out of its accustomed environment to dry land, it is not going to be able to live a long time. If a fisherman had to keep running after a fish to keep it still, it would become a nuisance to him. The fisherman I saw that afternoon on the pier, knew that once the fish was not in the environment that it was accustomed to, it was not going to be able to survive very long. It was created to live in water, not on land. There is nothing in this new environment that would be favorable to the fish for it to continue to live on land as it had in the sea.

The preaching of the cross is the net of the Gospel. The preachers who use that net will always catch souls for the glory of their Lord, Jesus Christ. The cross is the place where man will die to self. It's impossible for a person who is born again, and maintains his faith in Jesus Christ, to continue to live the same way he or she was living before their conversion to Christ. That person now has the transforming power of the Holy Spirit working within him or her to bring about change on the inside, and the outside.

It is written in the Bible: "And you have He quickened, who were dead in trespasses and sins; Wherein in time past you walked according to the course of this world, according to the prince of the power of the air, the spirit that now works in the children of disobedience: Among whom also we all had our conversation in times past in the lusts of our flesh, fulfilling the desires of the flesh and of the mind; and were by nature the children of wrath, even as others. But God, who is rich in mercy, for his great love wherewith He loved us, Even when we were dead in sins, has quickened us together with Christ, (by grace you are saved;) And has raised us up together, and made us sit together in heavenly places in Christ Jesus." (Ephesians 2:1-6)

Once this truth is embedded in the heart of the believer he or she will have no desire to continue to swim in the waters of this world. They will flee from the churches that have compromised with the world, introducing its music, its entertainment, and the like as means to attract the people of the world, while also ejecting "the preaching of the cross," the only way, provided by God for man to be born again.

▲   ▲   ▲

Remember the word of Jesus, *"And I, if I be lifted up from the earth, will draw all men unto me." (John 12:32)* No other gimmicks, programs or methods are going to work. By "All men" Jesus means everyone, from the youngest to the oldest, all over the world. There is nothing in the kingdom of God that resembles the world that would encourage a born-again believer to continue to live the same old way of life. The apostle Paul said this about those who are born again. *"Therefore if any man be in Christ, he is a new creature: old things are passed away; behold, all things are become new." (2 Corinthians 5:17)*

The born again believer is a new creation that was transported from the kingdom of darkness to the glorious kingdom of Jesus Christ. That new creation will be led by the light of the Holy Spirit since the environment of that new creation has changed its way of life must also change. If the fisherman that was fishing on the quay, had put some sea water in his bucket and had put the fish inside of it, the fish would not have died so quickly.

Nothing of this world has its place in the church. You cannot give these new born again believers a little bit of the environment that they came out of, and hope to have souls entirely dedicated to the Lord, Jesus Christ, but some people love these types of churches. It is to the detriment of your soul. The Lord will not be able to you use as He would like, if you are still swimming in the waters of this corrupt world. It is written: *"Love not the world, neither the things that are in the world. If any man loves the world, the love of the Father is not in him." (1 John 2:15)* Just as the fish cannot survive on dry land, it will be the same for a newborn again believer who has joined a church where the true gospel of Jesus Christ is being preached. It will not be long before that new Christian begins to resent the things of the world. The word of God will bring a change in Him. The passions of the world cannot remain alive in him because his environment has changed.

The world has greatly influenced how the church conducts its affairs. That's why there are so many carnal Christians in the churches. I was watching a Christian television program, and after a sermon on "The valley of the dry bones" in Ezekiel 37: 1-14. The pastor used the late Michael Jackson's "Thriller" music video to support his message. This is an abomination and it's a worldwide crisis.

When Jesus appeared to the disciples on the seashore, He said to them, *"Children have you any meat?" They answered Him, "No." (John 21:5) They* were hungry. Jesus had already prepared food for them. However, He had not given them to eat, until they were finished looking after the fish, He ordered the disciples to bring the fish to Him. It was a miraculous catch. They took the fish out of the net, **counted them and they brought them to Jesus** as He commanded them to. Then Jesus said to them, "come and eat breakfast, and He took the bread and gave it to them. And likewise the fish he had Himself prepared for them. Jesus wanted to teach His disciples that their priority was to take care of the souls he had miraculously saved from the world and placed in their care. That's a perfect example of a good Pastor. By preparing their meal for them, while they went fishing, Jesus was also reminding the disciples that He will always provide for their need. The Lord who provided for them for the past three and a half years, had not changed. "Jesus Christ is the same yesterday, today, and forever." (Hebrews 13:8) He is Jehovah-Jireh, our provider.

▲   ▲   ▲

When a fisherman catches fish, and puts them on his boat, there will always be fish of different sizes: small, medium and large. In this miraculous catch of fish, the Holy Spirit inspired John to write the number of fish that were caught, (hundred and fifty-three *large* fish) because they represented souls. When it comes to the souls of man, there are no small or average ones, they are all equal. They are all *large* in the eyes of God since they are all saved by the Blood of Jesus. The fish did not belong to the disciples anymore. Once the souls of man have entered the kingdom of God through the net of "the preaching of the cross," they do not belong to the pastor. Jesus counts them and knows the exact number of people that He has saved. Every pastor will stand before Him to give an account for each soul that he has placed in his care.

It is impossible for a pastor to know every person in his congregation when the church is large. But, Jesus knows them all, and He is asking every pastor to feed His sheep the sound doctrine of Christ. The souls that are fed the sound doctrine of Christ will always be pleasing to the Lord, because they will grow to know Him. They will seek a relationship with Him, and will direct their lives to be pleasing to Him. The pastor's job is then well done in the sight of the Lord.

The Holy Spirit did not reveal to us how Jesus disposed of the fish in this passage. Since they represented the souls of men, they belong to Him. He had done what pleased Him with them. God never reveals His plans for His children to others. It's a personal matter between God and each person that He has saved. There are also no verses that suggest that Jesus sent the disciples to sell the fish to take care of their needs. I strongly feel that the disciples didn't go back selling those fish. In the natural, there weren't enough fish to sell to provide for them throughout their ministry. After Jesus ascended to heaven, instead of going back to fishing or selling fish the disciples stayed in prayer in the Upper Room, awaiting the promise of the Holy Spirit.

In Jesus' conversation with Peter after the miraculous catch, recorded in the book of John chapter 21, He asked Peter three times if he loved Him. The first time Peter told Him yes, he loved Him, and Jesus replied, "Feed my lambs." The second time He told Peter, "tend to my sheep" and the third time He told him "feed my sheep." Jesus is the good shepherd, so, the well-being of His lambs and sheep is of utmost importance to Him. Jesus' main concern was the well-being of His sheep and lambs. They represent men, women and children whom Jesus is coming back to take with Him. Before asking Peter to feed His sheep, Jesus had Himself, fed the disciples to meet their physical need, and they were satiated. It was to remind them as well that He will always take care of their needs, so that they do not take advantage of the souls that He will later entrust to them. Jesus still does it to this day for His faithful servants who trust Him to meet their needs, and who continue preaching about Him, and His sacrifice on the cross, come "hell and high water."

▲　▲　▲

We read in the book of Isaiah: *"Behold, the Lord GOD shall come with a strong hand, and His arm shall rule for Him, and His work before Him. He will feed His flock like a shepherd; He will gather the lambs with His arms, and carry them in His bosom, and gently lead those who are with young." (Isaiah 40: 10-11)*

Jesus expects pastors to treat the born again believers He has put in their care with the same love and attention demonstrated in Isaiah. The lambs represent those that have just been born again. He gives them special care because they are the most vulnerable. They need to be protected from the influence of the world, so this powerful force does not drag them right back out. He expects the pastors to feed them the sound doctrine of Christ, and to never exclude Him from the gospel. As it is recorded in the above verses, as the great shepherd, "He gently leads those who are with young beside Him," meaning the sheep who have given birth. Even though they are mature enough to give birth, He still leads them gently beside Him. That's a very moving statement. Even those who have been in the church for years, although they may have matured spiritually where they are no longer in the milk of the word, and are themselves winning souls to Christ. They still need to be fed the sound doctrine of Christ and they still need the spiritual guidance of their pastor. Another way to look at this verse is in the sense that Jesus, as the great shepherd, does not leave the pastors (who are His sheep) with this monumental task without His guidance. They gently walk beside Him because they too need His strength, love, guidance, encouragement and peace of mind to continue to see souls being born again through the preaching of the cross and for them to maintain a victorious life in Christ through the preaching of the cross.

So when a pastor, instead of walking beside Jesus for strength, encouragement, and nourishment for his soul and the souls of the born again believers who are in his care, starts introducing the things of the world to the congregation and erroneous teachings to feed the lambs and the sheep. The result will always be emaciated Christians. In such case, the pastor chose his own path, his own methods, his own gospel, resulting in him being exhausted and eventually burning out. In summary, the pastors as well as the lambs and the sheep depend on Jesus' love and guidance to be spiritually healthy and to fulfill their assignment well in the eyes of the Lord. When the sheep and the lambs are fed the sound doctrine of Christ, they will not be blown away by every wind of doctrine and they will not turn away from the gospel. They will remain faithful to their Savior.

▲   ▲   ▲

The words that were addressed to the shepherds of the Old Testament, are still applicable to some of the shepherds of today. There is no difference between them as their behavior is the same. So, to them, the Lord would say, *"Woe to the shepherds who destroy and scatter the sheep of My pasture! Says the LORD. Therefore, thus says the LORD God of Israel against the shepherds who feed My people. You have scattered My flock, driven them away, and not attended to them. Behold I will attend to you for the evil of your doings, says the LORD."* (Jeremiah 23:1-2)

Those shepherds have scattered the flock and driven them away because they have not been fed the sound doctrine of Jesus Christ. Instead, they have been taught erroneous doctrines. They've been given promises that were never fulfilled. They were exploited, taken advantage of, and in some cases sexually abused. Discouraged, they left the faith. Fortunately for them, their heavenly Father has not forgotten about them. God also said: *"In the cities of the mountains, in the cities of the lowland, in the cities of the south, in the land of Benjamin, in the places around Jerusalem, and in the cities of Judah **the flocks shall again pass under the hands of Him who counts them,** says the LORD."* (Jeremiah 33:13)

Until the present time, God knows exactly how many of His children are in every church all over the world since He counts them. He will bring back to the fold those that have left because of the maltreatment of their pastor. He has made a promise to His people in the book of Jeremiah to those that have left that is still appropriate for His people today. God said: *"I will set up shepherds over them, who will feed them, and they shall fear no more, nor be dismayed, nor shall they be lacking says the LORD."* (Jeremiah 23:4) That promise is being fulfilled at this very moment by the pastors who are preaching the whole counsel of God with a greater emphasis on Jesus, the cross, and the power of His blood, which are the strength and the victory of Christians.

HEALING AT THE GATE

T HE FOLLOWING IS a beautiful story about the healing grace of Jesus that took place at the gate called beautiful, recorded in the book of Acts. *"And a certain man lame from his mother's womb was carried, whom they laid daily at the gate of the temple which is called Beautiful, to ask alms of them that entered into the temple; Who seeing Peter and John about to go into the temple asked an alms. And Peter, fastening his eyes upon him with John, said, Look on us. And he gave heed unto them, expecting to receive something of them. Then Peter said, Silver and gold have I none; but such as I have give I thee:* **In the name of Jesus Christ of Nazareth rise up and walk.** *And* **he took him by the right hand, and lifted him up:** *and immediately his feet and ankle bones received strength. And he leaping up stood, and walked, and entered with them into the temple, walking, and leaping, and praising God."* (Acts 3 2-8)

Indeed, it was an awesome miracle that occurred on that day. Peter and John, fixing their eyes on this poor, lame man, saw him as a son of the kingdom of God. They probably had money on them that they could have given to him. What I like the most in this passage is Peter's answer to him: "Silver and gold I do not have, but what I do have I give you; in the name of Jesus Christ of Nazareth, rise up and walk." The disciples of Jesus did the work of their Master unselfishly. They were not preoccupied by materialism. The message in a great majority of churches today, teaches the people how to believe God for silver and gold instead of taking them by the hand and lifting them up to a greater knowledge of Jesus Christ and the cross. Peter and John were interested in introducing the lame man to Jesus Christ—the giver of life, the healer. Then Peter said, "Look at us." So he gave them his attention, expecting to receive something from them." That means this man was focused, and at that moment, his eyes were not on his condition, but on Peter and John, with the expectation to receive something from them. But, he didn't receive "something," he received someone— the Lord Jesus Christ, I believe that encounter changed his situation forever, physically, materially and spiritually.

That's the difference between silver and gold and a personal relationship with the Lord Jesus Christ. This man was carried every day and placed at the gate, beautiful. He depended every day on people to carry him there. But that day, was his last day living a hopeless life, a life of dependency on others. Peter took him by the hand, and raised him despite his infirmity, and showed him the way to Jesus Christ, who died on the cross and was resurrected from the dead, not too long before the day this miracle took place. Jesus paid an enormous price to deliver this lame man from this condition, which he had inherited from his mother's womb.

This is the story of the entire human race. We have inherited the sin nature from our mother's womb, so we all have our own infirmities from which we need deliverance. A man or a woman who is enslaved by sin may be walking on their two feet and they may wear expensive clothing, but if they don't have a relationship with the Lord, Jesus Christ, they are spiritually, as poor as that beggar was. They may be addicted to things in their lives that they can't control, so they are as futile as that beggar was. Until they get a good dose of whatever they are addicted to, they can't function.

It was the lame man's day and his hour to receive this great miracle in the Name of Jesus. Maybe today is the day that Jesus Christ is going to perform a great miracle in your life. This could be your hour of deliverance! Everything is possible to the one who believes. If this story happened today this man would probably still be at the gate called beautiful begging for alms. Firstly, some ministers would not take time to speak with him, because there was nothing to expect from him. He was too poor to retain their attention. They probably would not have stopped and talked to him. He did not have any seeds to sow and could not contribute financially to their ministry.

Some modern ministers are shepherds who have no contact with the sheep. The sad fact is that they are interested in the money and the number of the people that are on their church roster, but they are not actually interested in the people. They have become the superstars of Christianity, and they are gods in their church, or their ministry. They may say, "Jesus Christ is Lord," but these are just words, that have no meaning to them. If Jesus was Lord in their church, He would be at the center of their sermons every week —not their own methods, not their erroneous teachings and not the riches of this world.

The pastors who are teaching the people to sow a seed for a need will say that "the money which you sow is not to buy a miracle from God, but to show your faith and that you should not appear before Him empty-handed." Again, this is reasoning based on Scriptures that have been distorted. Listen to what Peter, the disciple of Jesus Christ who took time to visit this man, had to say concerning his healing. *"Then Peter, filled with the Holy Spirit, said unto them, You rulers of the people, and elders of Israel, be it known unto you all, and to all the people of Israel, that by the name of Jesus Christ of Nazareth, whom you crucified, whom God raised from the dead, even by Him does this man stand here before you whole." (Acts 4:8, 10)* This is how the disciples of Jesus represented His kingdom. Let us analyze these verses: Peter reiterated, it is by faith in the name of Jesus Christ, who was crucified, that this man was healed. Only by the name of Jesus Christ, no seed was needed from this man who had a great physical need. The name of Jesus took care of his need.

▲   ▲   ▲

I heard a pastor testify on Christian television that God healed his son after he had given a ten-thousand-dollar seed. He was sincere in his testimony. But for those who are in a similar situation and cannot afford that amount of money to sow as a seed for a sick child they can become very discouraged when they hear such testimonies. It can even leave them with a feeling of hostility towards God. This type of teaching distorts the character of God, and questions His faithfulness. These pastors' teachings are erroneous, and in some cases, they don't even know it. They're just repeating what others have taught, without consulting the Bible to find out for themselves if what they are teaching lines up with the word of God. Any mother and father who have a sick child at home, and who cannot give such a large amount of money as a seed towards the healing of that child so that God can see their faith and heal their child, will tell you the negative impact this type of testimony has on them.

I can never understand the reasoning behind the seed offering for the healing of a child, since whatever we obtain from God is because of the sacrifice of Jesus on the Cross. The only requirement from God is that we believe in Jesus and His finished work on the cross. It is in His name we get our healing and it's free to us given that Jesus already paid the price for our healing. When Jesus went to raise Lazarus from the dead, He told Martha, *"Jesus said unto her, Said I not unto you, that, if you would believe, you should see the glory of God?" (John 11:40)* He didn't say, "if you sow a seed," or a large sum of money. It is the strategy of the enemy to encourage others to give money when they see what God has done for the Pastor. They then begin to think they, too, can obtain their miracle when they sow a large seed (money).

The enemy enriches these men with the money the people are giving to obtain favors from God. If a pastor had a sick child at that time, and he had asked Peter and John to pray for the child, they would have prayed in the same manner they prayed for this man: "In the name of Jesus Christ, who was crucified." He wouldn't have to plant a ten thousand seeds towards his child's healing. All he would have to do is pray and maintain his faith in Jesus and His sacrifice on the cross to obtain the healing of that child. The fact that the pastor planted the ten-thousand-dollar seed for the healing of his son shows his lack of faith in the finished work of Jesus Christ on the cross. He believed that the seed was necessary to move God's heart. Unfortunately for him, God never answers these kinds of prayers. A few years later, I received an e-mail from his ministry, asking for prayer for his son because the illness had manifested on him again.

It is a very sad situation. I wished that this pastor would have realized that if God had healed his son, it would have been because of the price Jesus paid on the cross for the healing of that young man. Then, Satan would have no power to put the sickness back on him. All that we receive from Jesus, by His blood, is sealed for eternity. He was deceived into believing a seed would make the difference in the healing of his son. He believed it with all his heart. If he didn't believe it, he would not have given that amount of money and testified afterwards. Most parents would do anything, even give their own life, to save their child, and that proved the sincerity of his action.

When the church abandons the cross, and subscribes to the false teachings inspired by the Jezebel spirit, you're going to hear things like that. This pastor was not the only one facing that kind of situation. Many Christians have fallen for the same lies of the enemy and have registered casualties. He preached it, he practiced it and it probably took him years to realize that the teaching doesn't work. I used the word ***probably*** because that spirit is a powerful seducing spirit. When you fall for her lies, you teach them, practice them and accumulate riches by them, then it's not easy to get out of her grip.

That's what Satan does to discredit God, and to throw His people into confusion. Let us hope that he is the first of many to see that this teaching, which excludes the sacrifice of Jesus on the cross, and replaces it with sowing a large sum or any amount of money for a need is not of the Lord. The cross doesn't need any money to help us obtain the miracles Jesus shed His blood to perform for us in time of need.

If it were the will of God that you give money before receiving His favors, if a seed (money) was continuously required with your prayer requests, to move heaven, then what would be the purpose of the cross? There are preachers who will send a piece of cloth or other articles in the mail and ask you to send them money in return to receive your miracle. The verses which these preachers exploit to validate their piece of cloth, or any other article they send as a point of contact, are in the book of Acts. Let's read these verses: *"And God wrought special miracles by the hands of Paul: So that from his body were brought unto the sick handkerchiefs or aprons, and the diseases departed from them, and the evil spirits went out of them." (Acts 19: 11-12)*

Paul preached no other doctrine but "Christ crucified." His messages were inspired by the Holy Spirit. He loved Jesus with every fiber of his being. He lived for Him, and it was reflected in his ministry. The Lord confirmed his ministry by performing signs and wonders through his hands. His ministry was at its Zenith when these miracles took place in Acts 19: 11-12, that we've just read about.

However, this did not remain so. Later in his ministry, in his letter to Timothy Paul wrote: *"Erastus abode at Corinth: but Trophimus have I left at Miletum sick. (2 Timothy 4:20)* This shows us that Paul was limited. The anointing that was on him, through which these miracles were happening belonged to the Holy Spirit. Therefore, he had no power to heal the sick himself. He could not do anything for Trophimus. If Trophimus had put his faith in Paul, because of his fame, and the great miracles, which were taking place in his ministry, he would have been disappointed. In order for Trophimus to be healed, he had to put his faith in "Jesus Christ and Him crucified," whom Paul preached with all his heart, and all of his soul. I am sure that Paul had prayed for Trophimus and left the situation in the hands of the Lord, who alone can heal.

▲   ▲   ▲

I am sure in our day, there are pastors that would have said to Trophimus "to get your healing brother it is necessary to plant a seed (money) for your need." In that situation, the need was healing. According to this teaching, if you don't plant a seed (money) for your need, you are doomed. Those who don't have any money to give are left with no hope. We are not healed by planting seeds in any men or women's ministry. We are healed by the stripes of Jesus. People of God! You don't ever need to "plant a seed for your need." Whatever the need may be; your heavenly Father knew about it before you became aware of it. Take it to Him, in prayer and watch Him perform your miracle because of the shed blood of Jesus on the cross.

I am almost sure there are people who have died of their illnesses, who could have been healed, if they had put their faith only in Jesus, and His sacrifice on the cross. If they had invoked the favor of God based on the great price paid on the cross by His Son Jesus for their healing. When you mix the word of God with erroneous teachings, everything comes to a standstill. It is also of utmost importance that we understand when it comes to divine healing, it doesn't matter how greatly anointed a person is; he or she doesn't have the final word on how a sick person is going to receive their healing. They can receive it instantaneously, or it can be manifested gradually. In the latter, a sick person must stay under their doctor's care until their healing is manifested. They have to trust the Lord and believe that their healing will be manifested, God will grant them that request to honor His Son's sacrifice on the cross. If you obtained your healing, by sowing seeds (money), by mixing the word of God with manipulation and lies that you've been taught, then you could always say, it's the money you gave that contributed towards this victory. In that case, God would not get all the glory. This mixture of the word of God with false teachings can make you a statistic for Satan, instead of a testimony for God.

THE FIRST LADY

ANOTHER PLAGUE THAT is in the church that cannot be overlooked is the pastors' wives being called "First Lady," from what we know, the First Ladies are in the White House, in palaces of the nations around the world, and in the mayors or the governors' mansions. In other words, the First Ladies are the wives of the heads of state. We hear, however, that title more often associated with the presidents' wives of all the nations around the world. There is no First Lady in the church of Jesus Christ. In the prophecy given to the prophet Joel, in the Old Testament God called us, ***"servants, and hand-maidens,"*** *(Joel 2:29)* which simply means male or female we are servants of the Lord. A handmaiden is a female servant.

In the New Testament, on the day of Pentecost when the Spirit fell on the disciples and they began to speak with other tongues as the Spirit gave them utterance. Peter reiterated the prophesy of Joel saying, *"But this is that which was spoken by the prophet Joel; And it shall come to pass in the last days, said God, I will pour out of My Spirit upon all flesh: and your sons and your daughters shall prophesy, and your young men shall see visions, and your old men shall dream dreams: **And on My servants and on My handmaidens** I will pour out in those days of my Spirit; and they shall prophesy:" (Acts 2:16-18)*

God called us "My servants and My handmaidens," meaning that we belong to Him. We are His possession. He foresaw the cross through which this prophecy was going to find its fulfillment at least in part. This began on the day of Pentecost and has not yet ended. Although He couldn't' officially called us sons and daughters because Jesus had not come yet to pay the debt of sin to reconcile us to Him. He used the words My servants and My hand-maidens or female servants in this context it's more like a son or a daughter who is taking care of the affairs of his or her father. Those of us who have put our faith in Jesus Christ are now sons and daughters.

God took the example of a loyal son who serves his father to explain to us how He will protect the one who serves Him faithfully. He sees us as sons and daughters who serve Him. He didn't take the example of a servant who serves his master, but rather a son who serves his father.

> *"And they shall be mine, said the LORD of hosts, in that day when I make up My jewels; and I will spare them, **as a man spares his own son who serves him.** Then shall you return, and discern between the righteous and the wicked, between **him who serves God** and him who serves Him not." (Malachi 3:17-18)*

This is a beautiful promise of God's protection for His loyal servants. However, the titles given to us by the Holy Spirit when He gave the word of prophecy to the prophet Joel (which was later reiterated by Peter) were "servants and handmaidens." That's what Jesus wants us to be **SERVANTS**! Male or female.

The First Lady is never a servant. On the contrary, she has many who serve her, and many who bow to her. Jesus Himself taught us to be a servant. He is our Lord yet He set the example before us. He came not to be served, but to serve. "And He sat down, and called the twelve, and said unto them, ***if any man desire to be first, the same shall be last of all, and servant of all." (Mark 9:35)***

God became Man to serve man —to teach us what we lost in the Garden of Eden: HUMILITY! However, after Jesus' resurrection, He ascended to heaven in glory. He appeared afterwards to John on the Isles of Patmos, He spoke of Himself in these terms: *"I am Alpha and Omega, the Beginning and the End, **the First** and the Last." (Revelation 22:13)*

According to the verse we just read, there is only one First in the church, and that is Jesus Christ Himself. There is no First Lady in the church of

Jesus Christ. In the body of Christ, we are servants in the service of our heavenly Father.

▲   ▲   ▲

As glamorous as this title may seem to be, it cannot be compared to that of being called a "servant of Christ." The late Jacqueline Kennedy, the wife of the late President John F. Kennedy said, "The one thing I do not want to be called is First Lady. It sounds like a saddle horse." Source: The Kennedys.

There are great First Ladies throughout the world who have made great contributions in their nation through the causes, which they have embraced. I am not putting down the First Ladies of the world. However, I feel there is no title on earth greater than that of "servant of Christ." The believers need to stop that nonsense of calling their pastor's wife "First Lady" this is worth repeating, you need to stop calling these women "First lady" it boosts their ego. They just want to be "rulers over you." (Mark 10:42-44) You are not Gentiles, you are sons and daughters of the Most- High God, by adoption through Christ. When you call them "First Lady," you put them on a pedestal if you are not careful, they may become a god in your eyes.

You are doing a disservice to yourself, when you let another woman bring you down to that level. Furthermore, they are not setting a good example for the younger generation. They are not teaching the younger pastor's wife to serve, but to be served. They are teaching them pride, instead of humility. That title carries pride with it. After a while, these First Ladies will behave according to the name that they have been called because they begin to think like the label, and this greatly influences how they interact with others. In addition, it can have a negative impact on the church in many ways.

You know very well those women who call themselves "First Lady" do not have a servant attitude in any way, shape, or fashion. They really feel, and act, like they are in the White House, or palaces of the world, not the church of Jesus Christ. And most do it out of pride. They are your sisters in Christ, they are your pastors' wives. You should love them, respect them and pray for them. The Bible tells us to obey those that God placed in authority over us. However, when they are asking you to do things that are contrary to the teachings of Jesus Christ, you must refuse, even if you have to leave their church.

They have no business asking the people of God to call them "First Lady" again, that's not the teaching of Christ. God calls them "handmaiden" (female servant) not "First Lady." That title was not inspired by the Holy Spirit. It is an attempt of Satan to bring inequality within the church of Jesus Christ. I pray the pastor's wife, who didn't know what she was doing when she embraced that tile because she was following a trend, or simply thought it was cool would come back to her senses, and have the courage and humility to tell her congregation not to address her as First Lady anymore. It takes humility to do that and that would be extremely pleasing to God. The others who are full of pride who deliberately choose to be called "First Lady" and who would not change it for anything you should be ashamed of yourselves for acting like "the ungodly rulers who rule over the Gentiles" —over the precious souls Jesus died for —with your self-appointed demonic- inspired title of "First Lady."

There is no First lady in the church of Christ. He calls us "servants," and we must remain that. Any pastor's wife who wants to change that is inspired by the Jezebel spirit, who is Satan. In fact, the pastor's wives should call themselves "Last Lady" because the servant who has a servant's heart will always put herself last. If they really cared for the souls, God entrusted to them, they would have a spirit of servant hood, and they wouldn't give themselves a title that is contrary to the teaching of Jesus Christ.

Some take that title, because they don't know who they are in Christ. They have low self-esteem, and a feeling of insecurity. So, that title becomes their covering. It makes them feel above everybody else in the church. In that case, they need to do some soul searching, and bring those feelings under the blood of Jesus. That way they can be free to take the servant mantle, to do the work God called them to do alongside their husband, which is far pleasing to God. Remember, people of God, your first and foremost priority is to please God. Calling your pastor's wife First lady is not honoring the teaching of Jesus Christ, and it's displeasing to God.

THE ULTIMATE DECISION

T HERE WAS A Pharisee, a leader of the Jews and a doctor of the law, named Nicodemus, who went to see Jesus in the middle of the night and He gladly received him. There is no inconvenient hour, day or night, for Jesus to receive a soul who is searching Him. Nicodemus wanted to know more about this person who was doing all these marvelous things. Jesus is always ready to help, and to guide. Nicodemus said to Jesus: … *"Rabbi, we know that you are a teacher come from God: for no man can do these miracles that you do, except God be with Him." "Jesus answered and said unto him, 'Verily, verily, I say unto you,* **except a man be born again, he cannot see the kingdom of God."** *'Nicodemus said unto Him, 'How can a man be born when he is old? Can he enter the second time into his mother's womb, and be born?" 'Jesus answered, Verily, verily,* **I say unto you, except a man be born of water and of the Spirit, he cannot enter into the kingdom of God."** *(John 3:2-5)*

Jesus also said to him, **"And as Moses lifted up the serpent in the wilderness, even so must the Son of man be lifted up: That whosoever believes in Him should not perish, but have eternal life."** *(John 3:14-15)*

Nicodemus asked this question to Jesus on behalf of the human race. It had to be a question that interested every man, woman, young child and teenager living on this earth, from the youngest to the oldest. **"How can a man be born again…?"** Jesus gave him the answer for every age category from the youngest to the oldest. The New birth is the only means by which man can see the kingdom of God and have a relationship with Jesus. His answer to Nicodemus pointed to the cross. Jesus said to him, *"And as Moses lifted up the serpent in the wilderness, even so must the Son of man be lifted up: That* *whosoever believes in Him should not perish, but have eternal life." (John 3:14-15)* Jesus was the first one to preach the cross to a man who wanted to know how to be born again. However, Nicodemus did not understand the answer that Jesus had given him because Jesus had not gone to the cross yet. To explain the "born again" experience that everyone must go through to see the kingdom of God, Jesus made a comparison between Himself, and the serpent that Moses had elevated in the wilderness.

The following passage is from the journey of the Israelites out of Egypt. Their journey across the desert was long, and exhausting and it had taken a toll on the people. They became discouraged along the way. They started complaining and had spoken unkind words towards God and Moses.

> *"The people spoke against God, and against Moses, wherefore have you brought us up out of Egypt to die in the wilderness? For there is no bread, neither is there any water; **and our soul loatheth this light bread.** And the LORD sent fiery serpents among the people, and they bit the people; and much people of Israel died. Therefore, the people came to Moses, and said, we have sinned, for we have spoken against the LORD, and against you; pray unto the LORD, that He take away the serpents from us. And Moses prayed for the people. **And the LORD said unto Moses, 'Make you a fiery serpent, and set it upon a pole: and it shall come to pass, that every one that is bitten, when he looks upon it, shall live'.** And Moses made a serpent of brass, and put it upon a pole, and it came to pass, that if a serpent had bitten any man, when he beheld the serpent of brass, he lived." (Numbers 21:5-9)*

They went as far as being ungrateful to God, after He had done wonders to set them free from the bondages of Egypt and had sent them manna (bread) every day from heaven to feed them. He had even sent them a double portion on Fridays, so that they would have enough food for the Sabbath, their day of rest.

The manna, the temporary bread from heaven, which fed their physical body, symbolized Jesus Christ, the bread of life, who had to come from heaven to feed the soul of man. When the Israelites called it "light bread" meaning that it had no value. They opened themselves up to every kind of evil to attack. And it has not changed to this day. When you reject Jesus Christ, the bread of life from heaven that can only satisfy your soul, and give you eternal life, you are going to feel an emptiness within that nothing in this material world can fill. In addition, you open yourself up to every kind of attack from Satan, the enemy of your soul.

▲　▲　▲

Generations later, when the true "Bread of heaven"— Jesus Christ— came down from heaven to the world many people rejected Him. *"**And Jesus said unto them, I am the bread of life**: he that comes to Me shall never hunger; and he who believes on Me shall never thirst. I am the bread of life. Your fathers did eat manna in the wilderness, and are dead. **This is the bread which comes down from heaven, that a man may eat thereof, and not die. I am the living bread which came down from heaven**: if any man eat of this bread, he shall live forever: and the bread that I will give is My flesh, which I will give for the life of the world."* (John 6:35, 48-51)

When the Israelites were in the desert they called "the manna," the bread from heaven "light bread," they faced the judgment of God. In the same way, anyone who rejects Jesus Christ, the true bread, which came down from heaven who gives eternal life will face the judgment of God before His great white throne.

"Moses made a bronze serpent, and put it on a pole and so it was, if a serpent had bitten anyone, when he looked at the bronze serpent, he lived." The serpent which Moses elevated was a type of Christ. Jesus is the only one who heals, and He is the giver of life. In this context, the serpent was not a type of Satan. It is us who should have been put on the cross, but Jesus was made to be sin for us. Our sins were placed on Him. Sinful man should have experienced the wrath of God, since he is incapable of meeting God's demands of justice with anything he can come up with. God's wrath was poured out on Jesus. He became a substitute in our place so we might become His righteousness. The Bible says, *"For He has made Him to be sin for us, **who knew no sin**; that* *we might be made the righteousness of God in Him."* *(2 Corinthians 5:21)* That's why everyone who looked at the serpent were healed because of who it represented Jesus, who took our place.

Jesus never became a sinner on the cross or at any other time. If he had become a sinner or had taken Satan's nature, He could not have atoned for sins. He would have become a sullied Being. He died a spotless Lamb and was resurrected a glorious Savior. It is written: *"How much more shall the blood of Christ, who through the eternal Spirit* **offered Himself without spot to God**, *purge your conscience from dead works to serve the living God?" (Hebrews 9:14)*

Jesus could not compare Himself with Satan. There is nothing common between them, near or far. Jesus has said Himself: *"Hereafter I will not talk much with you:* **for the prince of this world comes, and has nothing in me."** *(John 14:30)*

The pole was a type of the cross. Satan was never to be elevated on a pole. The bronze serpent that Moses elevated on the pole, was the shadow of what would take place at Calvary generations later when Jesus was elevated on the cross as a sin offering. It was at the cross Satan was brought down and was eternally defeated. The only appointment that God had with Satan, concerning the cross, was that it was going to be the place where the posterity of the woman, His Son Jesus, would crush Satan's head. If that serpent represented Satan, the children of Israel would have been wiped out. These fiery serpents in the wilderness would have killed them all. Man can look up to Satan in this world until eternity, if that were the case, he would never find healing, peace, and life and his soul would have been eternally damned.

Sin is like a fiery serpent; when it bites it kills. Adultery kills the marriage, theft kills good jobs, gossip kills friendships, and jealousy kills the bonds between parents or friends. Idolatry destroy nations that devote themselves to it. These are few sins, which are products of the sin nature. Indeed, there are a lot more sins that can kill whatever they touch. There is not a human being who does not know the pain of its bites. Our savior paid an enormous price for our freedom, so that we don't remain its victim forever. As stated before, the sin nature, is the nature in man that says, "I am my own god." It predisposes man to sin, to rebel against God, and to go his own way. It has been hurting man since the Garden of Eden. It is a dividing wall between man and God. The unregenerate man who is dominated by it is sullied in the eyes of God. No matter how well educated he is, how rich he is, or how poor he is.

The healing power of God healed the children of Israel when they looked at the bronze serpent. We are no longer in the shadow of a bronze serpent; we are now in the presence of the Almighty God who became man. *"Who His own self bare our sins in His own body on the tree that we, being dead to sins, should live unto righteousness: by whose stripes you were healed." (1 Peter 2:24)* The children of Israel obtained their healing through the shadow of what was to come. In the New Covenant we receive our healing through the manifested Savior, Jesus Christ, by whose stripes we were healed.

When Jesus spoke to Nicodemus using the serpent that Moses elevated in the wilderness as an allegory to explain how man is to be born again, He was then telling him that he would become our substitute, on the cross and die for our sins, so that we could have eternal life. We will never understand the amplitude of this great ransom that Jesus paid to give us this new life. Salvation is a gift to whoever will accept it, but it was pricey to Jesus. It cost Him His life.'

After the crucifixion of Jesus, Joseph of Arimathea asked Pilate permission to take His body. We read, *"And there came also Nicodemus, which at the first came to Jesus by night, and brought a mixture of myrrh and aloes, about a hundred pound weight. Then they took the body of Jesus, and wound it in linen clothes with the spices, as the manner of the Jews is to bury. Now in the place where He was crucified there was a garden; and in the garden a new sepulcher, wherein was never man yet laid. There laid they Jesus therefore because of the Jews' preparation day; for the sepulchre was near at hand." (John 19:39-42)*

The quantity of aloes and myrrh that Nicodemus brought to embalm the body of Jesus testified of his love, respect and deep gratitude towards the Lord. He could have gone his way and remained indifferent to the body of Jesus, for he must have been perplexed as to what had just taken place. Nicodemus esteemed Jesus so much that he had gone at night to see him, to inquire more about this man. He was persuaded that Jesus was an extraordinary Man, and that God was with Him.

The miracles wrought through Jesus's hands fascinated him. He mentioned this in their encounter when he went to see Him that night. It must have been difficult to see the same man beaten by sinners, carrying a cross, drenched in His own blood—He who had fed a crowd of people by multiplying five loaves of bread and two fish. Nicodemus likely also witnessed the moment Jesus was thirsty and He was not able to obtain water. And when He had asked the soldiers who were spitting in His face, mocking Him, and slapping Him, the only beverage they gave Him was vinegar. By then even His disciples abandoned Him. By looking at this spectacle, Nicodemus could have called the origin of Jesus into question.

Instead of looking at this reality as it was, Nicodemus rather looked at the cross. He probably remembered the encounter he had with Jesus who said to him: *"And as Moses lifted up the serpent in the wilderness, even so must the Son of man be lifted up: That whosoever believes in Him should not perish, but have eternal life." (John 3:14-15)*

When he looked at Jesus, nailed to the cross, these words spoken by Jesus came alive in his heart. He then understood what Jesus was talking about. The only way for anyone to be born again and have eternal life is by what he was looking at—Jesus' sacrifice on the cross. It was Jesus who would take the place of the bronze serpent elevated on a pole by Moses as a sin offering (Isaiah 53:10) He was made a substitute for us. Generations later, that shadow became a reality, when Jesus was nailed to the cross. Jesus was fulfilling His mission as "The Lamb of God who takes away the sin of the world." Nicodemus probably understood more than anyone that day what was transpiring, when he realized it, there was nowhere else to go, but back to the cross.

Although Nicodemus did not know how the death and burial of his Savior would conclude, he came with Joseph of Arimathea to embalm Him and to put Him in the sepulcher. That is true worship. It is love with a pure motive. Nicodemus was looking at a dead corpse. There was absolutely nothing to expect from Jesus. Nicodemus saw Jesus at His lowest and he continued to respect, and believe in Him. He honored Jesus. For the disciples of Jesus, it was all over they forsook Him. But, Nicodemus wasn't looking to the left, or to the right. He had made up his mind that he wasn't going to let the behavior of others affect his relationship with Jesus, even until death.

To love Jesus, the Son of God, until death—up to the tomb—that's faithfulness and loyalty! It is priceless, and it is divine. Nicodemus probably had said to himself, and resolved in his heart that men can say what they want, do what they want, believe what they want, and they can act as they want. But for me, I know what I heard about Him, I know what He said to me, I saw Him at work and I have seen the miracles He performed. I know in whom I have believed. If the crowd who cried "crucify Him, crucify Him" doesn't need the cross, I need it and my eternal life depends on it. I do not want to go burn in the fire of hell forever, the place that was created for Satan and the fallen angels, if I dare turn my back on the cross, and what it represents for the salvation of my soul. Nicodemus made the right choice. He had made up his mind to not let what took place around him distract him. The news of Jesus' resurrection spread three days later. It was joy from this day forward. The eternal life of Nicodemus was sealed forever, and so it will be for anyone after him who believes in Jesus, by confessing Him as their Lord and Savior. For it is written: *"If you shall confess with your mouth the Lord Jesus, and shall believe in your heart that God has raised Him from the dead, you shall be saved. For with the heart man believes unto righteousness; and with the mouth confession is made unto salvation." (Romans 10: 9-10)*

The same words that Jesus said to Nicodemus still resound two thousand years later. "Jesus answered and said to him, **"Most assuredly I say to you, unless one is born again, he cannot see the kingdom of GOD."** What is your choice? Where are you going to spend eternity? The answer to those questions is not found in religion but in a personal relationship with Jesus Christ. Religion is a mixture of the thoughts of man and of sorcery. Christianity is a personal relationship with Jesus Christ, the Son of the living God. The best decision you can make today is to tell the heavenly Father "I am sorry for my sins. Forgive me, Lord, from this day forward, I submit my will to you. Take my life Lord, Jesus and make it what you want it to be. Alive and in death, I belong to you. I will take up my cross daily, and I will follow you."

Thank you for the cross Lord Jesus!

About the Author

"You whom I have taken from the ends of the earth, and called you from the chief men thereof, and said unto you, you are My servant; I have chosen you, and not cast you away. Fear you not; for I am with you: be not dismayed; for I am your God: I will strengthen you; yea, I will help you; yea, I will uphold you with the right hand of my righteousness." (Isaiah 41: 9–10)

The Evangelist, Marie-Roberte Joseph was born in Jérémie, Haiti. She immigrated to the United States in 1970, with her mother, where she joined her father and her brothers. She obtained her nursing degree in 1986 from Queens Borough Community College in Queens, New York. In July 1994, she fell gravely ill of a skin disease, a condition that the doctors could not treat. With prayers and her faith in Jesus Christ, she was miraculously healed after seven months of suffering. On January 4, 1996 at five minutes to nine in the morning, while she was reading the Bible, Marie-Roberte did not have words to describe what she was feeling. It was like the words of these verses in the book of Isaiah had broken loose from the Bible and had become attached to her heart. She understood then that it was God who was speaking to her on that day to totally dedicate her life to Him. Shortly, thereafter, the Lord called her to serve Him in the ministry and she left her nursing career to dedicate herself to the service of the Lord.

▲　▲　▲

"Now unto the King eternal, immortal, invisible, the only wise God, be honor and glory for ever and ever. Amen." (1 Timothy 1: 17)

▲　▲　▲

www.ingramcontent.com/pod-product-compliance
Lightning Source LLC
Chambersburg PA
CBHW020847090426
42736CB00008B/274